THE KING'S ENGLISH

The King's English

Strategies of Translation in the Old English *Boethius*

Nicole Guenther Discenza

State University of New York Press

Published by
State University of New York Press, Albany

Printed in the United States of America

For information, address State University of New York Press,
194 Washington Avenue, Suite 305, Albany, NY 12210-2365

Production by Judith Block
Marketing by Michael Campochiaro

Library of Congress Cataloging-in-Publication Data

Discenza, Nicole Guenther, 1969–
The King's English : strategies of translation in the Old English Boethius/ Nicole Discenza.
p. cm.
Includes bibliographical references and index.
ISBN 0–7914–6447–4 (hardcover : alk. paper)—ISBN 0–7914–6448–2 (pbk : alk. paper)
1. Alfred, King of England, 849–899. Old English version of Boethius De consolatione philosophiae. 2. Alfred, King of England, 849-899—Knowledge—Language and languages. 3. Boethius, d 524—Translations into English—History and criticism. 4. Latin language—Translating into English—History—To 1500. 5. Translating and interpreting—England—History—To 1500. 6. English language—Old English, ca. 450–1100—Style. 7. Boethius, d 524. De consolatione philosophiae. I. Title.

PR1549.D57 2005
100—dc22

2004054173

10 9 8 7 6 5 4 3 2 1

CONTENTS

ACKNOWLEDGMENTS

This book would not have been possible without the encouragement and support of many others. First among these must be Katherine O'Brien O'Keeffe, my dissertation director, mentor, and friend, who helped greatly with both dissertation and book. I also thank my dissertation committee, Maureen Boulton, Stephen Gersh, John Van Engen, and Charles Wright, for all their comments and questions. Antonette diPaolo Healey aided my work on *cræft* and has always encouraged me. Paul Szarmach's interest and advice were indispensable. My work with the *Fontes Anglo-Saxonici* project led to additional material for the book, and I am grateful to Malcolm Godden and Rohini Jayatilaka for inviting me to contribute to *Fontes* and to two Boethius Project symposia, and especially for their specific questions, comments, and corrections. Joe Wittig answered many questions on the commentaries, provided me with a copy of a forthcoming item, and has always been friendly and encouraging. Judith Bealls, Sally Bormann, and Jana Schulman helped me to focus my ideas while I was at the National Endowment for the Humanities, Summer Institute, and Andrew Scheil made valuable comments then and after. James Peltz and Judith Block at the State University of New York Press have made my first experience with publishing a book a good one, and anonymous readers for the Press made many valuable suggestions.

Francelia Clark at the University of Michigan first started me on a study of Alfred's *Boethius* as an undergraduate, and the University of Michigan's Medieval and Renaissance program, and especially Cindy Sowers and Charles Witke, gave me a firm foundation for later work. I am very grateful for a Mellon Fellowship and dissertation-year grant from the Woodrow Wilson Foundation, as well as support from the University of Notre Dame. The dissertation was reconceived as a book during the 1999 NEH Summer Institute on Anglo-Saxon England at Western Michigan University, and I thank the NEH for support to attend. A summer leave grant from Hillsdale College funded the bulk of the additional research needed to turn the dissertation into a book. I was also fortunate to have help from two excellent interlibrary loan services: the Hesburgh Library of the University of Notre Dame and Hillsdale College's Mossey Library. The staffs at the British Library, the Bodleian Library, the Cambridge University Library, and Trinity College Library in Cambridge, England greatly facilitated my work with manuscripts. Part of chapter 4 is adapted with permission from Cambridge University Press from my "Power, Skill and Virtue in the Old English *Boethius*," *ASE* 26 (1997): 81–108.

Finally, I must thank my family and friends. My parents, Paul and Valerie Guenther, have always encouraged my love of both literature and history. Friends, especially John Somerville at Hillsdale College, and Laura Runge and John Fleming at the University of South Florida, lent moral support. My husband, Joe Discenza, provided an endless font of support and conversation about the book. He helped me talk through many of the ideas contained in these chapters (and many more that proved unworthy of inclusion) despite being a mathematician by training and an Anglo-Saxonist only by marriage. Completing the manuscript through a pregnancy and our daughter Catherine's earliest years would have been impossible without his great help. I thank Catherine too, although it will be some time before she knows why. Any remaining errors are, of course, my own.

INTRODUCTION

In the late ninth century, while the Danes were attacking England and the Anglo-Saxons were struggling to fight them off and rebuild, Alfred, King of the West Saxons, embarked on a startling program of translation and education. The king himself translated Gregory the Great's *Regula pastoralis*, Boethius's *De consolatione philosophiae*, Augustine's *Soliloquia*, and the first fifty Psalms into Old English.[1] He sponsored Wærferth's translation of Gregory's *Dialogues* and perhaps also the anonymous translations of Orosius's *Historiae aduersum paganos* and Bede's *Historia ecclesiastica*.[2] Alfred faced a more subtle threat than that of the Danes. He confronted competition from a much more widely known and prestigious culture: Latin language and traditions were accessible through much of the Mediterranean and Western Europe if only to the most learned. Latin was the language of learning, religion, and, for the most part, writing. English, by contrast, was widely accessible in England, but England was a small island in a corner of the known world; written English was accessible to few indeed, both on and off the island. Recent work by French sociologist and anthropologist Pierre Bourdieu, and in the field of Translation Studies, offers frameworks for understanding how Alfred's strategies mediated among the source text, the Latin traditions surrounding it, and the Anglo-Saxon culture that received the translation. These strategies legitimated the translation, enabled it to convey cultural capital to its readers, and helped it to inculcate a specific set of values into its audience.

Alfred had few models of how to render Latin into Old English and needed to authorize his own acts of translation. He had authority as king, but political authority is not the same as moral and literary authority.[3] Pierre Bourdieu would describe these as separate "fields": the political field is not equivalent to the spiritual field, and different kinds of authority and capital operate in each.[4] Even as a warrior-king, Alfred did not have absolute power; the *Anglo-Saxon Chronicle* records that in 893 A.D. an army dispersed because Alfred did not relieve it in time.[5] How much more difficult would asserting leadership in textual and religious matters be for this warrior-king? The Anglo-Saxons had kings who fought, not kings who wrote. No prior West Saxon king left extant texts in his name; the earliest, the laws of Ine, survive only as a part of Alfred's Law Code. Anglo-Saxon kings might assert power over the church, but that power was usually over church possessions and offices, not over texts and practices. Even so, church officials often disputed royal prerogatives. Bede's *Historia ecclesiastica* recounts many conflicts between royalty and clergy, and clerics usually emerge victorious if not downright heroic. In Alfred's own time, Pope John VIII wrote a letter supporting the bishops against Alfred in a land dispute.[6] Janet Nelson's recent work emphasizes how tenuous Alfred's authority was: while Alfred's father, Æthelwulf, may have been grooming him for a modest but still royal position in taking him to Rome, the rebellion of his eldest son left Æthelwulf's own position too insecure to ensure his youngest son a future leadership role.[7] When Alfred unexpectedly became the sole holder of the throne of Wessex (itself not a stable kingdom), "the gaining of authority was a priority."[8]

As Kathleen Davis notes, the Preface to the *Pastoral Care* asserts that "Alfred's role as a translator is also a negotiation of his role as a spiritual and secular leader."[9] Alfred's Preface affirms his roles as moral guide and translator precisely because they are not roles automatically attached to Anglo-Saxon kingship.[10] The Preface to the *Pastoral Care* links Alfred's kingship and translation to make support for one into support for the other. Although this Preface explicitly addresses bishops (each named in his own copy of the text), the program as a whole envisions a broader audience. The translations were not executed solely for the bishops. Alfred declares that the program will translate "sumæ bec, ða ðe niedbeðearfosta sien eallum monnum to wiotonne" ("some books, which are the most necessary for all men to know," *PC* 7.6–7)[11] and requires the education of "eall sio gioguð ðe nu is on Angelcynne friora monna, ðara ðe ða speda hæbben ðæt hie ðæm befeolan mægen" ("all the youth of free men which are now in England, who have the means and ability [*sped*] that they might devote themselves to it," *PC* 7.10–1).[12] The program prepares not only a clerical but also a lay audience to read these new English books. Those lay readers with leisure and means to acquire learning and materials would be the leaders and future leaders of Wessex—the *recceras* or "rulers" addressed throughout the *Pastoral Care.* Some few of Alfred's readers would be those learned bishops or monks who might avail themselves of his translations to read a difficult Latin text more quickly or to help less experienced pupils. A few others would progress through these English texts into the study of Latin and might eventually read the source texts. Most of Alfred's audience, however, would never encounter his source texts in the original Latin.[13]

Alfred needed to establish his authority as a writer and translator, then, for an audience that could include a few Latinists, but would primarily comprise clergy with poor Latinity and lay nobles. His strategies of translation drew on the high status of the Latin language and of his source texts to invest both his own work as translator and the developing medium of Old English prose with prestige and authority. He demonstrated thorough knowledge of the source text, Christian Latin traditions, and his own native language and literature, a display that should impress everyone from expert Latinists to neophyte readers of their native tongue. Every page of his translations displays his knowledge of Latin and opens an otherwise inaccessible text to a broader audience. The act of translation, moreover, engages in what Bourdieu calls "a strategy of condescension": even though Alfred knows Latin, he deigns to work in the vernacular for his people, much as the mayor of Béarn, in Bourdieu's example, speaks to his villagers in the local dialect not because he does not know French, but to demonstrate his ability and willingness to negate the hierarchy that elevates him above his people—although, as Bourdieu notes, the temporary negation ultimately reinforces the hierarchy.[14] Alfred works in the vernacular context both linguistically and at higher levels of the text: he injects Anglo-Saxon images and references to make his text more acceptable to his readers.

Not only must Alfred authorize himself, but he must also authorize his language. Bourdieu writes:

> only when the making of the "nation," an entirely abstract group based on law, creates new usages and functions does it become indispensible to forge a *standard* language, impersonal and anonymous like the official uses it has to serve, and by the same token to undertake the work of normalizing the products of the linguistic habitus.... The *normalized* language is capable of functioning outside the constraints and without the assistance of the situation, and is suitable for transmitting and decoding by any sender and receiver, who may know nothing of one another.[15]

Similarly, André Lefevere and Susan Bassnett write, "Translation...becomes one of the means by which a new nation proves itself, shows that its language is capable of rendering what is rendered in more prestigious languages....Translation, in this case, amounts to a seizure of power...."[16] Alfred's concerns for legitimating his writing and for more "bureaucratic" matters of kingship go hand in hand. Surely Alfred did not conceive of building a nation in the same way that modern scholars do; however, that his texts envision one England, a land whose speakers share a language and a history, has been well established.[17] This "abstract group" of the English is constituted by a newly written law code, and Alfred's program would produce readers and some writers of official correspondence.

Language unites Anglo-Saxons, but with great variations in style and dialect. Alfred began the process of establishing an official language. The process would not end with him; only later can we speak of a standard Old English.[18] Yet even as he authorizes himself as translator, Alfred begins to establish a legitimate language, adding to the cultural capital of his people. Indeed, his dual role as translator and king gives him unique authority to create this language as well as impetus to do so. Kathleen Davis argues that:

> Alfred never considers that the vernacular might be inappropriate or inferior, but suggests that Latin was retained only because "woldon ðæt her ðy mara wisdom on londe wære ðy we ma geðeoda cuðon" [they would have it that the more languages we knew, the greater would be wisdom in this land] (5,24–25). According to this formulation, translation is necessary, but it is not an unfortunate compromise. Rather, the English vernacular stands as one among many legitimate languages. . . .[19]

The Preface to the *Pastoral Care* indeed conveys the sense of English as a legitimate language, but this sense results from a strategy itself. As Bourdieu argues, struggle over definition and boundaries are key components of any field;[20] in writing his text, Alfred silently extends the boundaries of both written texts and religious discourse to the vernacular. Alfred could not help but be aware of the very different status English held from Latin and the risks of translating revered texts. Even as it asserts the value of the English language, the Preface reflects the association of Latin with learning, wisdom, and wealth. Alfred imagines the reason learned men did not translate texts in England's past: "Hie ne wendon ðætte æfre menn sceolden swæ reccelease weorðan and sio lar swæ oðfeallan . . ." ("They did not think that ever men should become so reckless and learning fall so far . . . ," 5.22–23). The languages he associates with learning are Hebrew, Greek, and Latin (7.1–3). He names no vernaculars except English because vernaculars do not have the same standing; his translations seek to attain that status for English. As Robert Stanton argues, "English as a literary language was born out of a program of translation, and defined itself largely in terms of differences between itself and the Latin language."[21] Stanton describes the age of Ælfric, a century after Alfred, as "a time when English is establishing itself as a written vernacular alongside the older, more prestigious tradition of Anglo-Latin religious writing."[22]

Alfred started a process of legitimation that was still not complete in Ælfric's time—and indeed would not be completed for many centuries. Yet

Alfred avoided explicitly acknowledging the inferior status of English to change that status. As a result, according to Stanton, "The stylistic innovations wrought by the ninth-century translators, including Alfred, helped to define English as a language of eloquence, worthy to be used not only for translations but for original composition too, as with Alfred's law-code."[23] As a king making his mark in a field that clerics dominated, Alfred could use the difference of English to his own advantage. Bourdieu writes, "the initiative of change falls almost by definition on the newcomers . . . in a universe in which to exist is to differ, i.e. to occupy a distinct, distinctive position, they must assert their difference, get it known and recognized . . . by endeavouring to impose new modes of thought and expression."[24] At the same time, Alfred's position as a king gave him the capital and confidence to take risks.[25] Alfred's assertion of English as a language that could convey authority helped him to stake out his own position in the field: he was not simply a Latin writer who had somehow missed being a cleric, he was a new kind of writer who simultaneously laid claim to tradition.

Bourdieu's ideas on legitimate language are especially challenging in the early Anglo-Saxon context, because his work concerns the way agents relate to an existing legitimate or official language. Alfred, however, must negotiate between existing norms of legitimacy drawn from a foreign language (Latin prose) and a different genre (Old English poetry), then craft a new legitimate prose vernacular for himself and his readers. This new language not only employs existing Old English vocabulary and grammar much more than it imports words and syntax from Latin, but it also draws heavily on Christian terms and imagery that may already have become established in English through poetry.

Alfred established a legitimate language through a series of strategies. Bourdieu uses the notion of "strategy" to avoid that of "rules," a rigid concept that neglects the element of time in human behavior. The term *strategy* recognizes the existence of a range of possible responses to problems within any given society; some may be more effective than others, but people within a society may choose from an array of options. Society limits the choice of strategies: what each individual considers possible and likely to succeed reflects what other individuals have done (and thus made conceivable) and what society accepts. At the same time, an individual chooses strategies. Bourdieu rejects a strong distinction between conscious and unconscious choice in strategy by referring to "habitus," an inculcated, "practical sense" or "feel for the game" of which speech and acts are appropriate and profitable to the individual in a particular society.[26] Davis argues against "assum[ing] Alfred's ability to escape and manipulate his own ideological framework."[27] Although Alfred indeed could not share a postmodern perspective on his era, he could not be blind to his own situation and that of his people. He was aware of different models other Anglo-Saxon kings followed as well as the Carolingians' modes of ruling and writing.[28] Bourdieu's idea of habitus avoids the problem because agents need not escape or fully recognize their "own ideological framework" to craft effective strategies within it, as Alfred does.[29] Although people do not consciously calculate every possible consequence of their choices in the way a computer selects chess moves, they do not simply behave reflexively either. How, when, and what an individual speaks, and thus how he or she enters into the social and cultural marketplace of a particular field, are matters of strategy.

All translators need strategies to negotiate between the source language and the target language. Translation Studies uses the terms *adequacy* and *acceptability* to describe how close to each of the languages and cultures an element of translation comes. *Adequacy* is the degree to which a translated text reflects its source at any level from that of vocabulary, style, and syntax to imagery, structures, and themes. *Acceptability* is the degree to which the work matches standards to which native texts are held, again ranging from vocabulary to higher structural and conceptual levels. Using similar terminology, Bourdieu explains, "The definition of acceptability is found not in the situation but in the relationship between a market and a habitus. . . ."[30]A translation may be more "adequate" to the source text in that it is a closer rendering, but to that extent it may be less "acceptable" to its audience, not reflecting native norms. On the other hand, a translator may choose a strategy that produces a less adequate text but one that is more acceptable to the readers or hearers. Alfred maintains substantial adequacy to the overall structure and most of the major arguments of the *Boethius*, but his linguistic choices reflect concern for Anglo-Saxon acceptability. The king also borrows several ideas and images from other Latin Christian texts, a third context in which the *Boethius* partakes, to forge a distinctive new English prose.

Alfred not only secures authority for himself and begins to craft a legitimate language for Old English prose, using his own West Saxon dialect as the basis for the legitimate language, but he also offers his readers valuable cultural capital. According to Bourdieu, social space is "constructed in such a way that agents or groups are distributed in it according to their position . . . based on the *two principles of differentiation* . . . economic capital and cultural capital."[31] Modern readers recognize economic capital as the possession of money and other financial goods that can be enjoyed or exchanged for other goods and services. Cultural capital likewise is the possession of commodities that can be enjoyed or exchanged for something else, but in this case the commodities are intellectual: one can trade on knowledge of certain subjects to secure a job or entrée into fashionable circles or, indeed, to establish the authority to speak. One must expend time and energy to acquire this capital, and then to demonstrate that one has it, in order to gain the things it can buy. One need not always spend capital for gain, just as a wealthy individual can command services simply by stepping into a casino without laying a single wager. On the other hand, one who spreads certain pieces of information—cultural capital—until they become common knowledge has spent that part of his or her capital and cannot keep using those pieces for his or her advantage.

Alfred invests cultural capital, drawn mainly from Latin, in his translations. The value of his cultural capital diminishes to the extent that he makes it more widely available, but from this expenditure he gains symbolic capital: recognition of his mastery of learning. His expenditure of time, labor, and capital helps both to establish his authority to speak in this literary and spiritual field and to enrich his audience with cultural capital. This study focuses on the *Boethius* because that text exhibits the full range of Alfred's strategies. Boethius's Latin *De consolatione philosophiae* is a difficult philosophical work and a prosimetrum, a text comprised of alternating prose and verse sections, testing Alfred's vocabulary, stylistic control, and understanding in Latin and Old English. The Latin text is never explicitly Christian but is in accord with Christian views; for the translation, Alfred draws on other Latin texts for Christian allusions and ideas to make the text more acceptable to his audience of Christian Anglo-Saxons. Alfred often explains classical allusions for his audience in more familiar or narrative terms. The *Boethius* becomes, in Alfred's hands, an encyclopedic text offering readers broad exposure to Roman mythology, history, and science; Christian theology and imagery; and a new Old English prose style.

The *Boethius* gave readers even more than they may have realized. While they learned, audiences would also be steeped in a model of society that Alfred valued. This model owed much to Gregory the Great, who emphasized the spiritual and eternal over the worldly and transitory but did not reject the latter entirely. Earthly rulers needed to use earthly goods and honors to fulfill their duties and lead their subjects to the higher kingdom. Furthermore, in Alfred's model, they needed exactly the kinds of knowledge and skills that his translations offered, ranging from practical advice for rulers (*Pastoral Care*) to an understanding of the nature and true home of the soul (*Soliloquies*). Rule is a responsibility rather than a right or even a privilege—and a responsibility owed ultimately to God. The translations thus seek to inculcate a certain habitus in readers, a certain disposition toward ruling and their own social roles. Not coincidentally, Alfred himself would be the very image of the ruler in this model, and his subordinates would do well to follow his lead. By reading the text, readers accept Alfred's authority in the field, making a place for him among the learned Latinists who dominate it.

The *Boethius*, then, provides rich opportunities for study of Alfred's strategies of translation. The text itself poses some problems. The *Boethius* exists today in two manuscripts. N. R. Ker dates manuscript C, Cotton Otho A.vi, to the mid-tenth century.[32] This manuscript contains a translation of the prose portions of the Latin source text into prose and the meters into Old English alliterative verse. The manuscript maintains the order of the source text, alternating prose and verse (although all modern editions to date put the verse sections together at the end of the text). It fell victim to the Cotton Library fire of 1731, and Walter John Sedgefield describes its condition thus:

> About three-quarters of the whole remain, mostly legible, though some leaves can only be properly read in a good light, and for a few even direct sunlight is necessary. The leaves vary in size from charred fragments a square inch or so in area to almost perfect specimens; but not one has quite escaped the action of fire or water. It seems that the latter element is responsible for most of the obliteration. . . .[33]

Although electric light has replaced "direct sunlight," Sedgefield's description remains accurate. Ker describes the script as "a well-formed Anglo-Saxon minuscule" in a single hand. The text is divided into books but not chapters, and each Old English Meter starts with a new line and space for an initial capital that was never written.[34]

Ker dates manuscript B, Oxford Bodleian Library Bodley 180, to the early twelfth century. It is divided into 42 chapters and contains initials in red, blue, purple, and occasionally green at the starts of chapters. A table of contents appears at the start and a prayer at the end.[35] Ker notes that the manuscript is "not well written" and that some of the letters are roughly formed. Although the manuscript is later, the text may be earlier because it contains only prose versions of the Meters, even though it contains as well a prose preface that refers to the composition of the Meters: "Ða bisgu us sint swiþe earforþrime þe on his dagum on þa ricu becoman þe he underfangen hæfde, 7 þeah ða þas boc hæfde geleornode 7 of lædene to engliscum spelle gewende, 7 geworhte hi eft to leoðe, swa swa heo nu gedon is. . . ." ("The cares which in his day came to the kingdom which he had undertaken were difficult to count, and yet he learned this book and translated it from Latin into English discourse, and then he worked it into song, as it is now done . . .," 6–10).

Other evidence for the text includes the Junius transcript of the B text and the C Meters, now the only testimony for some of the damaged parts of the C text.[36] Arthur S. Napier discovered a fragment from another manuscript in 1886 and his transcript was printed in 1887, but the fragment had been lost by the time Sedgefield made his edition.[37] Wanley mentioned a manuscript that Bishop Leofric presented to Exeter Cathedral in the eleventh century, but today whether this manuscript was one of the two now extant, the missing fragment, or one since lost is unclear.[38]

Walter Sedgefield's 1899 edition includes the prose found in both manuscripts and both the prose and the verse versions of the meters. For the purely prose portion, Sedgefield used the C text, citing the B text in the footnotes (except for recurring spelling variations).[39] Where the C text is damaged, the B text is printed, and readings from the Junius transcript of the C text are given in footnotes.[40] Sedgefield alternates the prose version of the prose text from C with the prose version of the meters from B, and he prints the Old English Meters together at the end of the text from C, noting the assistance of the Junius transcript. The edition has undeniable shortcomings. Malcolm Godden argues that the decision to print the prose version of the meters from B with the prose portions of the text from C results in a "hybrid" text that did not actually exist for readers in the Anglo-Saxon period.[41] Modern readers do not encounter the text the same way the original audience of either manuscript would have; as Godden notes:

> The new verse preface, the original introductory account in verse and then the first metre together mean that after the opening prose preface we have nearly 120 lines of verse before we return to prose, and then only twenty lines or so before we resume with verse. This is a work which announces itself, both in the prefaces and in the form of its opening, as a poem not a prose text.[42]

On the other hand, the existence of manuscript B demonstrates that an entirely prose version did circulate. In the absence of evidence against it, the tradition that the prose versions preceded Alfred's verse renditions deserves serious consideration. Sedgefield chose manuscript C as the earlier and more reliable witness to the original text, but used the form of B. Previous editions relied entirely on the B text plus the C Meters.[43] Two teams, led by Malcolm Godden and Kevin Kiernan, have begun working to produce, respectively, a new print edition and a CD-ROM containing images of the manuscripts themselves.[44] These welcome editions, expected within the next few years, will enhance the further exploration of the *Boethius* greatly, especially questions about the composition and relationship of the prose and the Meters. In the meantime, however, Sedgefield's edition continues to provide useful access to the text, and it is well suited to an investigation focusing on the prose translation.

This study is therefore based on Sedgefield's 1899 edition of the *Boethius*, supplemented by my own observations of microfilms and manuscripts B and C themselves and on Ludwig Bieler's edition of the *De consolatione*.[45] Although as yet we have no evidence for which manuscript Alfred used, the early texts of the *De consolatione* that Bieler edited have few and small discrepancies, indicating a relatively stable textual tradition, and the

Boethius matches the Latin very closely in many places.[46] Moreover, one of Bieler's base manuscripts, Vatican lat. 3363, is a ninth-century manuscript that Godden believes was produced in Wales, and later owned in England.[47]

The prose, not the Meters, form the basis of this study. The Meters represent a separate project of translation or transformation. The prose text is a translation from Latin into Old English; the Meters appear to transform Old English prose into Old English poetry.[48] Their authorship remains in some doubt. George Philip Krapp, in the introduction to his edition of the Meters, comments that the external evidence, style, and Proems all support Alfred's authorship, but none is conclusive.[49] The verse Proem's change of person at the end raises the possibility that Alfred and the translator are two separate people. Meter 26's use of "Þracia" three times for "Iþacige" would seem to indicate a versifier thought these the same, although Alfred knew better.[50] David Pratt writes, "If, *as seems likely*, the vernacular metres are not the work of Alfred himself, an anonymous poet seems to have versified the relevant prose sections in the first half of the tenth century."[51] If Alfred did not write them, their evidence could distort a study of his translation strategies. On the other hand, even if Alfred himself wrote them, as many now accept, his strategies would still differ from the prose. Intralingual more than interlingual translation would be at issue, but more important, the Meters would be subject to the well-established norms of Old English verse, not the norms being created for a new Old English prose.[52] The Meters pose a very different problem for the translator, one less revealing of cultural contacts and interaction between languages than the prose translation.

And it is these cultural contacts, and Alfred's interactions among them and with his audience, that this study seeks to illuminate.[53] In writing the *Boethius*, Alfred negotiates among three cultural contexts to authorize himself and appeal to readers: a Neoplatonic source text, Christian Latin traditions, and Anglo-Saxon expectations concerning language, religion, and literature. Chapter 1 explores the way Alfred maintained adequacy to the source text both to secure his own authority as translator and to make the wealth of difficult materials in the *De consolatione* available to his readers, who could then master cultural capital ranging from specific facts to a mode of reading new to them. Chapter 2 turns to Alfred's deployment of Christian Latin traditions, from which he selected those strands most useful for explicating the text—and most amenable to the values he sought to encourage in his readers, the current and future leaders of his people. Chapter 3 focuses on Alfred's use of native Anglo-Saxon elements of language and literature to make the text acceptable and accessible to his readers; and again, how his selection of elements reflected and reinforced particular values. The final chapter examines the confluence of these various contexts and strategies, illuminating the way Alfred wove these strands into a unified and effective text designed to inculcate an Alfredian model of society into his readers. At each stage, I read the *Boethius* both as a literary and as a political text. This unparalleled text imparts difficult philosophy in more accessible language with the help of fascinating imagery and anecdotes. Yet it also offers a model for Anglo-Saxon society in which its Christian leaders have the habitus, the knowledge, wisdom, and will to serve their people not only legally and martially, but also spiritually. The *Boethius* presents readers now, as it did in the days of Alfred and the years that followed, with a tremendously rich text. Let us now enter that hoard.

Chapter 1

Treasures from the Latin Hoard

Alfred's *Boethius* negotiates a deep cultural divide. The *De consolatione philosophiae* relies on familiarity with mythology, history, science, and philosophy that Alfred's readers simply did not possess. Because of the great differences between the source audience and the new target audience, changes in the text should come as no surprise. Yet the *Boethius* retains a wealth of classical and late-antique allusions and scientific ideas, a dialogue form popular centuries earlier, and much of a chain of arguments that followed a logic no longer strictly taught. The *Boethius* thus remains adequate to the *De consolatione* at several levels.

Alfred's strategic adequacy served first to authorize writer and text. The authority of a warrior-king, even once he had established it against foes both foreign and domestic, did not automatically translate into authority in the role of philosopher-translator; this was a different field and required a different form of capital. As the language of learning and religion, and one that had relatively standard grammar and spelling, Latin was the only "legitimate language," in Bourdieu's terminology. Bourdieu explains how French became "officielle"—both "official" and "formal"—in conjunction with the state: the legitimate language provided a measure against which dialects and solecisms could be found wanting and a means by which the less educated could be excluded.[1] In Alfred's England, the vernacular lacked standardization and had dialects; Old English had no legitimate form.[2] An author could not draw on an official form of Old English to legitimize his or her text as much later writers and speakers of vernaculars routinely do. Only Latin provided a standard by which to gauge good usage, and Carolingian writers viewed it as a valuable measure. Charlemagne's decrees sought to standardize language, especially the text of the Bible.[3] Yet for Alfred, Latin was not a viable option. Not enough of his people knew it.[4] Moreover, no evidence exists that philosophical or theological works had been composed in Old English before Alfred, and few works of any kind had been translated by the time Alfred wrote the *Boethius*. Old English had developed a poetic vocabulary, but Alfred did not use it much in his prose.

Both the *De consolatione* and the *Boethius* use the rhetorical and literary resources of the dialogue form, imagery, and stylistic variation to convey philosophical and religious ideas. Thus Alfred had to establish his authority, and the usefulness of his language, in the combined literary and spiritual field into which the *Boethius* entered. Universities did not exist to set credentials in Alfred's era; the church controlled the field, and members of the clergy dominated the production of spiritual literature.[5] A very small number of clerical readers would have some acquaintance with either late-antique literature or the specific source text; finding material in the translation that corresponded to norms of late-antique literature or to the *De consolatione* itself would inspire confidence in the text and its translator. Although few, these learned readers would carry great authority. Their attestation of Alfred's mastery of the Latin text would not survive in written form, but must have carried weight with some readers. As Bourdieu argues, unwritten sources of information, even rumors and gossip, play a role in shaping written fields as surely as writing itself because readers are formed by oral sources even more than by the texts they read.[6] In effect, Alfred's *Boethius* attempts to redefine the field, opening the category of Latin literary and philosophical works to include Old English literary and philosophical works.[7]

Most readers, however, would be unable to compare the Latin to the *Boethius*. Alfred's program of translation and education aimed at "eall sio giogud ðe nu is on Angelcynne friora monna, ðara ðe ða speda hæbben ðæt hie ðæm befeolan mægen" ("all the youth of free men which are now in England, who have the means and opportunity[8] that they might devote themselves to it," *PC* 7.10–1). Those with intellectual ability but no time could not be educated; a student was to be taught only "ða hwile ðe hie to nanre oðerre note ne mægen" ("as long as he is not capable of other employment," 7.12). The requirement for leisure assumed high birth; the expensive materials of tablets, writing implements, and perhaps even books, also point to a well-born audience. This program excluded men who were unfree or lacked means and opportunity, and women.[9] Thus Alfred's primary audience would be nobly born boys or young men, most lay but some destined for the clergy; they would not have a background in Latin or late-antique literature. Seeing unfamiliar textual elements handled consistently over a long text, however, they could conclude that Alfred followed the source text's ideas and usages. Alfred established his place in the literary field and, paradoxically, the usefulness of his West Saxon language, from his systematic adherence to Latin norms.

In the nineteenth century, Bourdieu finds "three competing principles of legitimacy" operating in fields: a specific legitimacy granted by other writers in an autonomous field, a bourgeois "consecration", and a popular "consecration."[10] In Alfred's era, the competing principles were somewhat different: educated churchmen comprised one small audience that might bestow legitimacy, whereas the high-born, mostly lay, originally illiterate audience Alfred sought to educate might also consecrate works using different criteria. Alfred's combination of Christian discourse with Old English reaches out to both groups.

The readers stood to gain cultural capital from the translation. The *Boethius* offers a compact library of Roman history, geography, science, theology, and philosophy. Alfred's retention of proper nouns helps to introduce these well-born readers (and future rulers) to mythology, history, and even science. The oral transmission of some of this information to nonreaders (hearers or relatives of readers) may have occurred as well. The adequacy of his imagery and dialogic structure does a less obvious service to new readers: Alfred's translation helps them learn to negotiate a text that still retains characteristics of difficult but important Latin texts. Finally, Alfred preserves the overall flow of arguments and themes, both in the general progression of arguments in both works and the specific case of the definition of eternity. Anglo-Saxon readers would not only gain specific knowledge, but also experience reading a complex and abstract text from a different milieu. Alfred's lay readers gained cultural and symbolic capital that could help equalize them with the clerical authorities who controlled Latin texts; now readers of the vernacular had access to information and strategies of speech and argumentation previously available only in Latin. According to Asser, Alfred required the *comites, praepositi*, and *ministri* (ealdormen, reeves, and thegns) to learn to read or get a son or trusted servant to read for them if they were to maintain their position.[11] Thus Alfred put the weight of his authority as king behind his authority as writer. The program may also have provided a way to ensure that those who held important posts were obedient to Alfred's orders, and it may to some extent have replaced an unlettered old guard with younger men literate in their native tongue. Clerical readers with poor Latin might also benefit, within the church or in service to the king, as their cultural and symbolic capital increased. All who learned to read would in turn owe any advancement and even confidence they gained from reading to King Alfred.

Alfred used the spoken language that readers already understood to initiate them into written texts. Acceptability to his audience governed Alfred's decisions more than adequacy does at the most basic textual level: the individual word.[12] Loan-words are often an important feature of translation in general, and they are most common when one culture has just begun translating from another.[13] Yet the *Boethius* uses very few Latin words. A few specifically Christian words include forms of *cristen, engel, papa, martyr,* and *arianisc*; these do not appear in the source text.[14] From the *De consolatione*, Alfred borrows several Roman political terms: *læden; consul*; the common *Rome, roman*, and related forms; and *casere or kasere*.[15] Three words name African and Asian animals: *leo, tigris*, and *elpend*.[16] Scattered other loan-words occur: *must, rosa, capitula, magister, gigant*.[17] *Æfweardnesse* and *þiofscole* appear to be calques, drawing at least one element from Latin.[18] For such a lengthy translation, however (142 pages in Sedgefield's edition), the *Boethius* has a very small set of loan-words. All these words are found elsewhere in Old English (although some are rarer than others); Alfred is not introducing any of the words to the language. The king relies heavily on words his audience would already know and exceedingly little on foreign words. Syntax and style also generally reflect developing Old English norms rather than Latin ones.[19] Alfred's handling of the most basic levels of vocabulary and grammar, then, generally reflect acceptability to his audience rather than adequacy. By making most of the language acceptable, Alfred relieves some of the inevitable conflict between native and foreign norms: his readers will encounter many new names, ideas, and rhetorical strategies, but he makes the text readable even if it remains difficult.

The *Boethius*'s handling of proper nouns thus contrasts with its treatment of other words.[20] Proper nouns from the source text almost always remain easily recognizable, although Alfred alters a few spellings in accord with Anglo-Saxon norms and does not use Latin declensions.[21] Alfred retains many Latin names. Sixty-six of the occurrences of proper nouns in the Old English come directly from the Latin text.[22] Seventy-three occurences of proper nouns are new to the Old English, nearly all to supply information that the late-antique audience of the *De consolatione* would already have known.[23] Most additions involve allusions clear only to highly educated readers; for instance, where Boethius gives a seven-line description of a season without naming it (I met. vi. 1–7), Alfred simply has "Agustes monðe" (12.7); where Boethius has "tergeminus . . . ianitor" (III met. xii. 29–30) Alfred names Cerberus (102.14).[24] Many of the added names gloss other names in the text, such as when Alfred keeps the name "Aetnae" (II pr. vi. 1) from the Latin text and adds "þam munte þe Ætne hatte, on þam ieglande þe Sicilia hatte" ("on the mountain that is called Aetna, on the island that is called Sicily," 34.8–9).[25]

Alfred does not blindly retain proper nouns from his source text; he invests labor in adding glosses ranging from a word to entire independent clauses. His retention of proper nouns indicates respect for the Boethius's text and in turn commands respect for the translation: the unfamiliar names promise fidelity to the source text. Alfred could have omitted or changed most names because they occur in illustrations. At one point he substitutes Weland for the source text's reference to Fabricius, demonstrating his skill with the strategy of replacement.[26] Yet Alfred often did not choose deletion and rarely used replacement, although either is easier than glossing.

By retaining and glossing so many proper nouns, Alfred increased both the prestige of his text (and therefore his own symbolic capital) and the cultural capital of his people. Alfred legitimated his language and his text by drawing clearly and overtly on the one legitimate language available, although he did not write in that language. He demonstrated that he was highly conversant with Latin, even where difficult matters of mythology, history, or science were involved. To the rare readers who had some acquaintance with the Latin text, that Alfred brought his own knowledge to bear on the Latin text would be clear. To the majority of readers, who lacked access to the Latin text, word of Alfred's investment might come from recommendations by those would could recognize it. Less learned readers would also recognize Alfred's comfort with unfamiliar names and references, and the high expectations he had of his audience.

Alfred's treatment of proper nouns not only legitimizes the translation, but it also introduces readers to classical mythology. Most of its mythological references appear in two meters, the Orpheus meter (101.19–103.21/III met. xii) and the Ulysses meter (115.12–116.34/IV met. iii). Alfred glosses both meters to explain several names and circumstances, but he keeps the main narratives intact. In addition to Christian interpretations of these stories, Alfred adds clear warnings that each meter is a "leasan spell" ("lying story," 103.14; see also 116.13 and .16) so that his audience did not understand them literally.[27] Boethius's original readers needed no such warning. These cautions also guide readers through other passages. Hercules (Erculus) is mentioned twice (36.33 and 127.11), both times as the son of Jove (Iob); thus when readers learn that Iob and Saturn (Saturnus, Iob's father) are also the figments of "leasunga" ("falsehoods," 99.4), they are prepared to consider all these references to Roman heroes and gods as no more truthful than stories of Orpheus and Ulysses.

The *Boethius* teaches its readers how to understand references to the classical pantheon and Greek and Roman heroes. Readers of the text acquired a small store of mythological knowledge, a framework into which they could put later additions to that hoard, and the tools to understand the mythological stories they encountered, not as fantastic tales from a distant world, but as moral stories relevant to their own lives and responsibilities. The *Boethius* not only offers cultural capital, it also inculcates the correct way to use this capital—a specific mode of reading. As Bourdieu writes, "Any legitimate work tends in fact to impose the norms of its own perception and tacitly defines as the only legitimate mode of perception the one which brings into play a certain disposition and a certain competence."[28] The ability to read correctly sets the reader apart from others, even as the ability to be read correctly sets the work apart. The demands the *Boethius* makes on its audience bestow privileged status on both text and readers even as the readers acquire a habitus of proper Christian reading. Alfred prepares readers in modes of thinking that had previously been a clerical monopoly.[29]

Alfred prizes history more than mythology as cultural capital. Names of figures in the distant past and of gods, winds, and constellations are occasionally discarded, particularly where Boethius uses them figuratively, but Alfred keeps many place names and most names of historical figures.[30] This practice accords well with his complaint that scribal error has caused men to lose their proper fame: "hi for heora slæwðe 7 for gimeleste 7 eac for recceleste forleton unwriten þara monna ðeawas 7 hiora dæda, þe on hiora dagum formæroste 7 weorðgeornuste wæron" ("On account of their sloth and carelessness and even recklessness [scribes] leave unwritten the behavior and deeds of men who in their days were most famous and most eager for glory," 44.2–4).[31] Alfred could only make such an accusation if he had taken care with most historical names himself.

Alfred's investment in glossing historical names would enable readers of the *Boethius* to make the acquaintance of historical figures from Tarquin to Nero.[32] Although the *Boethius* itself offers no sense of chronology, it would enable readers to recognize certain classical historical figures and their most famous (or infamous) deeds. The *Boethius* could thereby whet readers' appetite for the *Orosius.* If readers had already encountered the *Orosius*, these names would remind them of what they had already learned.[33] In either case, readers who found names they had learned from one text in another would see some profit from the time that they invested in the first text. Similarly, the *Boethius* offers the names of several classical writers.[34] Few or no Anglo-Saxon readers would encounter the works of Homer, Aristotle, or Plato, even in excerpts translated into Latin, but they could find further mentions of these authorities. They would be slightly more likely to encounter the works of Cicero and Virgil. Although the *Boethius* could not begin to offer its readers mastery of classical literature, it could offer them a sense of acquaintance. This pleasure of recognition rewards readers for work already done and promises future rewards as well. As Bourdieu explains, while readers become increasingly comfortable with texts and specific references and ideas those texts contain, they remain aware that most of their contemporaries lack the skills and knowledge they enjoy. They feel a sense of accomplishment in their ability to recognize and use names and concepts.[35] Readers also feel an investment in the text and so have a stake in believing in the authority and usefulness of Alfred's translation and language.

In addition to introducing readers to classical literature and history, the *Boethius* teaches natural science. The text names the four elements and explains their natural tendency to discord and the way God's power and love bind them together in several places. Although some of these explanations expand or repeat material from the source text, none are pure additions; all derive from the *De consolatione*.[36] Likewise, the *Boethius* offers observations about the weather and seasons; instructs readers about astronomy and cosmology; and teaches comparative physiology and psychology of plants, animals, and humans.[37] The *Boethius* exposes readers to some basic scientific terms and concepts, providing a foundation in classical scientific discourse.

Alfred thus not only asserted his ability to transmit Latin lore, he also gave readers entry into previously closed fields of discourse: classical mythology, Roman history, and the natural sciences. Providing this entrée did not much diminish Alfred's own dominance of these corners of the cultural market; even as he gave access to specialized learning, he clearly controlled that access. Adequacy in this regard strengthened Alfred's literary and linguistic authority, and the cultural capital whose monopoly Alfred relinquished by making it more widely available bought him symbolic capital in turn. The classical learning that readers acquired from the *Boethius* might not by itself make them successful. Yet it offered them encouragement and directions for future acquisitions. Most important, Alfred's own court valued this capital, providing a marketplace for those who had acquired the knowledge and skills that the books offered. Alfred set the standards and supplied the education, training future nobles and clerics in particular ways of thinking that he could then expect at court.

The *Boethius* did not simply hold out facts as capital. Both the Latin and Old English texts are rich in imagery, and Alfred frequently retains illustrations from his source text, although he sometimes develops his own metaphors. Again, adequacy underscores Alfred's authority by demonstrating his mastery of the source text and language even as it offers admittance to Latin literary culture, providing new readers with a stock of metaphors and the skills to understand them. In our technological age these may not seem to be useful skills, but when a king's court begins to value literature, being conversant with literature becomes very practical (much as when a U.S. president enjoys running, journalists buy track shoes and get in shape).[38]

Alfred keeps two key illustrations that would be unfamiliar to much of to his audience.[39] The first comes from the portion of the text that Alfred has most heavily abridged; he did not merely keep the image because it was there. Philosophy describes a rich library:

> non tam me loci huius quam tua facies mouet nec bibliothecae potius comptos ebore ac uitro parietes quam tuae mentis sedem requiro, in qua non libros sed id quod libris pretium facit, librorum quondam meorum sententias collocaui. (I pr. v. 6)

> Not so much this place as your appearance moves me; nor do I require a library with walls covered in ebony and glass but rather your mind as

> a seat, in which I once collected my teachings, not in books but in what makes the books precious.

The Old English sets a similar scene:

> ne me na ne lyst mid glase geworhtra waga ne heahsetla mid golde 7 mid gimmum gerenodra, ne boca mid golde awritenra me swa swiðe ne lyst swa me lyst on þe rihtes willan. Ne sece ic no her þa bec, ac þæt ðæt þa bec forstent, ðæt is, þin gewit. (11.26–30)
>
> Nor do walls worked with glass please me, or high seats ornamented with gold and with gems, nor do books written with gold please me as much as your right will pleases me. I do not seek here books, but what understands the books, that is, your mind.

Alfred adds fresh details appealing to Anglo-Saxons' love of treasure, but the concept of a library as a lavishly appointed room set aside for books would be foreign to his readers. The vivid image conveys effectively the value placed on learning, both in the form of rich books and in the form of what they confer on their readers. Cultural capital is associated with economic capital in the image of the library; a room fitted with glass, gold, and gems and set aside for reading would be the stuff of dreams for Anglo-Saxon readers. Yet, shockingly, Wisdom rejects the enticing physical setting in favor of the more valuable knowledge that lies inside the books—and the reader's mind. The image places an almost tangible value on the work that Alfred and his readers do in their engagement with the text, associating the more abstract cultural capital with highly desirable economic capital. Although Anglo-Saxons would not theorize the connection in the way Bourdieu does, the image of the library makes a powerful if implicit argument for the convertibility of cultural and economic capital.[40]

Even more surprising, Alfred chooses to keep a brief and obscure reference to late-antique disciplines. At one point Philosophy/Wisdom associates certain talents with certain professions: "sic musica quidem musicos, medicina medicos, rhetorica rhetores facit" ("so indeed music makes musicians, medicine doctors, rhetoric rhetoricians," II pr. vi. 17). The first two professions would be familiar enough to Anglo-Saxon audiences, but not the third. Alfred could have transformed it into something familiar, such as homilists preaching, but instead he keeps the rhetoricians: "Swa mæg eac se dreamcræft ðæt se mon bið dreamere, 7 se læcecræft þæt he bið læce, 7 seo racu deð þæt he bið reccere" ("So may also the art of music make a man a musician, and leechcraft a leech, and argumentation a rhetorician," 38.6–8).

Not only does this image demonstrate Alfred's faithfulness to his text, but the specific illustration also underlines Alfred's authority. Those few readers familiar with Augustine would recognize rhetoric and the figure of the rhetorician from late-antique learning.[41] Alfred's use of learned terms places his discourse within a patristic context. Bourdieu describes how the Homeric orator held the *skeptron* to demonstrate his authority to speak.[42] A writer too needs some form of authorization, and the use of recognized, authoritative discourse provides a symbolic *skeptron. Reccere* means both rhetorician and ruler; in this image, a *reccere* is learned in argumentation. The metaphor links Alfred's hard-won authorization as ruler in political and military matters with the less certain religious or rhetorical authority, securing both to Alfred. In Alfred's hands, the illustration proposes a connection between ruling and learning; it hints that Alfred is uniquely qualified to write this translation and that the learning that his translation demonstrates makes him uniquely qualified to rule. Even readers unfamiliar with Augustine could see the paronomasia that equated ruling with speaking well and suggested that the great warrior-king should be an equally great translator.

The impression of the authorized translator is borne out by the appearance of other important images from the source text, these more familiar to Anglo-Saxon audiences.[43] The recurring image of the doctor acts as an example of a particular skill or kind of knowledge as well as an illustration of the narrator's state as a sick man in need of the medicine of Philosophy/Wisdom.[44] Readers already initiated into late-antique Latin literature, directly or in translations, would recognize the image of the doctor as a favorite of Augustine and Gregory and feel the pleasure of recognition.[45] Readers who had not yet been initiated into Latin literature could enjoy the same pleasure later on finding the image in the Old English *Pastoral Care, Dialogues*, or *Soliloquies.*[46] Another Latin motif running through both texts is that of the spark or light as an image for knowledge and truth.[47] The connection of Alfred himself with medicine and with light becomes almost mythical; Asser writes of Alfred's prayers both for illness and for healing (he sought a less debilitating illness to replace a more difficult one) and of Alfred's invention of special candles to tell time and special lanterns to keep these candles from blowing out.[48] His translation is not purely intellectual; it affects court life.

The imagery changes between the Latin text and the Old English, and a few alterations are quite striking and significant, as the alteration from concentric circles to a wagon wheel (129.19–131.27) and from a labyrinth to a wood (100.4–9). Yet Alfred rarely omits images, and often instead of adding new images he displaces, repeats, or anticipates ones from the source text. This strategy, like his retention of the original people and places featured in anecdotes, indicates respect for the text and a recognition that arguments cannot be easily separated from the illustrations that support them.[49] Although not all the illustrations would have the same particular strategic value as that of the rhetorician, maintaining the source text's illustrations allows Alfred to demonstrate repeatedly his mastery of a source text authorized by the prestige of its original writer, a saint. Alfred also educates his audience in the reading of imagery. Readers would gain familiarity with some of the common patristic images they would encounter in other Alfredian translations or, in the case of a select few, in Latin texts themselves. Again, adequacy served both Alfred and his readers, yielding symbolic capital for the king and his language, and cultural capital for his audience.

The *Boethius* is even more adequate to its source text in dialogic structure. Out of nearly 500 turns in dialogue, only a handful has been reassigned. Where Alfred has abridged the text, he has generally taken lines from both characters instead of shortening the dialogue allotted to one or collapsing exchanges into one long speech, both of which would have been easy translation solutions to use. The narrator has lost only three turns and gained six responses relative to Wisdom over the course of the text.[50] His role in the dialogue remains as active as in the Latin, but no more so overall; the additional turns are few and small enough that they help compensate for the loss of the autobiographical material in I pr. iv, but do not tip the balance of the dialogue. The narrator is still the learner and his interlocutor the authority figure and dominant speaker.

The narrator of the Old English text agrees a little more often than the narrator of the Latin. On a few occasions questions are turned into affirmations, as when "Quidni?" ("Why not?" III pr. iii. 10) becomes "Ic wat þæt þu soð segst, þæt ic hi hæfde" ("I know that you say the truth, that I had [earthly goods]," 59.15–16).[51] Sometimes the Old English narrator's agreement is more enthusiastic than in the Latin: "Minime, inquam" ("'Not at all,' I said," III pr. ix. 4) becomes "Þa andsworede ic eft 7 cwæð: Ne secge ic no þæt he nauhtes maran ne ðyrfe, forðæm ic wat þæt nan nis þæs welig þæt he sumes eacan ne þyrfe" ("Then I answered again and said: 'I do not say that he does not need anything more, because I know that there is none so wealthy that he has no need of some increase,'" 75.3–5).[52] At 52.21–8, part of Philosophy's speech (III pr. ii. 3) on the highest good is given to the narrator rather than Wisdom, making the narrator a more active participant in this part of the dialectic, an equal partner who can correctly anticipate Wisdom's next lesson (which Wisdom then repeats in agreement, 52.28–53.3).[53] One major expansion occurs at 40.10–41.6 (roughly II pr. vii. 1) where the narrator delivers his speech on the ruler's need for tools to work his *cræft*. In that passage the balance is shifted in favor of the narrator.

Occasionally, it is the Latin narrator who agrees more. Once the Latin narrator almost fawns (V pr. i. 6–7) where the Old English narrator speaks more plainly (140.1–2), and once the Old English narrator merely agrees (107.26–7) where the Latin narrator summarizes (IV pr. ii. 24).[54] Yet most alterations in the dialogue also do not shift the balance between the characters. Where arguments are omitted, both lose turns.[55] Only the omission of Boethius's defenses of himself in Book I are significant in terms of characterization, and this loss is compensated in the dialogue by the extra turns and expanded replies that the narrator receives. The substitution of a different and much shorter argument in favor of free will in Book V also does not change the balance; Philosophy dominates the Latin text here as heavily as Wisdom does the Old English.

The translation also follows the source text's frequent use of rhetorical questions in the dialogue. Sometimes rhetorical questions are answered in the text; when both Philosophy and Wisdom ask whether bad fortune does not benefit the recipient by revealing true and false friends (48.5–15/II pr. viii. 6), only Wisdom supplies an explicit answer: "Ic wat ðeah þæt ðu hit woldest habban mid miclan feo geboht þæt ðu hi cuðest wel toscadan" ("I know, however, that you would have paid with great treasure to be able to distinguish them," 48.15–7). Similarly, Wisdom answers his own question regarding whether an individual can bring his honor to other nations (63.18–9).[56] However, the Latin, too, sometimes answers its own rhetorical questions: "At cuius praemii? Omnium pulcherrimi maximique; memento etenim corollarii illius quod paulo ante praecipuum dedi ac sic collige" ("But what prize? The most beautiful and greatest of all; for recall especially that corollary that I gave you a little before and consider thus," IV pr. iii. 8).[57] As in his translation of the preceding passage, Alfred sometimes changes rhetorical questions into simple statements.[58] Overall the same impression is given: both texts use rhetorical questions heavily, and sometimes they even answer them.[59] Again, the translation is not exact, but Alfred compensates to achieve adequacy. Learned readers would recognize Alfred's achievement, whereas the less educated would gain practice negotiating a sometimes difficult literary form.

Seeing what has been changed in the dialogue is easier than determining how much remains the same. The text runs 142 pages in Sedgefield's edition. By contrast, the changes can be listed in a few paragraphs here. The *Boethius* offers the characters the same turns in dialogue that the source text does and generally the same sentiments; the translation maintains the structure and balance of the source text. Alfred initiates his readers into particular modes of thinking and even disputation.

The aspect of the *Boethius* that diverges most from the source text is its treatment of the specific arguments and themes of the source text. Many scholars have emphasized difference at the argumentative level. Most prominently, F. Anne Payne views Alfred's work as less than coherent due to "a discrepancy between thought and style, between Alfred's ideas and the form in which they are presented."[60] In her view, fundamental philosophical differences with the source text prevent adequacy: Boethius believes in order and eternity; Alfred believes in freedom and contingency.[61] Kurt Otten points out that Alfred avoids the question of free will raised in Book V, and he concludes that Boethius ends his work on a philosophical high note, whereas Alfred instead finishes with practical Christian commands, giving his work a less powerful, more popular ending.[62] Otten also writes that in general Alfred simplifies the arguments of his source.[63] Alfred indeed makes some arguments that are not in his source text at all, and a few of these do not fit comfortably with the source. The changes strike the modern reader of both texts more than what is kept the same, but the similarities are profound, especially given how difficult and unfamiliar some passages must have seemed to Anglo-Saxon readers. The bulk of the *Boethius* has clear roots in the *De consolatione*.[64]

Alfred does omit arguments, cutting thirteen major passages. The *Boethius* also includes several significant additions. Besides glosses of existing ideas and names, the Old English contributes new arguments, primarily about the use of goods.[65] Despite these changes, which later chapters will treat, the central arguments of the *De consolatione* remain clear in the translation, and most proceed in the same way as in the source text. To list all the elements of the *De consolatione* that remain in Alfred's *Boethius* would be tedious. Although Alfred has made some significant changes, he has retained a great portion of his source text. It may seem obvious to modern readers that a translation would follow the source text closely, but this was not in fact obvious to Anglo-Saxons, as evidenced by some other Anglo-Saxon translations. Alfred's own *Soliloquies* omits large portions of Book II and adds an entire third book culled from several sources.[66] The *Orosius* and the *Bede* make deep cuts as well; most notably, the *Bede* omits much of the Easter controversy and much of the Latin documentation of Bede's *Historia ecclesiastica*.[67] Moreover, poetic texts such as *Genesis* and *Exodus* take such great liberties with their source texts that many scholars hesitate to dub them translations—but that kind of translation was clearly a viable option for Anglo-Saxons, even with sacred, more prestigious texts than the *De consolatione*. That Alfred retains so much of the *De consolatione* is significant, particularly in light of all the explanations and excuses scholars have produced for Alfred's changes: the Latin is difficult, Old English had never been used for such a work before, the philosophy is difficult and uses technical language, the mode of argumentation is foreign. All those claims are true, yet Alfred has retained most of the source text's structure and argumentation in spite of them.

Omissions fit a strategic pattern, coming almost entirely from the start and end. Several passages in Book I, especially those concerning the narrator's own life, are abridged or deleted.[68] The omissions at the beginning suggest impatience to get to argument and disinterest in the details of Boethius's imprisonment. Books II–IV are treated with the greatest respect, even reverence. The only other major omission before Book V is of II met. i, on the wheel of Fortune, which has been compressed into a very brief earlier reference in the Old English. The omissions near the end, combined with Wisdom's worry that, "Gif wit þæt eall sculon tosmeagan, þonne cume wit late to ende þisse bec, oððe næfre" ("If we must consider all that, then we will come to the end of this book late or never," 148.4–6), imply that more than philosophical and literary pressures impinged on translation. Indeed, Alfred's most substantial alteration to the arguments in the source text come in V, where the treatment of free will is greatly altered.[69] His alterations do not change the main point, that human beings all have free will, only the means of getting there. Alfred treats his source text not as something sacred and unalterable, but as something deserving great respect. Additions appear not as impositions on the text but expansions of the rich material already present. Alfred entered into conversation with Boethius. The evenness of tone and form over the course of his text would make it seem unified to readers unfamiliar with the source. They would see not divergence, but one coherent text.[70]

One issue provides a useful case study demonstrating both how Alfred made minor changes and how the bulk of the argument remains the same despite great differences in vocabulary and culture. The distinction among different kinds of eternity, although it is a supporting argument, has been hotly debated by scholars. Some think Alfred did not accept Boethius's distinction between perpetuity (unending time) and eternity (being outside time). J. M. Wallace-Hadrill writes that he is uncertain Alfred understood Boethian concepts of foreknowledge or eternity; "if he did, he rejected both in favour of something more up to date. He prefers the notion of the kingship of God and the personal dependence of every man, but especially the earthly king, upon that kingship."[71] Jerold Frakes has made stronger statements; he writes, "Alfred does not accept the ontological distinction between *aeternitas* and *perpetuitas*, which was essential to the Boethian order (147, 17–22)...,"[72] and F. Anne Payne declares, "Alfred omits completely Boethius's Platonic explanation about the states of eternity and time."[73] Payne views this difference as crucial to the translation: "The key to practically everything that goes on in the OE text...is that Alfred did not postulate Boethius' two separate and completely different states of existence, man's and God's...."[74] If Alfred truly did not understand Boethian eternity, his failure would have repercussions throughout the text.

Yet other scholars claim with equal vehemence that Alfred did in fact understand and translate the Boethian concept of eternity. Kurt Otten lists a series of antitheses from the Alfredian text, including time and eternity.[75] He remarks that these binary oppositions appear in the source text, but that both commentaries and Alfred's translation emphasize them more heavily than the Latin text itself. In direct response to Payne's book, Katherine Proppe argues that "Alfred certainly contrasts present time and eternity,"[76] and W. F. Bolton writes that Alfred distinguishes among *hwilendlic*, *ece*, and *ece buton ende*.[77]

Alfred faced a linguistic difficulty: he lacked individual words to match each Latin word dealing with time and eternity because *perpetuum*, a crucial term in Boethius's triad of limited time, perpetuity, and eternity, had no Old English equivalent. Instead, Alfred uses the word *ece*, "eternal," for both perpetuity and eternity. Fred Robinson finds that *ece* originally meant "lasting" and continued to be used in that sense both in poetry and prose, including Ælfric's first letter to Wulfstan.[78] Alfred explains perpetuity, "Oðer ðing is ece, þæt hæfð fruman 7 næfð nænne ende" ("Another thing is *ece*, that has an origin and has no end," 147.29–148.2). This explanation, while coming approximately where V pr. vi. 9 does in the Latin text, actually matches better the Latin in V pr. vi. 14, where the word used is *perpetuum*. Alfred then must use the word *ece* again for "aeternitas" (V pr. vi. 3): "Þridde ðing is ece buton ende 7 buton anginne" ("A third thing is *ece* without end and without beginning," 148.3).

Thus, when Alfred seems to use the word "eternal" where he should be using "perpetual," he may in fact mean "perpetual." He does not always supply "buton ende," his one clear way of distinguishing the two meanings for which he must use *ece*. He refers to the soul as *ece*: "monna sawla sint undeadlica 7 ece" (26.11) translates "mentes hominum nullo modo esse mortales" ("men's souls are undying and *ece*" for "the minds of men are in no way mortal," II pr. iv. 28). He also refers to the afterlife several times as *ece*: "symle bið se beag goodes edleanes ðæm godum gehealden on ecnesse" ("the jewel of good reward is always held for the good in *ecnesse*," 113.2–4) translates "corona non decidet, non arescet" ("the crown does not decay, does not wither," IV pr. iii. 5), and a number of other passages use the word *ece* similarly.[79]

These passages might appear to present a confused notion of eternity, but if one accepts that Alfred sometimes uses *ece* as an abbreviated form of *ece buton ende*, the problem vanishes. Alfred has precedent: Boethius himself does not always maintain the distinction, sometimes using *aeternitas* and *aeternus* to describe infinite time, not timelessness. Some instances clearly refer to *aeternitas* as a length of time and not a separate state, as in the question, "Quod si ad aeternitatis infinita spatia pertractes, quid habes quod de nominis tui diuturnitate laeteris?" ("Which, if you spread to the infinite space of eternity, what do you have to rejoice in the length of time of your name?" II pr. vii. 15; similarly, see II pr. vii. 18).[80] In Book IV Boethius explicitly speaks of an eternity that must have a beginning: describing how miserable the punishment of the evil would be if it had no end, he writes, "infinitam liquet esse miseriam quam esse constat aeternam" ("that misery is agreed to be infinite that is eternal," IV pr. iv. 9; see also IV pr. iv. 24).[81] Unless one wants to claim that the evil are co-eternal with God, one must read *aeternam* here the same way as Alfred's *ece* (*buton ende*). Finally, in IV met. vi Boethius refers to the courses of the heavens as eternal, although they are clearly created and inside time: "Sic aeternos reficit cursus / alternus amor, sic astrigeris / bellum discors exsulat oris" ("So mutual love reforms the eternal courses, so disharmonious war is banished from the shores of the stars," IV met. vi. 16–8).[82] Alfred does differentiate terms less often than Boethius does, using *ece* much more often that the Latin source text uses *aeternitas*; *ece* or forms of it occur forty-one times, whereas forms of *aeternitas* and *aeternus* occur twenty times.[83] Yet Boethius himself sometimes uses *aeternitas* for the more common sense of a long or endless period of time, and Alfred's usage of *ece* reflects this shifting sense.

In one key passage, both authors explain the restricted meaning of eternity. Boethius writes: "Quid sit igitur aeternitas consideremus; haec enim nobis naturam pariter diuinam scientiamque patefacit. Aeternitas igitur est interminabilis uitae tota simul et perfecta possessio" ("Let us consider therefore what eternity is; for this is made open equally to our nature and to divine understanding. Eternity, therefore, is the simultaneous and perfect possession of an interminable life," V pr. vi. 3–4). Alfred adds and repeats a little material, but the thrust of the passage is basically the same:

> Đa cwæð ic: Hwæt is ecnes?... Þridde ðing is ece buton ende 7 buton anginne; þæt is God.... Þæt an us is gewislice andweard þæt þe þonne bið; ac him is eall andweard, ge þætte ær wæs, ge þætte nu is, ge þætte æfter us bið; eall þæt is him andweard. (147.22–3, 148.3, 148.10–2)[84]

> Then I said, "What is ecnesse?"... [Wisdom answered]: "The third thing [of the triad limited time, perpetuity, and eternity] is *ece* without end and without beginning; that is God.... That alone is truly present to us which is then; but to him all is present, both that which was before, that which is now, and that which will be after us; all that is present to him."

Alfred clearly defines eternity as a separate state of being outside time just as Boethius does.

This case shows how Alfred negotiated linguistic obstacles he faced to achieve adequacy in philosophical argumentation. Although Alfred's usage is slightly freer, in that he employs *ece* more often and with less discrimination than Boethius among terms such as immortal, eternal, and unending, his usage is not substantially different from that of his source text. Ultimately he makes the same conceptual distinctions. The concept of eternity, and other arguments, show Alfred to maintain overall a fairly high degree of adequacy with some differences in specific terminology and some displacement and compensation in the text. At the level of argument as well as individual images, exchanges, and even words, Alfred proves himself an accomplished scholar of Latin and offers less-educated readers a way into a difficult philosophical discourse.

For adequacy in the *Boethius* always looks in two directions. On the one hand, it supports Alfred's authority in the field: by remaining close to the source text, he demonstrates that he is a reliable translator and secures symbolic capital for himself. For those with any familiarity with classical mythology, history, and science, or with Latin logical, philosophical, or theological texts, the *Boethius* would display Alfred's faithfulness to the source text and late-antique tradition, from the lowest level of the text, the word, to the overarching dialogue structure and major arguments. They would pass on their judgments to those unable to recognize the text's adequacy. For readers unacquainted with the Latin tradition, however, the very unfamiliarity could achieve the same end, indicating the use of a nonnative tradition.

On the other hand, Alfred offers cultural capital to his readers: readers at any level of learning stood to gain something, whether knowledge of particular names and facts or further mastery of difficult modes of thought, by working their way through the *Boethius.* The text provided a new kind of education for Anglo-Saxons. The training would be useful for those who read further in Alfred's program, especially readers who encountered the *Soliloquies*, a philosophical dialogue even denser than the *Boethius.* It was also an important step for those few who would proceed further to reading Latin texts in the original language and perhaps commenting on or translating those texts themselves. Because a king offered this cultural capital, readers could feel confident that it would be valued at court; in turn, they invested their own labor to earn it.

The *Boethius*, along with Alfred's other translations, opens the field of spiritual literature to West Saxon writers and readers. It also claims that field for the West Saxons. Mercia had produced many learned men and some literature, from glossaries to poetry, and Alfred's own helpers included Mercian clerics.[85] Cynewulf and other early, anonymous poets are thought to have worked in Mercia—although they can be difficult to date and locate.[86] Yet by using his own dialect for his own translation while maintaining much of the information, imagery, structure, and argument of the *De consolatione*, Alfred asserted West Saxon as the rightful heir to the Latin tradition. Alfred's texts were copied and recopied, and West Saxon became the language of many subsequent writers, a kind of "Standard Old English."[87] Today, students begin learning Old English with Alfred's early West Saxon. Nowhere does Alfred openly assert the superiority of his dialect or people. Indeed, by treating his language, a mixture of his own dialect and some Anglianisms, as the common language of the Anglo-Saxons, Alfred implicitly presents his text as the unified product of a unified tradition as he presents the whole program in the Prose and Verse Prefaces to the *Pastoral Care*.[88] He fabricates a singular Anglo-Saxon culture where there were in fact multiple cultures and quietly subsumes that culture under the authority that he is establishing for himself.[89]

Alfred translated the *De consolatione* with a sophisticated set of strategies: he maintained adequacy not only through close translation in many passages but also in the text as a whole through compensation and displacement, which allowed him more freedom while he kept reasonably close to the overall sense of the text. These observations suggest that Alfred did not make changes lightly and make it easier to see where Alfred made alterations at all levels of the text. The next chapter will examine alterations based on the Christian Latin tradition.

chapter 2

A Christian Art of Reading

Alfred's strategic adequacy to the Latin *De consolatione* demonstrated his command of the Latin language and the source text, and thus added to his symbolic capital and the value of his West Saxon prose, whereas the *Boethius* offered readers some cultural capital of their own. Yet contemporary Anglo-Saxons were not acquainted with Latin works of pure philosophy at this time; probably neither Alfred nor his audience would have recognized the Neoplatonic tradition or the *De consolatione*'s place in it.[1] The *Pastoral Care*, the *Dialogues*, and the *Psalms* form the cornerstones of Alfred's translation program. The *De consolatione* is substantially more philosophical, abstract, and difficult than those three crucial texts, each of which provide many anecdotes from and applications to daily life. In the course of translation, Alfred had to supply practical elements for the *Boethius* that the other source texts already contained.[2] His own reading in the Latin Christian tradition prepared Alfred to bridge the intellectual gaps between the *De consolatione* and other texts in his program. He knew more works than this chapter can explore, but examining a few of them will illuminate the overall conception of Alfred's program; how the *Boethius* might have fitted into that program; and specific strategies to render the text more inviting to Anglo-Saxon readers, including Alfred's explicit Christianization of the text by means of a Christian style of argumentation and his patristic approach to interpretation and pagan learning.

Alfred saw Boethius as part of the patristic tradition that encompassed Gregory the Great, Augustine, and others.[3] Moreover, as Deborah VanderBilt writes, for Anglo-Saxons, the *auctoritas* of an individual author extended beyond his own words: "It inheres just as much in the literate technologies that make up the context of the word—writing, books, and the Latin language."[4] Many of Alfred's alterations drew on this broader conception of *auctoritas*, synthesizing phrases, ideas, and imagery from other Latin Christian texts with Boethius's own authority. Alfred's addition of specifically Christian elements in turn helped make the translation more acceptable to readers. Those who had some acquaintance with patristic literature, whether they had read it in Latin, encountered it in other translations in Alfred's program, or heard its materials used in vernacular homilies, would find familiar modes of expression in the *Boethius*. As Bourdieu notes in a much later context, "The specialized languages ... are, as with all discourses, the product of a *compromise* between an *expressive interest* and a *censorship* constituted by the very structure of the field in which the discourse is produced and circulates."[5] Alfred's translations offer a Christian theological language that spans the cultural distance between Latin and Old English but sometimes sacrifices Neoplatonic elements of the *De consolatione*. Bourdieu goes on to explain, "The metaphor of censorship should not mislead: it is the structure of the field itself which governs expression by governing both access to expression and the form of expression, and not some legal proceeding...."[6]

For ninth-century England, Latin texts and their translations were with rare exceptions recognizably Christian in language and conception. Again, Alfred both conformed to the field and stretched its limits. Incorporating Christianity into the *Boethius* would help it achieve a place in a field of Latin spiritual literature controlled by educated clerics, but because that text was written in Old English, it would also appeal to Alfred's Christian lay audience. Alfred created a *Boethius* whose place in Christian tradition both kinds of audiences would recognize.[7] Patristic modes of expression would have carried a flavor of the Other to Anglo-Saxon readers, but a prestigious and relatively familiar Other. Demonstrating his command of patristic literature would further add to Alfred's symbolic capital and again help inculcate his readers with particular kinds of cultural capital, whereas his silent censorship of Neoplatonic elements would cost little and save much labor in explanation. In return for the investment of time audiences made in the *Boethius*, they would not only recognize a kind of language many of them had already encountered, they would receive a firmer grounding in the prestigious modes of patristic discourse. Finally, the text inculcated a Christian habitus, especially a sense of responsibility: the ruler must care both for his own soul and for those under him.[8]

Alfred's program had a relatively recent model in the Carolingian reform, and some of the reformers' work may also have helped to suggest the choice of the *De consolatione* for translation, because Alcuin brought it to Carolingian attention.[9] The Carolingian renaissance provided an important model of success in reinvigorating Christian learning, but Alfred's program did not duplicate the Carolingian one. While the Carolingian revival had vernacular aspects, it was primarily a Latin movement; royal policies prescribed Latin texts and a Latin renewal. Alfred's program produced vernacular texts.[10] Furthermore, although Charlemagne was a notable patron of the various efforts involved in that renewal and issued edicts supporting education and reform, he took no personal role in matters regarding specific texts. As Janet Nelson writes, "For an early medieval ruler, activity as an author is an astonishing fact, almost unprecedented—and unparalleled for centuries to come."[11]

Historical precedent for education could also be found within Anglo-Saxon history: Bede explicitly connects Theodore and Hadrian's success in teaching both religious and secular letters with the general success of the English in the years that followed.[12] Theirs was Latin and Greek learning, however, leaving little model for translation. Yet Cuthbert's letter on the death of Bede reported that at his death, Bede was engaged in turning part of the gospel of John "in nostram linguam ad utilitatem ecclesiae Dei" ("into our language for the utility of the Church of God," 582).[13]

Alfred invokes a tradition of scriptural translation in his letter prefacing *Pastoral Care*:

> Ða gemunde ic hu sio æ wæs ærest on Ebreisc geðiode funden, & eft, ða hie Creacas geliornodon, ða wendon hie hie on hiora agen geðiode ealle, & eac ealle oðre bec. & eft Lædenware swæ same, siððan hie hie geliornodon, hie hie wendon ealla ðurh wise wealhstodas on hiora agen geðiode. Ond eac ealle oðræ Cristnæ ðioda summe dæl hiora on hiora agen geðiode wendon. Forðy me ðyncð betre, gif iow swæ ðyncð, ðæt we eac sumæ bec, ða ðe niedbeðearfosta sien eallum monnum to wiotonne, ðæt we ða on ðæt geðiode wenden ðe we ealle gecnawan mægen. . . . (*PC* 5.25–7.8)

> Then I recalled how the law was first established in Hebrew, and again, when the Greeks learned it, then they turned it into their own language, and also all other books. And again the Latin people did the same; after they learned it, they turned it into their own language through wise translators. And also all other Christian peoples turned some portion of it into their own language. Therefore it seems to me better, if so it seems to you, that we likewise turn certain books that are most necessary for all men to know into that language that we can all know. . . .

It would be fascinating to know which Christian translations Alfred had in mind; he specifies "oðræ Cristnæ ðioda," so he does not seem to mean Old English versions, but what other translations might have been known to him is unclear.[14]

Alfred found models of Christian revivals of learning in Carolingian and English history, but he also found support for the vernacular goals of his program in Scripture itself. The translator of the Hebrew book of Sirach into Greek offers a long, self-conscious prologue, which was itself translated into Latin by subsequent translators. The prologue briefly reminded readers of the history and Scriptures of the Chosen People, introduced the translator and his motives for translation, and underscored the importance of wisdom—just as Alfred does in his Preface to the *Pastoral Care*, which is modeled on Sirach's.[15] Alfred thus had authority for the translation of a book of wisdom not only from historical precedents but from within Scripture itself, and a higher authority could hardly be desired.

As for a king's direct, personal involvement in a program, Alfred also had ample precedent from Scripture. He doubtless first became familiar with Scripture orally as his contemporaries generally did, starting at an early age and continuing throughout life. If Alfred was anything like the pious man that Asser presents, he was hearing religious texts constantly.[16] Small wonder if their vocabulary, their mode of expression and argument, and their themes and images became part of his habitus—and he expected the same of his audience. As Bridget Fowler explains, "The earliest tastes are formed through the family and take on an emotional bodily resonance which is ineradicable...."[17] Alfred translated the first fifty Psalms and so knew them intimately; he would surely have known the rest of the Psalms, as well as other Scriptural texts, from the mass, the hours, and extraliturgical reading, and they would have contributed to the young Alfred's habitus.[18] The impact of the Wisdom Books is evident throughout Alfred's work in quotations and echoes, especially from Psalms, Proverbs, Wisdom, and Sirach (also known as Ecclesiasticus).[19]

Alfred's beloved Scripture, especially the Wisdom Books, would encourage his royal program of spiritual education. Wisdom herself is the force behind every throne, she declares in her second address in Proverbs: "per me reges regnant et legum conditores iusta decernunt / per me principes imperant et potentes decernunt iustitiam" ("through me kings reign and the founders of laws discern right / through me princes rule and potentates discern justice," Prov 8:15–6). It is only fitting that kings should seek her themselves: "Gloria Dei celare verbum et gloria regum investigare sermonem" ("To conceal a word is the glory of God and to investigate it the glory of kings," Prov 25:2). The book of Wisdom offers Solomon as a model for kings. Solomon, as the first-person narrator, admonishes kings at the start of Book 6 that his words are intended especially for them (Wisdom 6:1–12); in Book 8 he explains why Wisdom is necessary for all rulers. Solomon was also reputed to be the author of Proverbs and Ecclesiastes, giving ample precedent for a king who wrote divine works. Asser describes Alfred as resembling Solomon in his desire for wisdom and learning: "in hoc pium et opinatissimum atque opulentissimum Salomonem Hebraeorum regem aequiparans..." ("in this equaling the pious and most highly regarded and most opulent king of the Hebrews, Solomon..." 76.43–5). Surely he conveyed this compliment directly to Alfred as well if Alfred did not himself suggest the parallel to Asser.

The New Testament too speaks of spiritual rulers. In Paul's epistles, the leaders of the Christian communities are the teachers. Their two roles overlap, and the responsibility of the leaders for the souls of their flocks is made clear in letter after letter. In I Corinthians 14, Paul writes of spiritual gifts, of which the most important is teaching; in Colossians he writes that they are to instruct one another continually:

> verbum Christi habitet in vobis abundanter
> in omni sapientia docentes et commonentes vosmet ipsos
> psalmis hymnis canticis spiritualibus
> in gratia cantantes in cordibus vestris Deo. (3:16)

> May the word of Christ live abundantly in you who teach and proclaim to each other in all wisdom with Psalms, hymns, and spiritual songs, singing in praise to God in your hearts.

Yet the *De consolatione*, although it provides the kinds of teaching that these Scriptures champion, is never explicitly Christian and does not itself recommend teaching. Philosophia, the voice of authority within the text, repeatedly instructs the narrator that he must focus on his own mental condition, and she discounts any responsibility to others or to society.

Where the *De consolatione* diverges from other Christian traditions Alfred would have known, he reads the text not as it asks to be read, for private study, but in a Gregorian context of spiritual leadership. The habitus he acquired through a lifetime of Christian reading informed his reading of the *De consolatione*. Whereas Alfred's Christian framework contradicted the *De consolatione* on the importance of teaching and responsibility for others, most major themes of the *De consolatione* otherwise fit into these traditions much as the rest of his translations do. The Christian themes throughout the Boethian text would only encourage Alfred to read the text as yet another call to fulfill one's duty in the world. The convergence of themes also probably influenced Alfred's choice of this difficult text for a program centered primarily around more practical advice and *exempla*. The program's translations all agree that God is the highest good and the goal of life, and they reject the world as an end in itself.

The problem of forgetting that opens both versions of the *Consolation*, and to which references recur throughout, can be found in the Prologue to the Gregory the Great's *Dialogi*:

forþon swilce beoð þæs mannes modgeþancas: þonne he ærest þæt god forleoseð, þæt þe he ær hæfde, he swa þeh æt fruman gemyneð, þæt he hit forleas, 7 þonne þæt mod feor gewiteþ ymbe oðre ðing, eac swilce hit forgyteþ his agnes godes, þe hit ær forleas, 7 þonne æt nyxstan hit geweorðeþ, þæt se mann na ne gemyneþ þæs þe he ær hæfde. (*Dialogues* 6.5–15)[20]

For such are the thoughts of a man: when he first loses that good, that he had before, he however forgets at the outset that he lost it, and then his mind departs far for other things, and so it forgets its own good, which it lost before, and then next it happens, that the man cannot recall through his mind that which he before held with deeds.

Wærferth's translation of the *Dialogi* of Gregory bears a letter in Alfred's name, linking this work more closely to the king than any other commissioned translation; he seems to have taken a personal interest in the text, and the *Dialogi* affected his approach to the *Boethius*.[21] Both require the faithful to recall their good. To a translator familiar with the Christian version of *anamnesis* found in the *Dialogi*, this passage in the *De consolatione* may have struck a chord:

Non omne namque mente depulit lumen
obliuiosam corpus inuehens molem;
haeret profecto semen introrsum ueri
quod excitatur uentilante doctrina. (III met. xi. 9–12)

For the body, carrying its oblivious matter, cannot repulse all light from the mind; indeed there remains within a seed of truth that is enflamed when learning fans it.

Although Alfred expands the image, the idea remains the same:

sio swærnes ðæs lichoman 7 þa unþeawas oft abisegien þæt mod mid ofergiotulnesse, 7 mid þam gedwolmiste hit fortio þæt hit ne mæge swa beorhte scinan swa hit wolde. 7 þeah bið simle corn þære soðfæstnesse sæd on þære saule wunigende, þa hwile þe sio sawl 7 se lichoma gederode bioð. (95.10–14)[22]

the heaviness of the body and the vices often distract the mind with forgetfulness, and with that mist of error it leads it astray so that it may not shine as brightly as it would. And yet there is always a grain of that truth dwelling as a seed in the soul, as long as the soul and the body are joined.

Another theme of the *De consolatione*, the concern that the evil seem to succeed and the conclusion that they ultimately do not, further links it to Christian literature and the Old Testament. The Psalmist prays: "Aris, Drihten, þy læs se yfelwillenda mæge don þæt he wille; and gedo þæt eallum folcum sy gedemed beforan ðe" ("Arise, Lord, lest the one willing evil be able to do what he wants; and make it so that all people are judged before you," 9.18). Why the good suffer is the fundamental problem of the book of Job. Ecclesiastes too laments: "haec quoque vidi in diebus vanitatis meae iustus perit in iustitia sua et impius multo vivit tempore in malitia sua" ("These things too I saw in my days of vanity: the just one perish in his own justice, and the impious live for a long time in his own malice," 7:16). The prisoner likewise mourns:

> Sed ea ipsa est uel maxima nostri causa maeroris quod, cum rerum bonus rector exsistat, uel esse omnino mala possint uel impunita praetereant; quod solum quanta dignum sit ammiratione profecto consideras. At huic aliud maius adiungitur; nam imperante florenteque nequitia uirtus non solum praemiis caret, uerum etiam sceleratorum pedibus subiecta calcatur et in locum facinorum supplicia luit. (IV pr. i. 3–4) [23]

> But this is even the greatest cause of my unhappiness, that, if a good ruler of things exists, either the evil are able to exist at all or that they remain unpunished; which you may consider indeed to be worthy only of great wonder. But another, greater matter is added to this: that while evil rules and flourishes, virtue not only lacks rewards, but even is trod under by the feet of the wicked, and in place of evil is suffers punishment.

Yet God has not abdicated from his role, as both Scripture and the *De consolatione* make clear, and the evil do not really succeed. That God still watches and rules is made apparent by the vindication of Job and the numerous triumphal Psalms that thank the Lord for conquering foes.

This Scriptural solution differs somewhat from the *De consolatione*'s conclusion that evil is simply nothing. Yet the *De consolatione* does say that God is watching constantly and adjusts Fortune for individuals according to what they can bear and what will make them better (132–5; IV pr. vi. 35–42). Both the Old and New Testaments also appeal to justice in the afterlife, a proposition that Philosophy accepts, although she declines to discuss it:

> Tum ego: Ista quidem consequentia sunt eis quae paulo ante conclusa sunt; sed quaeso, inquam, te, nullane animarum supplicia post defunctum

> morte corpus relinquis? — Et magna quidem, inquit, quorum alia poenali acerbitate, alia uero purgatoria clementia exerceri puto; sed nunc de his disserere consilium non est. (IV pr. iv. 22–3)
>
> Then I said, "Indeed, these [conclusions] follow those things that we concluded a little earlier; but I ask you whether you leave any punishment of the soul after the death of the body?" "Indeed, great punishments," she said; "I think some shall be exercised by harsh punishments, others, however, by a merciful purgatory; but it is not my plan to treat these now."

This passage needs little to bring it into harmony with a Christian understanding of the afterlife; Alfred merely adds a reference to reward as well as punishment and describes hell and purgatory in a little more detail (120.9–17).

The genre of consolation literature itself was readily identifiable with the Old Testament. The book of Job too features a good man suffering for reasons he cannot comprehend, a man who questions God but finally accepts his state after dialogues with his neighbors and then with God Himself. The Psalms have many consolatory passages as well. The speaker in this line from the Paris Psalter sounds strikingly like the prisoner in his opening scenes: "Ic swince on minre granunge, and ælce niht on minum bedde ic sice and wepe, and hwilum min bedd wæte mid tearum" ("I labor in my groaning, and each night I sigh and weep on my bed, and sometimes moisten my bed with tears," 6.5).[24] Psalm 108 concerns being wrongfully accused.

The *Boethius*, then, shares major themes with Scripture and patristic works in the translation program.[25] Scripture, patristic works, and the *De consolatione* all share the view of God as unity and highest good, the ultimate goal of humanity; the rejection of the world as an end in itself; the soul's forgetting and recollecting its own good; the fear that the evil are winning and the reassurance that they ultimately do not; and the very genre of consolation. The compatibility of the *De consolatione* with Christian texts authorized Alfred not only to translate it, but also to make the *Boethius* more overtly Christian and more acceptable to his audience. These Christian themes would in turn be recognizable to his audience as those of authorized church speakers such as bishops and pastors. Boethius's original philosophical language becomes a more theological language comprehensible to Alfred's readers through their contact with the church, although most laity would probably not use it themselves. Bourdieu explains that linguistic distinction arises in the gap between what a few can produce and many more can recognize.[26] Alfred claims distinction for his work by using a form of authorized language, a vernacular version of a Latin text with recognizable themes from the Scriptures.

The *Boethius* complements the other translations without duplicating their material to reinforce a Christian habitus in readers: the *Dialogi* provide *exempla* and miracle stories with its theme of how much faith can accomplish; the *Regula pastoralis* gives practical advice both for living and for advising others how to live; the *Orosius* and the *Bede* provide historical perspectives and numerous *exempla.*[27] The *Boethius* fits into this program neatly with its story of an individual reconciling his own fortunes with a broader perspective and the theme of free will, largely untreated by the other works in the program. Alfred made this valuable material more explicitly Christian by importing from other Christian texts ideas and motifs absent from the *De consolatione.* The *Soliloquies* would later provide abstract arguments for the immortality of the soul, placing the journey of the individual soul into an eschatological context.

These intertexts helped Alfred to make the *Boethius* more acceptable, to adjust its tenor to the structure of the literary field of his time. Gregory the Great offered the model of a man forced unexpectedly into a high office who accepted responsibility not only for governing, but also for edifying his people. Gregory's *Regula pastoralis,* on the disposition of the ruler and how he can best direct those under him for their spiritual advancement, was probably the first work Alfred himself translated and a driving force behind his conception of the program as a whole. The *Regula pastoralis* exhorts readers to accept the responsibilities that God imparts along with His gifts, whereas the *Dialogi* offers tales of people who did just that. Throughout his manual for rulers, Gregory admits that the world and its concerns are a distraction but insists that rulers attend to them, finding a way to strike the difficult balance between the demands of inner and outer life.[28] In translating the *Regula pastoralis,* Alfred broadened the application from pastoral office to all offices—including his own and his audience's—by translating *rector* as *se lareow* or simply *se reccere.*[29] Autobiographical passages in the *Dialogi* and the *Regula pastoralis* dramatize Gregory's desire to flee the world while much of the rest of these books explain precisely how to fulfill one's duty to the world.[30] These key texts then convey a Christian habitus, encouraging humility before God and a particular social relationship with specific responsibilities to those higher and lower in the hierarchy.

Alfred adopts the Gregorian notion of duty for the *Pastoral Care* and then introduces it into the *Boethius,* treating questions of the individual's responsibilities to others not as Boethius treats them, but as Gregory does.[31] The Latin narrator complains periodically throughout Book I that he has been badly repaid for the service he has given, and in Book II he explains his actions, "Scis... ipsa minimum nobis ambitionem mortalium rerum fuisse dominatam; sed materiam gerendis rebus optauimus, quo ne uirtus tacita consenesceret" ("You know... that ambition for mortal things has dominated me very little; but I wished for means of accomplishing things, lest virtue decay in silence," II pr. vii. 1). Philosophy gently but firmly tells him that fame was the only inducement that could tempt a mind such as his to leave its proper studies. The idea of responsibility to one's fellows deserves no consideration in the source text. Alfred, however, inserts his longest addition at this point. Mod gives a twenty-nine-line speech detailing the specific responsibilities of a ruler and what resources, both physical and intangible, he needs to carry them out (40.6–41.6). His interlocutor, here called Gesceadwisnes, cautions against "leases gilpes" (51.12)—*false* or *lying* fame—but allows most of the Old English narrator's speech to stand unchallenged: both speakers believe that a king has certain duties he must fulfill. Alfred's translation marks the *Boethius* as belonging to a Christian tradition of balancing engagement with this world and contemplation of the next. Although modern readers might consider such a translation inaccurate, Anglo-Saxon readers might have found a *Boethius* without this alteration unacceptable, and it would certainly not have fit Alfred's program as well. What Bourdieu calls "the censorship of the field" operates here: the *Boethius* conforms to "the social conditions of [its] production," fitting into the field of the few Old English translations then available and the Latin texts by Gregory and Augustine that a few readers might know.[32]

Treating the acceptance of office as a heavy responsibility rather than a right or an honor actually privileges the office and its holders. Bourdieu writes, "All aristocracies must expend considerable energy to convince the elect of the need to accept the sacrifices that are implied by privilege"; thus "the designated heir" receives a "different and distinctive treatment [that] can only encourage him to fulfil his essence, to live in conformity with his social essence."[33] Alfred's alterations not only place the text firmly into a Christian context, they also offer a mark of distinction to the audience. The current or future lord has important duties—including the reading of this text—which set him apart from others. David Pratt writes that the Carolingian reform redefined rule as a *ministerium*; "'Ministerial' rulership enabled ecclesiastical reform to be harnessed even more effectively to the needs of royal power, and it also enabled individual Carolingians to claim moral superiority over their relatives whenever dynastic disputes arose, as inevitably they did."[34] The Anglo-Saxons, operating in a very different ecclesiastical climate, did not undertake the same rigorous "ministerial" disciplines, he argues, but they were aware of Gregorian models (which writers such as Bede and Alcuin also championed) and the Carolingian ones.[35] Alfred need not require the same rigor some Carolingians practiced to inculcate in his people the disposition of a people set apart, given special gifts by God to answer special demands.

As the reader works through the difficult text, another problem of acceptability could arise from the mode of discourse in the *De consolatione.*

Modes of reading and interpretation are culturally marked, as Bourdieu notes, in accord with social rank and educational experience.[36] The rigorous logic and Neoplatonic philosophy of the *De consolatione philosophiae* would not attract Anglo-Saxon readers. Yet certain other types of discourse and exegetical methods would be recognizable in Anglo-Saxon England as specifically Christian. Alfred draws on these latter modes in his translation, although some are rarely deployed in the *De consolatione*. For that fraction of the audience with some familiarity with patristic Latin writers, the methods would seem even more familiar. Their recognition of Alfred's techniques and changes would impress on them Alfred's command of a difficult set of Latin texts, adding to his cultural capital and authority. The rest of his audience would gain familiarity with Christian modes of discourse and begin to practice a certain disposition toward texts.

By shifting the *Boethius* into an explicitly Christian context, Alfred enabled readers to place it in the same mental space as homilies and other Christian texts they might know.[37] Alfred's references to God in familiar Christian terms instead of Neoplatonic language would increase audience recognition and comfort, and his translation of *Philosophia* into the Old Testament *Wisdom* would also provide a frame of reference. Finally, Alfred's interpretive interventions offered readers a way through Boethius's allusive text. He explains some passages of Boethius's text in ways akin to Gregory and Augustine, although his explications are brief and uncomplicated, unlike Gregory's often extended allegorical readings. The *Boethius* is not an easy text, but Alfred has adapted it for an audience with little experience doing allegorical interpretation on their own.

A few of Alfred's specific additions would seem familiar to the small number of readers versed in Gregory's writings. For others, these additions may have carried the flavor of the Christian tradition, or they may simply have explicated the text. One of the additions to the *Boethius* is Alfred's assertion that the spirit can move while the body is asleep: "Swa eac ure gast bið swiðe wide farende urum unwillum 7 ures ungewealdes for his gecynde, nalles for his willan; þæt bið þonne þonne we slapað" ("So also our spirit is very wide-faring involuntarily and without our control because of its nature, not its will; that is, when we sleep," 93.6–9).[38] This passage recalls one in the *Dialogi*, when Benedict sends a dream to some monks to tell them where he wishes them to build.[39] Alfred could have read Gregory's explanation of this phenomenon either in Latin or in Wærferth's Old English rendering of the sentence: "gewisslice hit is cuð, þæt se gast is styriendlicran gecyndes þonne se lichama" ("Truly is it known that the spirit is of a more mobile nature than the body," Hatton 149.31–150.1).[40] In both versions of the *Dialogues*, Biblical examples of the spirit traveling in sleep are given. Although Gregory is not talking about involuntary motions of the spirit, the reference to the nature of the spirit, and the fact that (as Malcolm Godden remarks) this is the only time Alfred uses the word *gast* in the *Boethius*, make it seem likely that he was influenced by this text, and by the Old English version at that.[41] Alfred may have misread the source text, which refers to involuntary motions such as breathing in sleep; he seems to have taken *spiritum*, "breath," for its more common sense, "spirit." When he reached a passage in the *De consolatione* that confused him, he turned to another passage that also addressed sleep and motion (*mobilioris* in Gregory, *motibus* in Boethius, III pr. xi. 30) and contained the word *spiritus*.

Another surprising change follows. Boethius writes: "Nam uti cadauer hominem mortuum dixeris, simpliciter uero hominem appellare non possis, ita uitiosos malos quidem esse concesserim, sed esse absolute nequeam confiteri" ("For though you might call a cadaver a dead man, you could not call it simply a man; thus you might concede the vicious to be bad, but you could not profess absolutely that they exist," IV pr. ii. 35). After stating that the evil are nothing, Alfred adds:

> ne magon we næfre gereccan ðone yflan mon clænne 7 untwifealdne, ðon ma ðe we magon hatan oððe habban deadne mon for cwucone; ne bið se cwuca ðonne nyttra ðe se deada, gif him his yfel ne hreowð; ac se þe ungereclice liofað 7 his gecynd nyle healdan, ne bið se nauht. (109.26–31)

> Nor may we ever account the evil man pure and undivided, any more than we may call or hold a dead man for a live one; nor is the live one more useful than the dead, if he does not repent his evil; but he who lives unthinkingly and will not restrain his nature, he is nothing.

Alfred's point is now the uselessness of the evil, whether living or dead. This harks back to Gregory and the *Pastoral Care*:

> Ða ðe libbende bioð, hi witon & ongietað hwæt ymb hi gedon bið; ða deadan ne magon nanwuht witan. Ða bioð genemde deade, & ða stigað on helle, ða ðe nyton hwonne hi untela doð; ac ða ðe hit witon, & swaðeah doð, ða gað libbende & witende on helle. (429.24–8)[42]

> Those who are living, they know and understand what is done around them; the dead can know nothing. Then those are called dead, and they descend into hell, who do not know that they do evil; but those who know it, and yet do it, go living and knowingly into hell.

The ideas are not identical, but the idea of the ignorance of the dead, and the declaration that those who do evil are really dead, are similar.[43] Again,

Alfred explicates a difficult passage in the *De consolatione* with help from a patristic source.

Alfred also draws on Augustine to elucidate the text.[44] The *Soliloquia*, an early Augustinian text, has a strongly Neoplatonic flavor and refers to God in many of the same ways that Boethius does, but Augustine uses overtly Christian terms. Boethius ordinarily simply uses the term *deus*, a term referring equally well to the Christian God or the Neoplatonic. Boethius's God is the highest good, the greatest happiness (*beatitudo*), the unity of all goods, self-sufficiency without lack: "Est igitur summum, inquit, bonum quod regit cuncta fortiter suauiterque disponit" ("'It is therefore,' she said, 'the highest good that rules and disposes all things strongly and gently,'" III pr. xii. 22). Augustine uses similar language: "Deus beatitudo, in quo et a quo et per quem beata sunt, quae beata sunt omnia. Deus bonum et pulchrum, in quo et a quo et per quem bona et pulchra sunt, quae bona et pulchra sunt omnia" ("God, happiness, in whom and by whom all things are happy [or: blessed] that are happy. God, the good and the beautiful, in whom and by whom and through whom all things are good and beautiful that are good and beautiful," *Soliloquia* 24, I.3); "ubi nihil deest" ("where nothing is lacking," 26, I.4). Unlike Boethius, however, Augustine introduces the Christian term *pater*, father: "Deus pater veritatis, pater sapientiae, pater verae summaeque vitae, pater beatitudinis, pater boni et pulchri, pater intelegibilis lucis . . . " ("God, father of truth, father of wisdom, father of true and highest life, father of happiness, father of the good and beautiful, father of intelligible light . . . " 24, I.2). Augustine employs a term deeply familiar from the Christian *Pater Noster*, a prayer well-known to Anglo-Saxons even in Latin; texts ranging from Old English charms to the vernacular homilies of Ælfric and Wulfstan refer to it by the Latin name.[45]

Alfred has ample authorization to take Boethius's "deus" as the Christian "Dryhten" and to note that "an God is fæder eallra gesceafta" ("one God is the father of all creation," 69.20). Using Christian words or phrases common in Anglo-Saxon religious texts would reduce the inherent tensions between Anglo-Saxon and late-antique habitus and avoid the possible confusion that a series of references to a "god" who was simply the greatest "gesælð" ("good" or "happiness") might engender. Augustine's *Soliloquia* offered a mix of Neoplatonic and Christian terminology that Alfred maintains in his translation of the *De consolatione*, even though Boethius's text avoids Christian terms. Readers who reach III met. ix. 22 will encounter the words, "Da, pater . . . " ("Grant, Father . . . "), the Christian notion of God as Father—but Alfred did not make his readers wait that long. The brief biography of Boethius on 7.1–24 refers explicitly to Christians and Arians (7.6) and the pope (7.11). The Wisdom who visits the narrator in his prison is "heofencund" ("divine," 8.16). God is referred to as "Dryhten."[46]

Alfred's adaptation of the text to more explicitly Christian language does not end with references to God. Other overtly Christian references are also incorporated as Alfred brings angels, martyrs, theological virtues, and the Old Testament figure of Wisdom into consideration in his text. Alfred's language thus becomes distinctive, using terminology and categories from Christian thought that would be recognizable to his audience, even though many could not deploy that kind of learning themselves.

Alfred's references to angels clearly come from a Christian context. A passage from Alfred's translation of the Psalms is typical of that book's mention of angels:

> 5. Drihten, hwæt is se mann þe þu swa myclum amanst, oþþe hwæt is se mannes sunu þe þu oftrædlice neosast?
> 6. Þu hine gedest lytle læssan þonne englas; þu hine gewuldrast and geweorðast, and him sylst heafodgold to mærðe; and þu hine gesetest ofer þin handgeweorc.
> 7. Ealle gesceafta þu legst under his fet and under his anwald . . . (8.5–7)[47]
>
> Lord, what is man that you care so much for him? Or what is the son of man that you so often visit him? You make him little less than the angels; you glorify and honor him, and give him a crown for his glory; and you set him over the work of your hands. All creation you lay under his feet and under his rule. . . .

Matthew (22:30) and Mark (12:25) both say that human beings will be like angels at the resurrection, and Paul uses phrases such as "et angelis et hominibus" ("both angels and men," I Cor 4:9) and "si linguis hominum loquar et angelorum . . ." ("if I spoke with the tongues of men and angels. . . ." I Cor 13:1).[48] A passage in the *Dialogues* (263.11–22; Latin III.3.1) similarly includes reference to angels as well as men. Alfred too takes care to include angels in his considerations. Boethius gives them little attention, with just one, brief mention at IV pr. iv. 13, "seu angelica uirtute seu daemonum uaria sollertia" ("either angelic virtue or various aptitudes of daemons"). Alfred translates the reference "goodan englas . . . scuccena mislice lotwrencas" ("good angels . . . various demons' wiles," 129.4, 6), taking the Neoplatonic *dæmones* as Christian demons.

Alfred develops this one brief allusion in Boethius into several comparisons of human free will with angelic. These references to angels in the *Boethius* do not change the text dramatically, but they do add to the overall Christian tone of the translation. Elsewhere Boethius is much more circumspect on the topic of angels; the closest he comes to mentioning them again is "Nam supernis diuinisque substantiis et perspicax iudicium et incorrupta uoluntas et efficax optatorum praesto est potestas" ("For the power of perspicacious judgment and incorrupt will and ability to effect what they wish is possessed by supernal and divine substances," V pr. ii. 7). Alfred renders this: "Englas habbað rihte domas 7 goodne willan, 7 eall þæt hi wilniað hi begitað swiðe eaðe, forðæmþe hi nan wos ne wilniað" ("Angels possess correct judgment and good will, and all that they will they obtain very easily, because they will no evil," 140.28–30). The identification of "supernis diuinisque substantiis" as "englas" was conditioned by Christian literary tradition and in turn set Alfred's *Boethius* squarely in the Christian tradition in which he sought to educate his readers. Boethius continues this passage with a consideration only of human souls, but before translating that sentence (140.31–141.1), Alfred inserts, "Nis nan þe hæbbe friodom 7 gesceadwisnesse buton englum 7 monnum . . . " ("There are none who have freedom and discernment except angels and men . . . " 140.30–31), extending consideration of angels. Alfred also introduces angels into several other passages where Boethius gives no hint of them.[49]

Alfred likewise makes the *Boethius* more Christian through overt mention of martyrs. Where Boethius declares, "Quodsi multos scimus beatitudinis fructum non morte solum uerum etiam doloribus suppliciisque quaesisse . . . " ("but if we know that many have sought the reward of happiness not only from death but even from sorrows and torture . . . " II pr. iv. 29), Alfred exhorts, "Hwæt, we gewislice witon unrim ðara monna þe þa ecan gesælða sohton nalles þurh þæt an þæt hi wilnodon ðæs lichomlican deaðes, ac eac manegra sarlicra wita hi gewildnodon wið þæm ecan life; þæt wæron ealle þa halgan martiras" ("Listen, we know with certainty countless men who sought eternal good not only through this, that they willed bodily death, but also they willed many sorrowful tortures in return for that eternal life; these were the holy martyrs," 26.17–21).[50] Boethius's text allows a range of interpretation from Christian martyrs to pagan men of virtue who died or were tortured for their principles—men like the "liberum quendam" ("certain free man," II pr. vi. 8) whose bravery in the face of a tyrant's torture Boethius cites a little later in his text. Alfred, however, is steeped in a tradition rife with lives of martyrs; the Old English *Martyrology* may have been part of his program or at least known to him.[51] Moreover, Alfred constructs Boethius himself as a martyr; the opening of the translation presents Boethius as a Christian taking a courageous stand against the Arian Theodoric (7.6–24). This understanding of Boethius's life was consistent with his status as a saint (Saint Severinus) and allied the difficult *Boethius* with the popular Christian literature of saints' lives.[52]

Several changes in the mode of discourse complemented Alfred's specific Christian alterations to the text. His translation practice follows patristic precedent in its use of authority, its style of exegesis, and its attitude toward pagan learning. Boethius's text makes relatively little use of authority, relying instead upon logic; the *De consolatione* is renowned for its clear logical style.[53] The argument proceeds somewhat like a Socratic dialogue in which the prisoner, as the student, is slowly led, step by step, to irrefutable conclusions. Philosophy carries more of the weight of the argument and asks fewer questions than Socrates in Plato's dialogues, but the effect is still that of logical progression with one character learning from the other. Some support derives from generalized, abstract cases, and some from appeals to the prisoner's own history, but the prose argument relies overwhelmingly on logic, not experience. Many of the meters then offer figurative illustrations of the points in the prose.[54]

In several places Philosophy does cite an authority such as Plato (e.g. III met. ix. 15; III pr. xii. 1; III pr. xii. 38) or Aristotle (e.g. V pr. i. 12). Yet citations from these thinkers are not taken on faith but fitted into a logical argument and subject to evaluation, as when the narrator announces, "Platoni, inquam, uehementer assentior" ("'I vehemently agree with Plato,' I said," III pr. xii. 1). Boethius's text aims to persuade pagans and Christians alike, relying only on logic and not on authorities, although silent quotations and allusions drawn from many sources, both pagan and Christian, ornament the text and provide a special pleasure to the most educated readers. Bieler's learned notes reveal that Boethius draws on a great many more sources than he acknowledges, including several Scriptural texts, but they are all adapted for the context and fitted together into a logical framework.[55] The text's reliance on formal logic is much more evident than his literary debts, but such logic would appeal only to those with the necessary training. As Bourdieu explains, later philosophy specifically addresses the initiated and excludes those who have not learned its form of discourse; his notion of internal reading explains how a group, such as nineteenth-century German philosophers, develops a specialized language, then practices self-censorship on their own writings, making certain that any texts they produce follow the rules of the genre and the language.[56] The same principle lies behind Boethius's language and an internal reading of Heidegger.[57] Comprehension of the text rewards students in the field and distinguishes them from other readers, who are frustrated and even repelled by the difficulty of the text. One must be initiated to read and write the language, even as one becomes initiated only by reading and writing the language.

Alfred's *Boethius*, however, addresses specifically those not initiated into logic and philosophy, and Alfred does not need a text that can persuade pagans. Thus, although much of the logic is kept, sometimes the argument takes different paths and employs different modes of discourse.[58] Pagan authorities are still subject to evaluation: "Platoni, inquam, uehementer assentior" ("'I vehemently agree with Plato,' I said," III pr. xii. 1) and "Ða cwæð ic, Ic eom geðafa. . . ." ("Then I said, 'I am in agreement. . . .'" 95.24); both suggest that the narrators could dissent. Yet a Christian preference for authority and plausibility over logical proof is frequently reflected in the different formulations the characters of Philosophy and Wisdom use to refer to their argument: "crebras coaceruabo rationes" ("I will assemble many reasons," IV pr. ii. 26) expresses overwhelming logical force, whereas the corresponding "forðy ic ðe wolde gegaderian manigu spell 7 manega bisna be ðæm þæt ðu meahte ðy eð ongitan hwæt ic secgan wille" ("thus I want to gather for you many sayings and many examples so that you might more easily understand what I will say to you," 108.1–3) implies an argument based on *exempla* and trust in the speaker.

When the arguments do not all proceed on a strictly logical basis, the reason for the prisoner, and the reader, to accept them changes. They no longer persuade because they are logically irrefutable; now they convince both because they sound true and because they have the support of *auctoritas*. Alfred's looser logic can be quite persuasive to those less concerned with the rigor of the argument and more interested in the authority of the speaker than Boethius's original audience were. Scriptural texts and church teachings are, in Alfred's treatment, not subject to criticism or dissent. For medieval Christians, these writings and beliefs are part of what Bourdieu calls *doxa*: what everyone knows without question.[59] In the field of Christianity, doubting the Scriptures or patristic writings is outside the realm of thought. Merely quoting or referring to them establishes the point at hand. This mode is largely typical of early Christian discourse that, when addressed to believers, works less to prove or justify than to explicate.

Near the end of the *Boethius*, Alfred seriously curtails the arguments about free will and instead substitutes imagery and the language of the church (see 141–9). He also introduces a Scriptural quotation into a passage that lacked it in the source text (133.11–13) and adds Augustine's "cum dilectione hominum et odio vitiorum" ("with love for the man and hatred of vices," Epistle 211, 365.11–12): "lufie þone man, 7 hatige his unþeawas" ("love the man and hate his vices," 124.16).[60] Alfred does not offer explicit attributions for these borrowings, nor does he attribute any of the material he may have gleaned from sources outside the *De consolatione*.[61] Either he relies on audience recognition, he is satisfied that the borrowings fit the argument and so need not be justified, or he has internalized them so much that he reproduces them unconsciously. His silent adoption of other sources, sometimes so transformed that determining exactly where his debts lie is difficult, actually parallels Boethius's silent use of many texts, including Scripture.

A kind of "internal reading" different from the purely philosophical one occurs here. This internal reading involves texts written by and for a group of people who have accepted certain fundamental assumptions about the universe, its governance, and the revelation of these assumptions in Scripture. Alfred's text invites nonphilosophers and nonlogicians; it would exclude non-Christians, but the king does not anticipate any of those among his audience.

Alfred constructs a model of authority based on other texts that he knew. The Scriptures, of course, have the highest possible authority: divine inspiration. Arguments within Scripture can be based only on appeals to other parts of Scripture or to divine revelation itself. The brief prologue to Sirach cites the law and the prophets twice. More often, however, the Scriptures simply assume their own authority and proceed without logical proof. This is not to say that the content does not make sense or that it is not convincing, but that the arguments are as much intuitive or associative as strictly logical, and they rely on the faith of the readers more than on any system of proofs. Wisdom's speeches in Proverbs do not make any explicit claim to authority, but implicitly she claims the authority of God. This authority ultimately makes her words convincing. Alfred's Wisdom proceeds similarly. Wisdom never explicitly claims divine authority, but in his arguments for free will he explains God's reasoning (142.1–22). In the passage in which Philosophy explains the way different kinds of fate are given to people for different reasons (IV pr. vi. 35–42), Philosophy comes close to explaining a portion of the workings of God, but Wisdom uses the word *God* repeatedly, even explaining the way God operates (132.20–135.21). As Otten notes, Wisdom is closely associated with God; the prisoner says at one point, "ic ongite þætte eall ðæt þu me ær reahtes me reahte God þurh ðe . . ." ("I understand that all that you told me before, God told me through you . . ." 103.27–8).[62]

Alfred's appeals to Scripture would have been influenced by similar practices among patristic authors. At the outset of Book IV of his *Dialogi*, Gregory the Great explains the need to rely on authority for things we cannot know personally (IV.1 in the Latin, 260.7–262.13 in the Old English). For example, one must accept authority for the existence of heaven and its habitation by angels. Gregory cites no particular authorities here but simply relies on the doxa or common knowledge of the faithful. He often makes free use of his predecessors' work; sources or influences outside Scripture often appear without citations of any kind.[63] Gregory quotes the Scriptures with clear references wherever it might help his argument. Alfred only adds one definite (although uncited) Scriptural quotation to the *Boethius* (at 133.11–13, where he substitutes Psalm 16:8 for a Greek quotation, IV pr. vi. 38).[64] Yet the very idea that Scripture would be fitting here is significant. Boethius writes a few passages reminiscent of the Scriptures, the most obvious being the image of the metal and wood vessels (IV pr. i. 6) and the house on the heights (II met. iv), which recall respectively Romans 4:21 and 2 Timothy 2:20, and Matthew 7:24–7 and Luke 6:48–9.[65] As Henry Chadwick notes, however, the Latin work is characterized "by an evidently conscious refusal to say anything distinctively Christian."[66] Boethius wanted his arguments to be based on logic, not authority; Alfred employs both, following not only Boethius, but also patristic tradition. In calling on patristic authority in this way, Alfred authorizes himself. Bourdieu speaks of "the alchemy of *representation*... through which the representative creates the group which creates him: the spokesman endowed with the full power to speak and act on behalf of the group...."[67] Alfred makes himself the recipient of the authority passed from Boethius, Gregory, and Augustine, a group he has himself marshalled.[68] He has been authorized by the authors he translates.

The freedom with which Alfred uses other authorities also finds grounding in Augustine. Augustine might seem to be an exception to the Christian tendency to prefer authority. The *Soliloquia* is so similar to the *De consolatione* that it has been suggested the former was a model for the latter, or even that Boethius thought of his work as a sequel to Augustine's; the text attempts to argue a potentially religious issue, the immortality of the soul, in the same purely philosophical mode that Boethius later adopted for his work.[69] Yet Augustine abandoned the *Soliloquia* unfinished; he never wrote the projected third book, and Alfred supplies it for his translation from a variety of sources. Augustine's answer to the question of whether the soul is immortal comes instead in a later work, *De videndo deo* (Epistle 147), which he built entirely on a foundation of authoritative texts. Alfred clearly knew the letter and explicitly referred to it in his *Soliloquies* as his source for Book III of that text (see 92.5, .12, and .18–20). Epistle 147 begins with an appeal to the necessity and the reliability of arguments based on authority (especially Scriptural) and to the reader's internal sense of what is true:

> Nolo auctoritatem meam sequaris, ut ideo putes tibi aliquid necesse esse credere, quoniam a me dicitur: sed aut Scripturis canonicis credas, si quid nondum quam verum sit vides, aut interius demonstranti veritati, ut hoc plane videas.[70]

> I do not wish that you follow my authority, so that you think it is necessary for you to believe something, because it has been said by me; but believe either in the canonical Scriptures, if you see anything that does not yet seem true, or in the demonstration of truth within, as you see it clearly.

The brief letter contains several such passages; not logic but Scripture persuades the reader here. Alfred's text does not have the authority of Scripture, but it does have a figure of authority drawn from Scripture: Wisdom. Other changes carry the ring of Scripture as well. The combination enables Alfred to argue authoritatively. Alfred's free and often unacknowledged borrowings from others' texts, and his reliance on authority, can thus be traced back to patristic forebears.

Alfred's debt to patristic thought is also evident when he introduces interpretations of Boethius's historical and mythological anecdotes and images. Most readers, of course, would not realize that Alfred had added the interpretive level to the text; they would have thought it Boethian. If they had any familiarity with homilies or patristic texts, providing interpretation of an anecdote or an image would have seemed quite normal. Yet Boethius does not generally inject his own interpretations of images or allegory into his text.

The best example of Alfred's nonmythological explication is his translation of II met. iv. This brief meter (only twenty-two short lines in Latin) uses the image of the house on safe ground; although Boethius also mentions building a house on a mountain (7), the central image contrasts the house on sand with the house on rock. The Latin offers no explication. Alfred's prose adds sixteen lines of pure explication (26.26–30 and 27.2–13): the house on the heights represents boastfulness, whereas the sand is the sand of a man's mind when it is not founded in Christ.

One probable inspiration for this trait of Alfred's translation is the commentary tradition. Although Alfred's use of commentaries to translate the *De consolatione* was highly selective, he had clearly seen glossed texts.[71] Alfred could possibly have seen non-Christian commentaries (the Servian commentaries on Virgil were much copied, and one extant manuscript is ninth-century Irish), but surely the most familiar examples would be glossed Biblical or liturgical texts.[72] Both glosses and freestanding commentaries employ the same methods Alfred uses in the *Boethius.* Commentaries add information about unfamiliar words and about figures of all types whose literal meaning may not be immediately clear. They also frequently Christianize texts that are not (explicitly) Christian. They interpret passages in moral terms, sometimes developing explanations evident already in the main text, sometimes adding them completely.

Alfred's more overt interpretations within the text have further precedent within patristic literature. The interpretation of Scripture lies at the heart of much patristic writing, and writers normally proceed by quoting a short passage that they then explicate, often in much the same way Alfred explains the Orpheus tale.[73] Homilies often select one parable or Scriptural narrative to explicate. Alfred's *Soliloquies* shows the king clearly knew Gregory's *Homily on Luke*, which begins by quoting Luke 16:19–31, the story of Lazarus and Dives. The homily then goes on to expound the significance of the details, modeling allegorical interpretation for Alfred.[74]

Gregory frequently explicates Scriptural texts elsewhere as well. The paraphrase of an image from one of the Wisdom Books is explained thus in Alfred's *Pastoral Care*: "Đære wambe nama getacnað ðæt mod, forðæm sua sua sio wamb gemielt ðone mete, sua gemielt ðæt mod mid ðære gescadwisnesse his geðeahtes his sorga" ("The word 'belly' betokens the mind, because just as the belly digests the food, so does the mind digest with discrimination the thoughts of its sorrows," *PC* 259.5–8).[75] Gregory even explicates his own figures, and Alfred retains such explications: "Hwæt is ðonne ðæt rice & se ealdordoom butan ðæs modes storm" ("What is then that kingdom and that lordship, except the storm of the mind?" *PC* 59.3–4)?[76] Thus the explication of a myth or addition of a moral might well seem to Alfred to be less an intrusion on a text than a necessary completion of it.

Yet the mythic content and allusive nature of the meters presented particular problems for Alfred. Boethius had learned classical mythology and techniques for deploying and interpreting it, but the Anglo-Saxons did not share his education. The Old English text must therefore carefully explain at the outset who the figures are and then how and why mythical or literary *exempla* can be used. Alfred moralizes much more frequently and overtly than Boethius.

Alfred first explains how his audience should read mythical material, an explanation Boethius need not provide because his initiated readers already know the required mode of reading. Alfred instructs readers that these tales (and others like them) are "false [or lying] tales" ("leasan spell," 103.14, for *fabula*, III met. xii. 52). The myth of the giants (98.30–99.3, III pr. xii. 24) contrasts with the "true tale" ("soðspell," 99.5) of the Scriptures, exemplified by the story of the Tower of Babel (99.6–20). An addition to IV met. iii describes the story of Circe and Odysseus as a *spell* made up by *lease men* (116.13). The text tells readers not to take these stories too literally, a problem that did not worry Boethius. Yet despite Alfred's criticism of the myths, he sees their usefulness and preserves them according to a Christian formula summed up in Augustine's *Soliloquia*: "est fabula compositum ad utilitatem delectationemve mendacium" ("a fable is a lie composed for utility or delectation," 96, II.19). Augustine deals with the problem at some length in the *Soliloquia*, giving examples of stories such as that of Daedalus and what lessons can be drawn from them. Alfred did not translate this section (or most of Book II) in his *Soliloquies*, but Augustine's was an influential definition of myth. The usage Alfred makes of the *leasan spell* demonstrates this instrumental understanding of fable. As Wisdom says at one point, "We sculon get of ealdum leasum spellum ðe sum bispell reccan" ("We shall yet reckon some example from these old false tales," 101.21–2).

The *De consolatione* gives its readers no advice on the way to read the mythical material in the meters. The story of Orpheus, for example, is susceptible of several readings, and its relationship to the prose remains somewhat ambiguous.[77] This meter in fact contains the most overt reading Boethius offers of his own work in the whole text; III met. xii concludes:

> Vos haec fabula respicit
> quicumque in superum diem
> mentem ducere quaeritis;
> nam qui Tartareum in specus
> uictus lumina flexerit,
> quicquid praecipuum trahit
> perdit dum uidet inferos. (III met. xii. 52–8)

> This fable addresses you who seek to lead your mind into supernal day; for whoever turns back from the light to look into Tartarus loses whatever excellence he drew [from above] when he looks down.

Boethius makes the overall meaning fairly clear but leaves the reader to determine the sense of individual elements: Orpheus is presumably the seeker; Eurydice appears to be the excellence that he lost. Yet even his interpretation allows for ambiguity: What is Tartarus? What constitutes looking down? Moreover, later commentaries presented Orpheus as the soul returning to its vices, Eurydice.[78] This treatment does not seem entirely in line with the concluding verses, but Boethius's interpretation is suggestive rather than conclusive, making space for such a reading. Boethius has excluded naïve readers who might not know what to make of such tales at all, leaving him no need to explain how to interpret it.

Alfred's conclusion is much more explicit and less likely to admit variant interpretations:

> Ðas leasan spell lærað gehwylcne mon ðara ðe wilnað helle ðiostro to flionne 7 to ðæs soðan godes liohte to cumanne, þæt he hine ne besio to his ealdan yflum, swa þæt he hi eft swa fullice fullfremme swa he hi ær dyde. Forðæm swa hwa swa mid fulle willan his mod went to ðæm yflum ðe he ær forlet, 7 hi ðonne fullfremeð, 7 hi him þonne fullice liciað, 7 he hi næfre forlætan ne þenceð, ðonne forlyst he eall his ærran good, buton he hit eft gebete. (103.14–22)[79]

> This false story teaches each man who wishes to flee hell's darkness and come to the true light of God, that he not look back at his old evils, so that he again accomplish fully that which he did before. For whoever returns his mind with full will to those evils that he left

> before, and then accomplishes them, and they please him fully, and he never thinks to leave them, then he loses all his earlier good, unless he again improve.

Alfred does not completely forestall readers' interpretations, but he directs them more strongly than Boethius does: looking back means returning to one's old sins.

Book IV met. iii, where Circe turns men into beasts, is juxtaposed with the notion that vice makes men beasts, but the meter lacks overt explication. It concludes that such an external transformation does not harm the internal man, but internal "uenena" ("poisons," IV met. iii. 35) alienate a man from himself. Alfred reads the meter as figuring the dependence of the mind on the body: "Be swilcum 7 be swylcum þu miht ongitan þæt se cræft þæs lichoman bið on þam mode, 7 þætte ælcum men ma deriað his modes unþeawas" ("By this and that you may understand that the strength [or virtue] of the body lies in the mind, and that the mind's vices harm each man more [than the body's]," 116.30–32). Just as notable as Alfred's divergent reading is the fact that this reading is performed explicitly: Alfred tells his readers how to understand the story. The *Boethius* initiates its audience into a particular Christian mode of reading. The Neoplatonic language of the source text would exclude such readers, but the *Boethius* introduces them to a kind of "internal reading" that may later enable some of them to perform such interpretations on other mythological texts. The *Boethius* imposes norms of interpretation for itself and helps produce in readers a disposition to read other texts similarly.

Alfred's interpretation of the mythological meters also negotiates another problem that patristic writers faced, but one less likely to surface in vernacular sources: the use of pagan stories to illustrate moral or religious points. Gregory generally restricts himself to Scripture or other Christian sources, but Augustine treats the problem directly. The narrator of the *Soliloquia* asks:

> A. Movet me tamen, ne per istam cuipiam videatur etiam illas fabulas veras esse; nam et has discimus et tenemus.
> R. Numquidnam magister noster nolebat nos credere, quae docebat, et nosse? (II.20)

> A[ugustine]: I am concerned, however, lest it seem to anyone even through this [the discipline of grammar] that these fables are true; for we both learn and retain them.
> R[eason]: But did our master not want us to believe and to know what he taught?

The speakers then discuss the falsity of fables and what truth they actually carry. These stories are memorable, Augustine concludes, and so are useful for conveying important meanings despite the anxiety that the unlearned might misunderstand the purpose of the stories (II.20).

The issue returns in *Soliloquia* II.29 when the two characters discuss the truth or falsity of the story of Medea flying on snakes. The language that Augustine consistently uses—of truth, falsehood, and fables—is well-suited to an Anglo-Saxon writer likewise concerned with the truth and falsehood of what Boethius also calls a "fable" and Alfred generally simply calls a story.[80] Alfred introduces the terms *soð* and *leas* (or *leasung*) into his use of Boethius's mythological stories, most notably the Orpheus and Circe meters (III met. xii and IV met. iii); Boethius never applies these terms himself.

Augustine thus provides Alfred with a model for understanding mythological stories: Augustine understands the story of Daedalus as a "ficta fabula" ("fictional fable," II.20) and the story of Medea as untrue, not so much a falsehood but an "imitationem veri" ("imitation of the truth," II.29). Both have their uses, Augustine indicates, and Alfred too finds uses for Boethius's mythological stories. Anglo-Saxon Christians, however, might not welcome Roman mythology with open arms.[81] Here Alfred expends some of the capital he has accrued: having offered readers some familiar and valuable elements so far, he may be able to convince them to continue through the most difficult mythological passages, which begin nearly two-thirds of the way through the text. The *Soliloquia* envisions a reward for this labor in the learning readers retain from the memorable tales.

Alfred thus invested effort in his people's cultural capital as well as ensuring his own symbolic capital. If he overcame the resistance that might be activated by stories both unfamiliar and un-Christian, he could initiate readers into distinguished modes of discourse. Readers of Old English would now share a mode of internal reading with a broader audience of Latin-educated readers and writers throughout the Christian world who interpreted myth in the ways that Alfred does. He would also have exposed readers to material they would encounter later if they pursued learning further. Those who reached a measure of comfort with this material would be better equipped to deal with Augustine's *Soliloquia.* Some few might ultimately venture even further, perhaps such work as Virgil's, where pagan narratives could present great barriers to Anglo-Saxon study.

Any lingering hesitation Alfred had about investing energy in perpetuating pagan myth and Christian readings thereof might have been assuaged by Augustine's handling of pagan learning in *De doctrina christiana*, which deals extensively with the topic. Although no concrete evidence exists for Alfred's direct knowledge of this text, Luke Reinsma notes, "*De doctrina* I–III presents, on the one hand a content so traditional, and on the other an exegetical methodology so pervasive throughout the Middle Ages, that we cannot argue for Aelfric having known the treatise on the basis of his exegesis alone.... Few escaped its influence; no one would have had to study the *De doctrina* to discover its principles."[82] Likewise, Teresa Webber writes, "Secular learning as an essential preliminary to sacred studies formed part of the programme of study advocated by Augustine in the *De doctrina christiana*, and set out in detail by Cassiodorus in the two books of his *Institutiones*: two texts which formed the principles for all subsequent early medieval programmes for study and learning."[83]

If Alfred did know the text or at least its methods, surely the image of "gold out of Egypt" would have informed his thinking. The Israelites taking Egyptian gold as they left in their Exodus to the Promised Land and melting it down for reuse indicates, for Augustine, that Christians need not abandon music, natural science, or letters if they can help in the understanding of Scripture; Christians must simply adapt these pagan disciplines to their own uses (II.18.2–19).[84] Although the "gold out of Egypt" metaphor provides some legitimation for Alfred's careful use of pagan mythology as allegory, Augustine emphasizes primarily how the liberal arts could aid comprehension of the Scriptures. He clearly affirms the value of history and, to a lesser extent, geography, biology, botany, and even geology as legitimate forms of study (II.29.1–5); medicine, where it does not include the "superstitious" use of amulets (II.29.5–21); and astronomy, where it does not include astrology (II.29.22–45). A list of Alfred's expansions in the *Boethius* would match this list of disciplines very closely.[85] As John Brinegar notes, a list of topics with which wisdom is concerned can be also found in Wisdom 7:17–21.[86] This list includes constellations and the nature of animals, as Augustine does; it also includes the nature of the elements and the weather, which Augustine does not specifically mention. Augustine's influential methodology, combined with Wisdom's embrace of the arts and sciences in the Old Testament, could inform Alfred's treatment even if he had not read the *De doctrina christiana* himself.

Alfred's program, then, draws on models from both history and Scripture to forge the idea of an educational and translational effort led actively by the king himself—an idea unique in its time. Christian tradition, through specific scriptural and patristic texts, affected both Alfred's choice of texts to translate and his methods of translation. The *De consolatione* supported major themes of Alfred's other translations such as God as the highest good, the end of all creation, and the ultimate source of fortune. It offered a specific, detailed portrait of one man's turn back to God to complement the many *exempla* of other translations. Yet Alfred altered his source text to include a Christian disposition of duty toward others, in place of Boethius's focus on the self, and teachings about the role of the ruler.

The *Boethius* contains a few additions and changes indebted to specific Latin Christian texts. Moreover, the *Boethius* employs Christian modes of interpretation and authority to provide readers an acceptable and yet prestigious language and style while teaching them methods of thinking and reading that would be useful in further study. In place of a difficult and foreign text aimed at Roman readers with sophisticated philosophical training, Alfred offers readers a work that could inculcate and reinforce Christian ideas in a less-educated Anglo-Saxon audience. Such changes made this unusual text more recognizable to Anglo-Saxons as part of the Christian Latin tradition, simultaneously demonstrating Alfred's own familiarity with that tradition and initiating readers into vernacular versions of its modes of discourse. Alfred would, however, make other changes even more geared toward ensuring the acceptability of the work by drawing more heavily on native traditions. To these we now turn.

Chapter 3

The Making of an English Dialogue

Alfred stayed close to his source text in many ways and introduced elements from other sources in Christian Latin culture to achieve adequacy and prestige. Yet every translator adapts his or her source text to render it comprehensible and attractive to the target audience, giving it what Translation Studies calls *acceptability*.[1] At the most basic linguistic level, a translator must use words and phrases that the audience knows instead of leaving words untranslated or rendering idiomatic expressions literally.[2] At higher levels of the text, passages or even whole works may be restructured according to the tastes of the target audience.

Although translators cannot guarantee that particular adaptations will lead to the text's acceptance within society, they seek to meet many of the expectations of their audiences. As Pierre Bourdieu writes, a discourse is only effective:

> so long as it is not simply grammatically correct but also, and above all, socially acceptable, i.e. heard, believed, and therefore effective within a given state of relations of production and circulation. . . . In reality, the conditions of reception envisaged are part of the conditions of production, and anticipation of the sanctions of the market helps to determine the production of the discourse.[3]

As king, Alfred was immune to many possible market sanctions; he was not likely to lose his position because of his techniques of translation![4] Yet he needed to win and retain the confidence of his subjects, officials, and counselors, not just in the military and political fields, but also in spiritual and intellectual ones. In his unprecedented program of translation and education, Alfred had to be sensitive to his audience's expectations for a work in Old English. If he failed to meet them, the *Boethius* would not retain that audience for long, and it would not accomplish its work of increasing symbolic capital for Alfred and his language, granting cultural capital to his elite group of readers, and inculcating certain modes of discourse and values.

Bourdieu adds that this "sense of acceptability" in discourse, even when it does not result from rational calculation, "determines corrections and all forms of self-censorship—the concessions one makes to a social world by accepting to make oneself acceptable in it."[5] Alfred's concern for acceptability affects elements of the *Boethius* ranging from the individual word and word pair to the treatment of illustrations, logic, and characterization, and even to the introduction of two new themes: friendship and kingship.

The paucity of loan-words in the *Boethius* has already been noted in chapter 1: Alfred uses native Anglo-Saxon vocabulary, not borrowings. A second characteristic of the text that marks the *Boethius* as fitting Anglo-Saxon norms is its use of doublets. Scholars often use the terms "doublet" and "word pair" specifically to mean two Old English words that replace one Latin, presuming that doublets serve only adequacy, never acceptability.[6] Yet when a 'doublet' is defined purely in terms of Old English, as two or more words joined by a conjunction that fill the same syntactic function without significant distinction in meaning,[7] it becomes clear that doublets advance acceptability even more than adequacy.

A surprisingly high number of doublets occur in the *Boethius*. Of its 745 doublets:[8]

300 (40.3 percent) do not correspond to words in the Latin text;
51 (6.8 percent) differ in meaning from the corresponding word or words in the Latin text;
104 (14 percent) have one word corresponding to the Latin and another with a different meaning;[9]
110 (14.8 percent) render a Latin pair of words;[10]
204 (27.4 percent) match one word in Latin without significant changes in meaning.

Doublets in the *Boethius* do not primarily offer precise translations of the Latin. Forty-seven percent of the Old English doublets differ in whole or in part from the corresponding Latin words; these make no attempt at direct adequacy to the Latin text.[11] On the other hand, where doublets occur in the Latin, the Old English preserves them.[12]

Even where two words in Old English replace one in Latin, both words are not necessarily required to render the Latin word precisely. In some cases, two specific words are used to translate one general word when Alfred elsewhere uses a single term for the same Latin word. For instance, Alfred usually translates "bonum" with "god" ("good," for example, as at 62.20), but when "bonum" occurs at II pr. ii. 2 he specifies "ægþer ge þinra welona ge þines weorþscipes" instead of "god" ("both your wealth and your worship," 17.7).[13] The two most common doublets, "andwyrde 7 cwæð" and "andswarode 7 cwæð" ("answered and said"), hardly seem necessary to replace the Latin "inquit" or "inquam" ("said"). Even in places where no one Old English word could be found to represent one Latin word, Alfred could still simply define a word as he did at the outset of the *Boethius*, writing, "Þa wæs sum consul, þæt we heretoha hatað" ("There was a certain consul, which we call a war leader," 7.11–2), not "Þa wæs sum consul 7 heretoha" ("There was a certain consul and war leader").

Alfred's strategic use of doublets presented Anglo-Saxon readers with a familiar technique and even familiar word pairs.[14] At least 13.3 percent of the *Boethius*'s individual doublets appear elsewhere in Old English texts.[15] Nearly half the doublets are repeated within the *Boethius* in whole or in part, sometimes for particular effects.[16] At 17.12–3 (II pr. ii. 4) Wisdom, speaking for worldly goods (Philosophy for Fortune in the Latin), says that the goods have "getydde 7 gelærde" ("educated and raised [or taught]") Boethius.[17] This must remind readers of how Wisdom earlier said she "afed 7 gelæred" ("nourished and raised," 8.18) Boethius, and when she says that she took him in "untydne 7 unlæredne" ("uneducated and untaught," 20.6), the point is unmistakable. The *Boethius* contrasts the false tutelage of worldly goods with the valuable upbringing Wisdom offers.

Antitheses work much like doublets. In an antithesis, two words fulfill the same syntactic function and are joined by a conjunction, but they have opposite meanings (as in "ægðer ge innan ge utan," "both inside and outside," 36.12). Of 167 antitheses in the *Boethius*:

93 (55.7 percent) do not match words in the Latin text;
11 (6.6 percent) of antitheses have different meanings than the Latin;
16 (9.6 percent) have one word corresponding to the Latin and another with a different meaning;
31 (22.2 percent) match Latin antitheses;[18]
16 (9.6 percent) specify two opposed words where the Latin has a blanket term that covers both;
101 (60.5 percent) are repeated at least once in the *Boethius*.

Although they help preserve adequacy to the Latin text, antitheses as well as doublets offer Anglo-Saxon readers familiar textual elements, from the technique of alliteration to the specific word pairs invoked.

That antitheses and doublets further acceptability becomes most apparent where they actually obscure arguments in the text. Before both the Latin and Old English texts have explicitly shown that the highest good, the greatest happiness, and all their earthly manifestations are one (82.18–83.19; III pr. x), Old English doublets unite these concepts syntactically where the Latin does not. For example, at 84.4–5 "þæt hehste good 7 þa selestan gesælða" ("that highest good and the best wealth") replaces "beatitudinem in summo" ("the summit of happiness," III pr. x. 10); at 84.9–10 the phrase "ælcere fullfremednesse 7 ælces godes 7 ælcere gesælðe" ("each perfection and each good and each wealth") occurs where the Latin has only "boni summi" ("the highest good," III pr. x. 11). After the concepts have been shown to be identical, the Latin text employs only one word at a time, usually *bonum*, as in "ipso bono" ("that good," III pr. x. 43); the Old English continues to use doublets: "his god 7 sio his gesælð" ("his good and his wealth," 89.1). This tactic may help keep the concepts together in the reader's mind, but it reduces the drama of Boethius's realization that they are identical, an important stage in the argument. Furthermore, at 131.11–2 an antithesis makes a distinction that should not be operative in the text: "his walde, næs seo wyrd" ("his power, not fortune"). The text has already established that "þios wandriende wyrd þe we wyrd hatað færð æfter his forþonce 7 æfter his geþeahte, swa swa he tiohhað þæt hit sie" ("This wandering fortune that we call *wyrd* follows his forethought and his thought, as he has designed that it be," 128.28–30). The antithesis actually obscures a point in the argument, that *wyrd* is part of God's plan. In these cases, verbal acceptability has clearly taken precedence over conceptual adequacy.

Old English did not require doublets, but they were commonly used in both poetry and prose.[19] Many doublets and antitheses alliterate as well, helping the *Boethius* meet audience expectations formed by Old English poetry, the dominant vernacular literary form.[20] The use of doublets in poetry is evident from the poem *Christ*, which makes a convenient comparison because of its length (1,664 lines in the Anglo-Saxon Poetic Records edition) and the fact that its three parts reflect multiple poets and ages, not just the taste of one.[21] Of the eighty-four doublets in *Christ*, sixty-one (72.6 percent) alliterate, and eight (9.5 percent) are repeated within the poem.[22] Of its twenty-nine antitheses, thirteen (44.8 percent) alliterate, and five (17.2 percent) are repeated within the poem. Although the frequency of specific characteristics varies from the *Boethius*, the use of doublets and antitheses is similar, right down to the four word pairs *Christ* and the *Boethius* share.[23] As Bourdieu notes, "The value of the utterance depends on . . . the speakers' linguistic competences, understood both as their capacity for production and as their capacity for appropriation and appreciation. . . ."[24] Alfred demonstrates such "capacity for appropriation and appreciation" by using the techniques of doublets and antitheses common in other translations (particularly the *Dialogues*, probably complete at this time) and, more important, Anglo-Saxon poetry. The use of doublets also conforms reasonably well to the Latin source text, although their frequency in Old English is much greater.

Elsewhere Alfred's strategies of acceptability diverge more from the source text. The self-consciousness the *Boethius* exhibits as a text certainly meets Anglo-Saxon rather than late-antique expectations. Both the Latin and Old English texts make references to previous or anticipated speeches, such as "memento etenim corollarii illius quod paulo ante praecipuum dedi ac sic collige" ("recall also that corollary that I gave particularly a little before and consider thus..." IV pr. iii. 8), "swa we ær spræcon" ("as we said before," 30.14, etc.), "gehere get sum bispell, 7 geheald þa wel þe ic ðe ær sæde" ("hear yet some story, and then retain well what I said to you before..." 114.1–2). Both texts also refer to other books, as in: "Aristoteles meus id, inquit, in Physicis et breui et ueri propinqua ratione definiuit..." ("'My Aristotle,' she said, 'defined it in his *Physics* with a reason brief and near the truth..." V pr. i. 12), rendered "Aristoteles min diorling hit gerehte on þære bec þe Fisica hatte..." ("My darling Aristotle explained it in the book called *Physics*..." 140.8–9).

The *Boethius* cites other books more pointedly, however: "sicut Ptolomaeo probante didicisti" ("just as you learned from Ptolemy's demonstration," II pr. vii. 4) becomes "on Ptolomeus bocum, se towrat ealles þises middangeardes gemet on anre bec" ("in Ptolemy's book, he wrote the measure of this whole world in one book,..." 41.27–8) because an audience unfamiliar with Ptolemy might take the Old English as a reference to oral teaching. "Atqui plena est exemplorum uetustas, plena etiam praesens aetas..." ("But history is full of examples, even the present age is full,..." III pr. v. 2) becomes "Hu ne wasð ðu þætte ealle bec sind fulla þara biesena þara monna þe ær us wæren?" ("How do you not know that all books are full of the examples of those men who were before us?" 65.12–13).[25] An intense awareness that these ideas come from books informs the allusions and references in the *Boethius*, adding a slight note of awe appropriate to a people for whom books are precious—and sometimes ornamented with gold to give concrete representation to their metaphorical hoards.[26]

Furthermore, the *Boethius* makes much more explicit reference to its own status as book than the *De consolatione* does. The Latin work occasionally refers to previous points in the discussion, but it never calls itself a book; the dialogue maintains the illusion that the characters are people having a real conversation. The writer and readers of the *De consolatione* had easy access to books and had been reading since childhood in a society where people of rank were expected to be literate. Indeed, Seth Lerer argues that the *De consolatione* celebrates the ability of the mind to synthesize and rewrite the books it has read.[27] Early in the text, Philosophy declares that her interest lies not in the books but in Boethius's mind: "non tam me loci huius quam tua facies mouet nec bibliothecae potius comptos ebore ac uitro parietes quam tuae mentis sedem requiro, in qua non libros sed id quod libris pretium facit, librorum quondam meorum sententias collocaui" ("Not so much this place but your appearance moves me; nor do I require a library with walls covered in ebony and glass but rather your mind as a seat, in which I once collected my teachings, not in books but in what makes the books precious," I pr. v. 6). The Latin work makes its offhand citations with the casual comfort of the *litterati.* The learned need not make explicit the fact that they are citing books because each recognizes what the other is doing; Boethius and Philosophy speak in this manner, and readers of the text are expected to respond appropriately.[28] The difficult Neoplatonic concepts and wide-ranging allusions demand a target audience with a classical education strong in logic, philosophy, and Greek and Roman literature. Bourdieu's idea of an internal reading, in which specialists develop their own terminology and style to exclude nonspecialists, fits this situation; the Latin text participates in a form of discourse that only the initiated can fully enter.[29]

The Old English text, on the other hand, addresses primarily readers who are by definition not qualified interpreters of the source text. Alfred opens the discourse to a new audience and celebrates the act of reading that Boethius takes for granted. The characters in the Old English work do refer to their own discussions as a book: "swa swa we lange ær sædon on ðisse ilcan bec" ("as we said long before in this same book," 94.11–2); "Gif wit þæt eall sculon tosmeagan, þonne cume wit late to ende þisse bec, oððe næfre" ("If we must consider all that, then we will come to the end of this book late or never," 148.4–6). The *Boethius* makes a dozen references to itself as a book.[30] Alfred and his audience struggled not to recall books from earlier intimacy but to acquaint themselves with books that were hard to obtain and often difficult to understand. The Anglo-Saxons could not reach the level of comfort with Latin that Boethius's education had given him with his own language and the books of his youth. Yet, with Alfred's help, they could read Boethius. The references of the *Boethius* to itself as a book mark a victory over the difficulties of acquiring and using books in Anglo-Saxon England.

Bourdieu notes that the form of discourse varies according to the distance between speaker and hearers and the sensitivity of the speaker to this distance. A tactful speaker reduces tension through politeness; for instance, as a request becomes more insistent, polite formulas increase: "Will you?" or "Would you?" instead of "Do this." Often this takes the form of using colloquial language or calling attention to the linguistic nature of the question itself (in Bourdieu's example, "May I ask you to come?").[31] Thus we find that as the *Boethius* makes greater demands on its audience's understanding and good will, Alfred adjusts the form. The *Boethius's* references to itself as a book cluster at crucial moments. For instance, they occur when Wisdom cautions that false goods, however beautiful and pleasurable, lead one away from the true good and are therefore in some sense evil (73.13–16), and when he explains that the good always have power and the evil never do (105.29–111.12). More references occur in the meter describing how apparently powerful tyrants are actually suffering (111.12–112.12); the related point that the good never lack their prize and the evil never lack their punishment (112.13–115.11); and the narrator's objection that people should not be able to do evil and Wisdom's answer that if they could not, their punishment would be incomplete (117.1–124.2). The penultimate reference comes when Wisdom explains that human reason cannot approach the divine (143.4–145.32), and the final reference comes in the distinction between perpetuity and eternity (147.10–149.10). The conclusion at the heart of the text that the highest good is unified and is God, who governs the world in goodness, and that evil must therefore be nothing, comes over several pages that contain five of the references (89.24–101.18). Passages that are difficult to comprehend or accept make explicit reference to the book as book.

Alfred turns an illusionistic dialogue that requires an audience familiar with specific conventions into a text that acknowledges the presence of a reading or listening audience and asks them to read further. This strategy defuses tensions that may be growing as readers or listeners struggle with an increasingly complex text. The references recall how much the audience has already learned and point to what is to come, and they create a closer bond between translator and audience by acknowledging the nature of their shared labor. Boethius need not call attention to his book as book or acknowledge his audience explicitly because less tension exists between his text and his audience.

The *Boethius*'s references to itself as book also establish connections with its audience by recalling native poetry.[32] Anglo-Saxon poetic formulas such as the often-repeated "hwæt," or variations on "we have heard" or "we have learned," reassert the poetic frame and the process of learning the audience enact as they hear or read a poem. The poets insist on the truth of the material or the tradition by which it was passed down even as they remind the audience that these are artistic creations. Finally, the references to the book as book acknowledge the concrete reality of the physical object in the hands of the reader in a way that the Latin text does not. Books were rarer and more valuable for Anglo-Saxons than for late antique readers, and Anglo-Saxon awareness of the book as object is reflected in riddles concerning books and bookmaking.[33]

At the same time, Alfred's vernacular translations, including the *Boethius*, supplement and even replace native Old English poetry and values, and his program privileges literacy and written texts over oral learning. Although the *Boethius* rewards familiarity with Old English alliterative poetry and uses some of its conventions, such as doublets and sometimes alliteration, it also ties itself to the more prestigious Latin and Christian traditions (as indeed some of the poetry does, but some does not). The frequent references to books remind readers that what they hold when they hold the *Boethius* has both physical and symbolic value that oral poetry lacks. It is no accident that Asser's probably mythical or mythicized story of Alfred memorizing Anglo-Saxon poetry presents him as quite a young boy, and Alfred's miraculous learning to read involves Latin texts when he is an adult.[34] Asser's *Life* constructs native poetry as children's play and religious texts as adult. Alfred himself uses Old English poetry to ornament his works, writing a Verse Preface to the *Pastoral Care* and possibly the *Meters of Boethius*, but a prose text conveys the heart of the argument in the *Boethius*, and a complete prose text probably preceded the Old English prosimetrum.[35]

Besides reminding readers of its nature as a book, the Old English *Boethius* displays a drive for concreteness in the illustrations used for points in the argument. Both the Latin and the Old English texts elucidate points through imagery and anecdotes, but even where the *Boethius* retains the source image or story, it often makes the illustration more concrete, narrative, or rational.[36] Many of the illustrations throughout the source text are abstract and elusive. Alfred uses two strategies for such passages. He systematically omits (or abridges) the handful of meters that rely heavily on abstract images or allusions.[37] More often, however, Alfred expands such difficult passages to explain them, make them more narrative, or add concrete details.

II met. vi on Nero demonstrates all four tactics. The Latin meter alludes to Nero's story in seventeen lines of verse; the Old English prose version of the meter is twenty lines in print (39.16–40.4), each line much longer than Boethius's pentameters. The Latin meter assumes knowledge of the story, offering readers brief allusions and memorable lines. Indeed, the first word explicitly activates readers' memories: "Nouimus quantas dederit ruinas" ("We know how many ruins he gave . . ." II met. vi. 1). The second line, "urbe flammata patribusque caesis" ("with the city burning and the leading men slain," II met. vi. 2), recalls stories and images connected with Nero's tyranny, evoking through dense imagery the narrative it does not tell. Alfred tells the story for readers who do not already know it: "Se het æt sumum cyrre forbærnan æalle Romeburg on anne sið æfter þære bisene þe gio Trogiaburg barn. Hine lyste eac geseon hu seo burne, hu lange, 7 hu leohte be þære oðerre; 7 eft he het ofslean ealle þa wisestan witan Romana" ("He ordered that all the city of Rome be burned at one time at a certain signal after the example of how old Troy burned. He wanted to see how it burned, how long, and how light, in comparison with the other; and again he ordered slain all the wisest assembly of the Romans," 39.19–22). Soon after that, ". . . sed esse / censor exstincti potuit decoris" ("He was able to be judge of the dead beauty," II met. vi. 6–7), would require telling the story of Nero's dissection of his mother. Alfred replaces this detail and its requisite explanation in favor of the blunt, "ge furðom his agen wif he ofslog mid sweorde" ("and he even killed his own wife with a sword," 39.23–4), which also arouses pathos. The meter's closing image becomes both more narrative and more concrete in Old English: "Heu grauem sortem, quotiens iniquus / additur saeuo gladius ueneno!" ("Alas the evil lot, such a wicked sword is added to savage poison!" II met. vi. 16–7) becomes "Eala, eaw, hu hefig geoc he beslepte on eallæ þam þæ on his tidum libbende wæron on eorðan; 7 hu oft his sweord wæron besyled on unscyldegum blode" ("Alas, alas, how heavy a yoke he placed on all those who were living on earth in his time; and how often his sword was soiled in guiltless blood," 39.31–3). Alfred omits some details, but more often he adds narrative, explanation, and more tangible imagery.[38]

Prose passages become more concrete and acceptable to Alfred's readers as well. A brief reference to giants (III pr. xii. 24) becomes in Alfred's hands a tale leading from giants to the Flood, a Biblical genealogy, and the tower of Babel (98.25–99.20). Anglo-Saxon audiences apparently relished tales of giants: the giants and the Flood appear in *Beowulf*; giants also appear in other poetry, the Paris Psalter (18.6 and 32.14), Psalter glosses, and several homilies and saints' lives.[39] The king's expansion affords the audience a moment of delight in recognition; in the midst of a difficult text, they find anecdotes familiar from both Scripture and vernacular poetry. The story gives readers a moment of rest and enjoyment before they plunge back into difficult arguments.[40]

Alfred also rationalizes images that do not make sense at a literal level; an audience already struggling with the text may be less willing to entertain such images than the original audience. Boethius's illustration of the man who has forgotten how to see (IV pr. iv. 31) becomes the life story of a virtuous and talented child who grows up, later becomes blind, and then forgets his gifts as he ages (122.1–12).[41] Alfred's version works at both literal and metaphorical levels, whereas Boethius's does not.[42] Nearly as difficult is Boethius's image of human nearness to God as a series of concentric circles (IV pr. vi. 14–6). Those who are occupied with worldly goods are in the outer circles; those who have given up temporal things move to inner circles, nearer God, who is the center. In Alfred's version, the illustration becomes that of a wagon wheel (129.19–131.27). The wise move up the spokes to the center, God, but they are always in contact with others in other positions on the spokes.[43] The image no longer derives from geometry, a discipline with which few Anglo-Saxons were acquainted; Alfred's image reflects readers' experience.[44]

Making illustrations more dramatic, concrete, and rational accommodates contemporary expectations. That such imagery was a contemporary norm is demonstrated by the work of other translators—despite the fact that their source texts are less abstract and allow less opportunity for such modification.[45] To the start of each book of the *Dialogues*, Wærferth adds the image of a font pouring forth water.[46] The translator of the *Orosius* expands the narrative component, elaborating the story of the Sabine women and the founding of Rome (38.31–39.24), the description of Babylon (43.33–44.6), the story of Alexander's wounding (73.18–27), and the description of the Carthaginians' mourning (89.16–29).[47] The account of what befell St. Alban's executioner takes on new vividness in the Old English *Bede*: "namque oculi eius in terram una cum beati martyris capite deciderunt" ("for his eyes fell to the earth together with the head of the blessed martyr") becomes the even more graphic "ac him ða eagan of his heafde ascuton 7 ætgædere mid þæs martyres heafde on eorðan feollan" ("but the eyes shot out of his head and fell on the earth together with the martyr's head," 40.9–11).

Further evidence of contemporary norms comes from poetry. Old English poetry may be allusive, difficult, even obscure, yet the imagery remains highly concrete. Although we cannot ascertain all the details of narratives implied in *Wulf and Eadwacer* or *The Wife's Lament*, the images are clear and vivid: "Wulf is on iege, ic on oþerre. / Fæst is þæt eglond, fenne biworpen" ("Wulf is on one island, I on the other. Secure is that island, divided by swamp," *Wulf and Eadwacer* 4–5); "Heht mec mon wunian on wuda bearwe, / under actreo in þam eorðscræfe" ("One ordered me to dwell in a grove of trees, under an oak tree in that earth-cave," *The Wife's Lament* 27–8). Boethius's images would presumably elicit immediate recognition from the late-antique audience, but Alfred's readers would have stopped and puzzled over some of them as twenty-first-century readers puzzle over those in Old English. Alfred's changes made stories and images clearer and fit prevailing norms better than a more adequate translation would. Alfred refers to objects from the Anglo-Saxon world, and he adds details we might expect in narrative poems such as *Beowulf* or *Elene.*

Concrete imagery and narrative aid comprehension; they both help explain the arguments and offer some relief from the demanding mental work of rigorous logic. The *Boethius* also assists readers by previewing and reviewing arguments in a way the *De consolatione* does not, reinforcing through repetition the meaning of important passages.[48] It also sometimes diverges from the formal logical structures and technical language of the source text to make the text easier for an audience not trained in philosophy.

Boethius's Philosophy often delays important points, producing tension and even frustration for the narrator,[49] but Alfred's text frequently hints at the direction the argument will take. By the second page of text proper his narrator has already admitted, "Me ablendan þas ungetreowan woruldsælþa" ("The false worldly goods blinded me," 8.9). Aside from this addition, the passage corresponds to I met. i, but the Latin narrator only recognizes his blindness at the end of Book II—50.7 in the Old English. A reference to "ðam hehstan freodome" ("the highest freedom") appears as early as 11.24–5, although the argument about freedom only emerges in the last ten pages of the Old English (Book V of the Latin). The Old English text does not usually preview arguments so far in advance; more often, it mentions a point coming up in a few lines. For instance, at 68.29–31 Wisdom declares that praise for a noble family is worthless "forðam þe ælc mon wat þæt ealle men of anum fæder comon 7 of anre meder" ("because every man knows that all men come from one father and from one mother"). This speech otherwise corresponds to III pr. vi. 6, but the Latin only addresses the issue of shared ancestry in III met. vi (69.16–32).[50]

The *Boethius* uses repetition more often than anticipation. Over three dozen times part of an argument, usually the conclusion, is repeated.[51] Wisdom and Philosophy each conclude that created beauty does not belong to the admirer or owner, and so the latter derives no honor or glory from it (29.20–5/II pr. v. 11). Alfred likes this argument so much that he runs briefly back through it as soon as it is done (29.25–30.2) and then repeats it again, or alludes to it, at 30.27–30, 31.5–8, and 32.25–8 as well. He occasionally repeats illustrations from an argument; having told the stories of Nero and Seneca, Papinianus and Antonius at 66.23–67.1 (III pr. v. 10–11), he repeats them at 67.1–7.

Repetition and anticipation assist in the processes of dictation and reading aloud. Walter Ong's "psychodynamics of orality" include a tendency to be "redundant or 'copious'": "Since redundancy characterizes oral thought and speech, it is in a profound sense more natural to thought and speech than is sparse linearity. Sparsely linear or analytic thought and speech is an artificial creation, structured by the technology of writing."[52] One cannot always hear everything the first time in a recitation, and redundancy ensures that important points will not be missed. Reading aloud was the norm in the early Middle Ages, both to groups and to individual listeners; the habitus of writers and readers was geared toward oral delivery. A speaker or writer who knows what points he or she is about to make can make them in advance as well as repeat them later, and both strategies improve audience comprehension, so anticipation and repetition become ingrained as well.

Alfred also faced the hurdle of presenting a text written by a trained logician to a people with little knowledge of formal logic, and indeed Alfred himself probably had minimal acquaintance with the discipline as such. Alfred frequently disrupts the form of the syllogism, leading some scholars to charge him with illogic.[53] A few changes are radical enough to produce a different or even defective sense. Yet the relationship between the two texts is sometimes more complicated than that. In a passage on the highest good, a clear syllogism is transformed into something else:

Si beatitudo est summum naturae bonum ratione degentis nec est summum bonum quod eripi ullo modo potest, quoniam praecellit id quod nequeat auferri, manifestum est quin ad beatitudinem percipiendam fortunae instabilitas aspirare non possit. (II pr. iv. 25)

If happiness is the highest good of a being with reason, that is not the highest good which in any way is able to be taken away; since that which is not able to be taken away excels it, it is obvious that the instability of fortune cannot aspire to seizing that happiness.

Forðæm ic ðe mindgige þæt þu ongite þætte nan gesælð nis on þis andweardan life ac onget ðæt nauht nis betere on þis andweardum life[54] ðonne seo gesceadwisnes, forðæm hio þurh nan þing ne mæg þæm men losian; forðy is betere þæt feoh þætte næfre losian ne mæg ðonne þætte mæg 7 sceal. Hu ne is þe nu genoh sweotole gesæd þæt sio wyrd þe ne mæg nane gesælða sellan? forþæmþe ægþer is unfæst, ge seo wyrd ge seo gesælð; forþam sint swiðe tedre 7 swiðre hreosende þas gesælþa. (25.24–31)

Therefore I remind you so that you understand that there is no good in this present life, and understand that nothing is better in this present life, other than discernment, because men may not lose her in any way; for that property is better which cannot be lost than that which can and will. How is it not clearly enough said that *wyrd* may not give you any goods? For either is unstable, both *wyrd* and goods; for goods are very fragile and very ephemeral.

The Old English does not make quite the same argument; while still arguing against faith in fortune, it adds an argument in favor of the faculty of discernment, a transformation (or mistranslation) of the Latin *ratione degentis*. The passage does not constitute a logical progression at all like that in the Latin passage. Yet not only is the conclusion (that earthly goods are not worthwhile in the end) the same, but the reason is similar: that they are too short-lived to be valued. This point seems to be achieved more by verbal repetition than by rigorous argumentation. The negatives and the words *wyrd* and *gesælð* are reiterated often. Here Alfred does not simply break a syllogism; he transforms the argument, adding a new point and persuading through a different strategy, that of repetition.[55]

Thus Alfred does not always keep the terse, syllogistic logic of the original. Instead, he occasionally omits steps, produces a different argument with the same or a similar conclusion, summarizes an argument, or adds evidence. The *Boethius* departs from the strict logic of the source text for a looser logic of its own frequently enough that an Anglo-Saxon reader or listener would find its style of argumentation consistent, and he or she would probably not notice a difference between those points that came from the source text and those that were added. The translation is not a piece of Latin dialectic, but a hybrid of late antique logic rendered in Old English and less formal reasoning. Alfred's modes of argumentation may seem foreign to modern readers, but the new readers that Alfred's program was designed to produce were unprepared for the logic of Boethius.[56] Moreover, dictation was the normal means of composition in early England.[57] Alfred most likely read aloud or had read to him passages from the Latin, then dictated his translation among a small group of helpers and scribes.[58] He may well have discussed the material and incorporated others' suggestions as he went. The *Boethius*, once finished, would often be read aloud as well. The Anglo-Saxon habitus was much more oriented toward oral communication than to the silent, private experience of letters on a page, whether in reading or writing.

A related and more pervasive change is the use of less technical language in the *Boethius*. Alfred had to translate not only Boethius's Latin, but also his philosophical and logical vocabulary, a language unfamiliar in ninth-century England. Bourdieu's notion of an internal reading works for late-antique philosophy as well as modern: practitioners develop a specialized language and genre with its own rules for reading and writing.[59] Alfred had to invert such an operation: he removed a text from a Neoplatonic hermeneutic circle and made it accessible to an audience that did not speak their language. He did so by removing or altering some of the argumentative structures and by his treatment of logical markers in the Latin text. Although these markers might have an important role in the formal logic of the source text, they were of questionable value in the less formal Old English text and did not necessarily have strict equivalents in the vernacular.[60]

Alfred again uses strategies of omission and substitution to make the text acceptable. Latin terms with technical meanings are either simply omitted or translated less rigorously; Alfred does not create equivalents to use consistently for each Latin term. "Necesse est, inquam" ("'It follows necessarily,' I said," III pr. ix. 15) marks the necessary, logical conclusion of a syllogism. Alfred supplies instead, "Ða andsworede ic 7 cwæð: þisses ic eom ealles geþafa" ("Then I answered and said, 'I am in agreement with all of this,'" 76.10–1). This latter assent is weaker; the speaker was not compelled to accept the conclusion. "Ne mæg ic ðæs oðsacan, forðæm þe ic his wæs ær geþafa" ("Nor can I forsake this, because I consented to it before," 85.9–10) is stronger, but it still does not have quite the same logical force as the corresponding "Nec propositis, inquam, prioribus refragari queo et illis hoc inlatum consequens esse perspicio" ("'I cannot dispute those things that were said before,' I said, 'and I see that this conclusion follows from them,'" III pr. x. 17). Alfred tends to change impersonal logical phrases with set meanings such as *corollarii illius, necesse est,* and *concessum est* into a variety of more subjective expressions of agreement.[61] Similarly, *ita est, monstratum est,* and forms of *concludere* are translated in a variety of ways.[62] *Ratio* and *rationes* are often rendered by the more general *spell, bispell,* or *bisn,* all of which mean speech, story, or example.[63] The word *racu* perhaps comes closest to *ratio,* as in this passage: "Nam ne illud quidem adquiescent quod aeque ualidis rationum nititur firmamentis . . ." ("For indeed they will not agree to that which is similarly shown with valid foundations of reasons . . ." IV pr. iv. 32); "Ic ðe wolde giet reccan sume swiðe rihte raca; ac ic wat þæt þis folc his nele gelyfan . . ." ("'I would yet tell you some very true reasons; but I know that this people will not want to believe them . . ." 122.17–8). However, Alfred generally does not use *racu* but *bispell* and similar words. He instead translates those words and phrases that punctuate stages in the argument not as markers of logical steps but as turns in a conversation. In place of using technical terms to signal conclusions, the *Boethius* reiterates who has said what ("Hwæt ic þonne ær sæde . . ." "What I then said before . . ." 85.6) or has the narrator accept the conclusion for himself and, by implication, for the reading or listening audience ("þisses ic eom ealles geþafa," "I am in agreement with all of this," 76.11, with many variations in other passages). To those who had never learned dialectic, this would have seemed a clearer, more natural way for a dialogue to proceed than a closer translation of the Latin, with its technical and impersonal expressions, would have.

The Old English terms offer reasonable equivalence without having the same history of usage that the Latin terms have. Alfred must establish approximations, for no ready-made Old English vocabulary of logic awaits him. Alfred's approximations begin the work of creating a standard language, a language that can be used, in Bourdieu's definition "outside the constraints and without the assistance of the situation."[64] Alfred takes a step toward the objective vocabulary of Latin logic, yet he cannot yet truly distance his characters from personal circumstances. As Bourdieu explains, writers "play their part in constructing the legitimate language by selecting, from among the products on offer, those which seem to them worthy of being consecrated and incorporated into the legitimate competence through educational inculcation. . . ."[65] Readers may not be able to wield the words themselves, but they must be able to recognize the vocabulary and usage to accept it.[66] Alfred cannot introduce an entirely new set of logical terms or even significantly redefine available words in Old English. Instead of developing a set of regular, analytical substitutions, as modern translators of logic might, he takes a flexible approach.

The phrasing becomes consistently more personal in Old English: instead of having objective, logical relationships, the steps in the argument exist in relation to the speakers.[67] Where the Latin argues in the third person or in impersonal terms, the Old English often employs the second person.[68] "Quae est igitur haec potestas..." ("What therefore is this power..." III pr. v. 7) becomes "Hu þincð þe nu, hu þe se wela 7 se anwald licige..." ("How does this seem now, how do this wealth and power please you..." 66.1–2). To translate "maneant modo quae paulo ante conclusa sunt" (III pr. xi. 4), Alfred not only replaces the logical marker "conclusa sunt" with a more personal reference, he changes the third-person plural subjunctive, referring to the previous conclusions, into a second-person singular command to the narrator: "ne forgite þæt þæt ic ðe ær tæhte" ("Let those things remain now that were concluded a little earlier" becomes "Do not forget that which I taught you before," 90.1). He transforms the impersonal response "Manebunt" (III pr. xi. 5) into "Ða cwæð ic: Nese, na forgite ic hit no" ("They shall remain" becomes "Then I said, 'No, I will not forget it,'" 90.1–2). First-person expressions also introduce arguments in the Old English but not in the Latin, as in the addition of "þonne ic secgge" ("then I say," 54.9) in a passage that is impersonal in the source text (III pr. ii. 9).

Furthermore, Wisdom makes personal remarks more freely than Philosophy. In one addition, he complains about the difficulty of the arguments: "Nu ðu miht ongitan hu hefig 7 hu earfoðe þis is eall to gerecanne" ("Now you might understand how heavy and how difficult it is to tell all of this," 127.21–2). In another, the narrator's interlocutor explains his or her motives, but there is a significant difference in tone between the two: "Faciam, inquit illa, tui causa liberter..." ("'I will do this,' she said, 'freely for your sake..." III pr. i. 7). The Latin is relatively emotional and personal for Boethius, but the Old English goes even further: "Ða cwæð sio Gesceadwisnes: Ic wille forlustlice for ðinum lufum..." ("Then said this Discernment, 'I will most gladly for your love...'" 51.18–19).

Alfred retains the personal references typical of oral cultures even as he moves toward a more logical language in a compromise with Latin. Separating the style of argumentation completely from the characterization in either the Latin or the Old English text is difficult. Because arguing is precisely what the characters do throughout both texts, how they do it defines them. The characters in the Old English text are less argumentative and debate in politer terms than in the Latin.[69] Ruth Waterhouse's comments on the *Soliloquies* describe the *Boethius* accurately as well. She writes that Alfred makes the dialogue's participants more friendly to draw in the audience: "Together, they build up a tone or relationship between writer and audience characterized by its immediacy and friendly intimacy."[70] Alfred has not radically changed either of the characters but simply given their relationship a more personal and less scholastic tone.

In the Latin text, Boethius and Philosophy are first and foremost student and teacher, and their logical vocabulary reflects this hierarchy. In the Old English, the relationship is less strictly defined. Wisdom is still a teacher, but he and the narrator speak more as fellow men. The relationship in the Old English text is also more dynamic: Wisdom shows increasing sympathy for the narrator as the text progresses. Both are more emotional, more cooperative, and less aggressive; the atmosphere is less that of a debate or disputation than of a friendly discussion. This sort of relationship would be more familiar to an Anglo-Saxon audience that had never been trained in dialectic. Anglo-Saxons were taught at home or sometimes in monastic settings. Parents would teach, and on the rare occasions when children had tutors (doubtless limited to the upper reaches of society), they would have been members of the household.[71] The idea of Wisdom as a parent or foster parent makes a great deal of sense within the Anglo-Saxon social context, and Alfred translates Boethius's "nostro quondam lacte nutritus, nostris educatus alimentis" ("I once nursed you with my milk, raised you on my food," I pr. ii. 2) easily as "fostermodor" ("fostermother," 8.27) and "agne modor" ("own mother," 9.1). Moreover, Alfred drops the first three references to the narrator's family (I pr. iv. 40–1, II pr. iii. 6–8, and II pr. iv. 1); the first reference to them finally appears at 22.1–26 (II pr. iv. 4–7). At the start, Wisdom seems to be the only family the narrator has—and that, in fact, is the case. Boethius has been irrevocably separated from rest of his family, although he does not yet know it; the preface tells readers that he will never be freed but executed.

At first, however, Wisdom shows little sympathy. The Latin narrator's protestations at I pr. iii. 3 that he has been falsely accused are not translated at all, and his defense, which occupies I pr. iv, is severely abridged (9.18–30) in favor of generalizations about the triumph of the unjust (10.1–27). Philosophy's agreement that Boethius has been unjustly accused is missing from the Old English (I pr. v. 8–9), and biographical material in I pr. v. 20 is also eliminated. These omissions change the relationship between the narrator and his interlocutor as well as the audience's perception of him. The character is still suffering unjustly: the preface has made clear that he acted in the interests of the true religion in sending his letters (7.19–20).[72] His deeds should make him a martyr; he stood up for religion, and now he must pay the price. He is unwilling to pay it, however, unlike most saints.[73] Accordingly, in the beginning he may seem less sympathetic to Wisdom and to the audience.

Wisdom and Philosophy share the same first criticism of the narrator: both tell him he is responsible for his own exile (11.9–12/I pr. v. 3). Yet in the Latin, Philosophy asks whether the narrator thinks misfortune is new because he never suffered it before. She says that Fortune has always been changeable; therefore, Fortune has always been the same for him (I pr. vii. 9). Wisdom changes the question to whether he thinks it has not happened to others and tells him that everyone shares the same fortune (15.20–3). The two authors repeat their respective points a little later (II pr. iii. 12 in the Latin, 20.17–9 and 21.22 in the Old English). These two criticisms strike different chords. Philosophy's advice that the narrator learn to accept his fortune is fairly mild, and many readers can sympathize with a reversal of fortune. Wisdom, on the other hand, implies that the narrator has been privileged for a long time and will have to adjust to living like other people, an accusation that hardly elicits sympathy, especially from Anglo-Saxons reading about a late-antique, privileged Roman. The fact that Philosophy's criticism is repeated once but Wisdom's twice also increases the force of the Old English admonitions.

The Latin text is not wholly sympathetic to the narrator, sunk as he is in self-pity. In one passage, the narrators' interlocutors in both texts are unmoved by the character's suffering: "illa uultu placido nihilque meis questibus mota" ("placidly, with her face moved not at all by my complaints," I pr. v. 1); "se Wisdom þa 7 seo Gesceadwisnes him bliðum eahum on locodon; 7 he for þæs Modes geomerunge næs nauht gedrefed" ("Then Wisdom and Discernment looked on him with blithe eyes; and he was not at all disturbed by Mod's groaning," 10.29–11.2). In a second, the interlocutor has become impatient: "Sed delicias tuas ferre non possum" ("But I am not able to bear your whims…" II pr. iv. 11) becomes in Old English: "Ac ic ne mæg adreohan þine seofunga for þam lytlan þe þu forlure" ("But I cannot endure your lamentations for that little which you have lost," 23.21–2). In both cases Wisdom seems even further removed and less sympathetic than Philosophy.

At the same time, differences appear both in the narrator's self-representation and in the interaction with his interlocutor.

> Tum ego: Speciosa quidem ista sunt, inquam, oblitaque rhetoricae ac musicae melle dulcedinis tum tantum cum audiuntur oblectant, sed miseris malorum altior sensus est; itaque cum haec auribus insonare desierint insitus animum maeror praegrauat.—Et illa: Ita est, inquit; haec enim nondum morbi tui remedia, sed adhuc contumacis aduersum curationem doloris fomenta quaedam sunt; namque in profundum sese penetrent cum tempestiuum fuerit ammouebo. (II pr. iii. 2–4)

> Then I said, "Indeed those things are beautiful, and smeared with the honey of sweet rhetoric and music that please so much while they are heard, but for the miserable there is a deeper sense of evils; and thus when these things cease to sound in my ears, sadness weighs down my soul inside." And she said, "Thus it is, for these are not yet remedies

for your disease, but are certain salves for the contumacious sadness that resists a cure; I will make things penetrate you more deeply when the time is right."

The narrator in the Old English is more humble; instead of complaining about the lack of a cure, he admits his own guilt. Wisdom is then more accusing and shifts the context from illness to sin:

> Đa cwæð þæt Mod: Ic me ongite æghwonan scyldigne, ac ic eom mid þæs laðes sare swa swiðe ofðrycced þæt ic inc geandwyrdan ne mæg. Þa cwæð se Wisdom eft: Þæt is nu giet þinre unrihtwisnesse þæt ðu eart fulneah forþoht. Ac ic nolde þæt þu þe forþohte, ac ic wolde þæt ðe sceamode swelces gedwolan; forðæm se se ðe hine forþencð se bið ormod, ac se se ðe hine sceamað se bið on hreowsunga. (19.26–20.1)[74]

> Then Mod said, "I understand myself to be guilty in every way, but I am so greatly oppressed with the sorrow of this pain that I cannot answer you." Then said Wisdom again, "That is still your unrighteousness, that you have very nearly despaired. But I would not want you to despair about yourself, but I wish that you were ashamed of such errors; because he who despairs is proud, but he who is ashamed of himself is in sorrow."

Mod is not portrayed here with kindness, either in his own account or Wisdom's, and the tone is markedly harsher than that of the Latin. Yet Mod's acknowledgement of sin paves the way for the narrator's redemption.

Wisdom and the audience both have some small sympathy with the character from the start on which the text later builds. The prologue tells us, "se wæs in boccræftum 7 on woruldþeawum se rihtwisesta" ("He was in booklearning and worldly matters the most righteous," 7.12–3)—an admirable man. After the narrator's first admission of guilt (19.26–20.1) Wisdom gradually warms to him. Where Philosophy merely begins to lecture on the evils of fame (II pr. vii. 2), Wisdom introduces his speech, "Eala, Mod, eala . . ." ("Alas, Mod, alas," 41.8). The narrator accepts both his guilt and his fate: "ac ðeah me giet mare frecenes on becume, ne cwiðe ic næfre ma þæt hit butan gewyrhtum sie; forðæm ic wat þæt ic maran 7 hefigran wyrðe wære" ("though yet more misfortune come upon me, I will never again say that it is without desert; for I know that I am worthy of more and heavier," 50.18–20). Soon after, Wisdom addresses him by name for the first time: "Geþenc þu nu be ðe selfum, la, Boetius" ("Think now about yourself, indeed, Boethius," 58.24–5). The Latin has only pronouns here ("te ipsum," "you yourself," III pr. iii. 5), not names; in fact, Philosophy never addresses Boethius by name.

Wisdom even comes to express camaraderie with the narrator, including them both in "we" statements that have no parallel in the Latin. Introducing a new stage in an argument, Philosophy says, "Atqui hoc quoque pulchrius nihil est quod his adnectendum esse ratio persuadet" ("But there is nothing more beautiful than this, which reason persuades should be joined to these things," III pr. x. 27). Wisdom declares: "Nis nan wuht wynsumre ne gewisre þonne þæt ðing þæt þis spell ymbe is 7 we nu embe sprecan willað; forðæm me þincð good þæt we hit gemengen to ðæm ærran" ("There is nothing more winsome nor wiser than that thing about which this speech is, and we now desire to speak concerning it; for it seems good to me that we add it to the previous," 86.12–5). Philosophy speaks of the argument proceeding independently of the participants; Wisdom aligns himself with the narrator as a seeker of knowledge. The Latin makes clear that the ignorance is the prisoner's: "Quo fit ut, tametsi uobis hunc ordinem minime considerare ualentibus confusa omnia perturbataque uideantur, nihilo minus tamen suus modus ad bonum dirigens cuncta disponat" ("As it happens, even if all things seem to you, who are not at all strong enough to consider the order of the universe, confused and perturbed, nevertheless, however, each thing disposes itself towards the good, its own manner directing it," IV pr. vi. 21). The Old English not only changes the second-person *uobis* to *us*, it uses the first-person plural pronoun four times: "Ac se godcunda foreþonc hit understent eall swiðe rihte, þeah *us* þince for *urum* dysige þæt hit on woh fare; forðæm *we* ne cunnon þæt riht understandan. He demð þeah eall swiðe rihte, þeah *us* hwilum swa ne ðince" ("But the divine foreknowledge understands it all very rightly, though it seems to *us* in *our* foolishness that it goes badly; for *we* cannot understand the right. He, however, judges all very rightly, though sometimes it does not seem so to *us*," 131.16–9, emphasis added). Whereas Wisdom speaks of "our" difficulties here, his discourse does not truly lack authority; Wisdom himself never questions God's actions but always seems to understand them, and for the next two pages he explains how various fates are really for the best. Instead, this rhetorical gesture brings his audiences—the narrator and the audience of the text—closer to him. He does not lose any authority when he momentarily puts himself on the same footing with the prisoner or his readers, casting the work of seeking the truth as shared labor, but he gains good will.[75]

At the same time, the narrator's responses to Wisdom also emphasize their relationship. Even when the Latin narrator agrees strongly—"Firmissime, inquam, uerissimeque conclusum est" ("'This is most firmly and truly concluded,' I said," III pr. x. 6)—the Old English narrator casts his affirmation in more personal terms: "Ða andsworede ic 7 cwæð: Swiðe rihtlice 7 swiðe gesceadwislice þu hæfst me ofercumen 7 gefangen, þæt ic ne mæg no wiðcweðan ne furðum ongean ðæt þencan, buton þæt hit is eall swa swa þu sægst" ("Then I answered and said, 'Very rightly and very discerningly you have overcome and taken me, so that I cannot argue nor even think contrary to that, but that is all just as you say,'" 83.15–9). In the Old English, the emphasis is on the speakers as much as on the argument, and the repeated pronouns call attention to the cooperative nature of the endeavor.

The narrator agrees both more emphatically and a little more often. Twice Alfred substitutes agreement for another question: "Quonam, inquam, modo?" ("'In what way?' I said," III pr. ix. 17), the narrator's question about how in seeking the parts people lose the whole, becomes "Ða cwæð ic: þæt is soð" ("Then I said: 'That is true," 76.23–4). The narrator's objection to Philosophy's declaration that all fortune is good, "Et qui id, inquam, fieri potest?" ("'And how is that possible?' I said," IV pr. vii. 2), becomes: "Ða cwæð ic: Ic wene þæt hit eaðe swa bion mæge, þeah us hwilum oðer þynce" ("Then I said: 'I know that it easily may be so, though it sometimes seems otherwise to us,'" 137.4–5). In each case Wisdom continues his explanation of the assertion he has just made, recognizing that the narrator's response indicates neither capitulation nor full understanding but a less competitive mode of dialogue and a faith that explanations will follow. The Latin characters almost invariably just speak (often without a verb of speaking); the Old English duo speak with emotion: "smearcode . . . 7 cwæð" ("Then . . . smiled and said . . ." 91.11, 137.28–9, etc.) and "wundrode . . . 7 cwæð" ("Then . . . wondered and said . . ." 98.17, 122.19–20, etc.) are used for each speaker at least once. Near the end, Alfred writes, "Ða onsac se Wisdom sarlice, 7 cwæð . . ." ("Then Wisdom denied it sorrowfully, and said . . ." 138.15). The emotional element appears most strongly in the last third of the work as the characters come to understand each other better and the audience is brought closer to both of them.[76]

Students trained in dialectic may bark out questions as abruptly as the Latin narrator does, and modern scholars used to such dialogues will not be surprised, but Anglo-Saxons educated by family members or clerics might be taken aback at such brusqueness. Pierre Riché notes that the dialogue remained a form of teaching in post–Roman Europe, but it did not have the same character as in earlier times.[77] Alfred makes the narrator a more obviously cooperative partner in the dialogue, reflecting differences in social situation between a late-antique student and master and an Anglo-Saxon one.[78] As Bourdieu notes, "Form [in a discourse] and the information it imparts condense and symbolize the entire structure of the social relation" between the speakers; Alfred's alterations make the exchanges more acceptable to the "social sense" of the audience.[79]

The relationship between the Old English characters is still centered primarily on teaching, but a less formal kind of teaching than in the source text. No longer are the two simply student and teacher confined to a purely academic discourse; sometimes they speak as student and teacher, sometimes as child and parent, and sometimes as two friends. To an audience without a tradition of dialectic or philosophy, this conversational tone would have been easier to understand and to relate to than the source text's mode of argumentation and characterization. Alfred makes no radical changes here; most of what he does in the characterization has some roots in the Latin. Alfred's modifications of emphasis away from philosophical argumentation to a friendlier relationship also complement his alteration of themes: his version emphasizes the importance of friendship or comradeship more than the Latin text does.[80]

Nearly all of Alfred's passages on friendship are expansions, not free additions. Boethius too considers friendship a positive good and not a gift of fate, but the difference between the writers emerges in their terminology. Boethius uses the word *sodalis* ("companion") once, but otherwise generally employs the terms *amicus* ("friend") and *amicitia* ("friendship"), locating his work in the classical tradition for which Cicero is best known.[81] Such friendship involves men who are social equals and free to choose friends based on virtues or common interests. Boethius uses the words *familiaris* and *familiaritas*, implying a more formal bond between friends or associates and the powerful, only in III pr. V.

Alfred uses a wider variety of terms, including *freond, freondscipe, geferræden, geferscipe*, and *gefera*. Bosworth-Toller defines *freond* in terms of both the Modern English "friend" and the Latin *amicus* (335), but the *Supplement* adds:

> (3) a relative, kinsman; (3a) where the duties or benefits consequent upon kinship are referred to;...(5) one who wishes well to another, favors, supports, helps; (5a) in the laws, one who undertakes responsibility on behalf of another. (266)

These ideas of duty and legal status are not present in the Latin *amicus*; they are specific to an Anglo-Saxon conception of friendship. Bosworth-Toller links *geferræden* to both *amicitia* and *comitatus* (391), which places the term in a context not just of friendship but association in war. *Geferscipe* is initially defined as "society, fellowship, brotherhood: societas, comitatus, clerus" (391), and the supplement adds "(1) a collection of persons (a) in a general sense, a company (b) in special senses: a society of ecclesiastics (α) an association, a guild (β) a profession, order (γ) a class, social order (ε) a retinue, court; comitatus" (326). Again, we see less a sense of personal choice than in the Latin *amicus* and more a sense of legal and social status and obligation. The related *gefera* is even further from *amicus.* Bosworth-Toller defines it, "A companion, comrade, associate, fellow, colleague, fellow-disciple, man, servant" (391). The *Supplement* adds specifics:

> (1) a companion, associate; (2) an associate in work, partner, assistant; (2a) an associate in office, a colleague . . . (3) an associate in the execution of a plan, a confederate . . . (4b) a comrade, brother in arms; (4c) a fellow-servant . . . (8) a follower, adherent, one of a retinue. (325)

This word carries even stronger connotations of specific legal and social status. The text has come quite far from *amicus.* These terms are closer to the Latin *familiaris,* and Alfred translates accordingly, using *freond* where Boethius uses *amicus* while using *gefera* in other passages.[82] The connotations of mutual responsibility and legal status attached to the Old English words give the *Boethius* a different charge from the Latin.

Other alterations are more dramatic. When Boethius mentions false friends of fortune, Alfred changes the passage. Both texts have been discussing whether the king's friendship is of value, a point illustrated by tales of Seneca and Papinianus's deaths at the hands of their powerful "friends." The Latin text addresses the disadvantages and presumes that such a relationship is not true friendship but friendship brought about by fortune: "An praesidio sunt amici quos non uirtus sed fortuna conciliat? Sed quem felicitas amicum fecit infortunium faciet inimicum. Quae uero pestis efficacior ad nocendum quam familiaris inimicus?" ("Are not those friends a danger whom not virtue but fortune attracts? But those whom good fortune made friends, misfortune shall make enemies. Truly, what plague is more effective at harming than an enemy who is a close associate?" III pr. v. 12–4). Alfred not only expands the passage, he presents a more positive view of the relationship between the ruler and his associates:

> Oððe hwæt forstod seo menigu þara freonda þam deorlingum þara cyninga? oððe hwæt forstent hio ænegum men? Forðon þa frend cumað mid þæm welum 7 eft mid ðæm welan gewitað buton swiðe feawa. Ac ða frend þe hine ær for ðæm welan lufiað þa gewitað eft mid þæm welan, 7 weorðað ðonne to feondum, buton þa feawan ðe hine ær for lufum 7 for treowum lufedon; þa hine woldon þeah lufian ðeah he earm wære, þa him wuniað. Hwylc is wirsa wol oððe ænegum men mare daru þonne he hæbbe on his geferrædenne 7 on his neaweste feond 7 freondes anlicnesse? (67.14–24)

> Or what did a retinue of friends avail the darlings of the kings? Or what does it avail any man? For friends come with wealth and again

> depart with this wealth, except for very few. But the friends who loved him before for the wealth then depart again with the wealth, and become then enemies, but for the few who loved him before for love and for truth; then they would love him although he were wretched, and they remain with him. What is a worse plague or greater harm to any man than that he have in his retinue and in his presence an enemy and the likeness of a friend?

Although Alfred does not omit or change what is present in the source text, his additions mitigate its impact. Boethius leaves no possibility that the powerful might have genuine friends; Alfred admits that genuine friendship under such circumstances is the exception more than the rule, but he emphasizes the value of those exceptions. His use of *geferrædenne* and *neaweste* also change the context. Seneca was Nero's tutor and Papinianus was Antoninus's favorite; their status at court was entirely based on their personal relationships with the emperors, and they were therefore subject to the emperors' whims. Alfred writes about different relationships. He speaks of the retinue, men with official duties and recognized, mutual social and political obligations with the king. The Boethian comments still apply; many of these men are not in the retinue because of friendship with the king but simply because he is the king and to have enemies among them is dangerous. Yet Alfred evokes a more formal, legal relationship than the one described in the source text.

The difference between Alfred's circumstances and conception of friendship and Boethius's appear more fully in other passages. One Latin prose opens with Philosophy's rhetorical question: "An uero regna regumque familiaritas efficere potentem ualet?" ("Does kingship or association with kings suffice to make one powerful?" III pr. v. 1). In the source text, Philosophy continues uninterrupted to answer her own question in the negative. In the translation, the narrator answers the corresponding Old English question: "Ða andsworede ic 7 cwæt: Forhwi ne magon hi? Hwæt is on ðis andweardan life wynsumre 7 betere þonne þæs cyninges folgað 7 his neawest, 7 siððan wela 7 anweald?" ("Then I answered and said: 'Why may they not? What is more pleasant and better in this present life than the king's retinue and his presence, and after that wealth and power?'" 65.5–7). Wisdom then gives the same anecdotes that Philosophy does, but he never directly challenges the narrator's answer. When Alfred explicitly raises the possibility of real love and loyalty for one's king, he opens the way for an entirely different relationship between a king and his followers than Boethius admits, one that may allow the kind of benefits the narrator mentions.

Alfred seems to be reflecting less on friendship between equals, freely chosen, and more on hierarchical relationships based on loyalty and love. As Otten notes, the shift is from a Roman to a Germanic value system.[83] This kind of relationship can be seen throughout Old English literature—for instance, between Beowulf and Hygelac or Wiglaf and Beowulf, and in the loyalty of retainers to their lords in poems such as *The Battle of Maldon* or *The Fight at Finnsburg.* A religious version of the relationship is evident in the Cross's devotion to Christ as its lord in *Dream of the Rood.* Alfred's changes align the themes of the translation more closely with Anglo-Saxon literature and culture and represent a social reality far different from that of the source text.

Friendship or comradeship is an important part of a social structure that culminates for Anglo-Saxons in the king.[84] The problems of good and bad kings, and of how a king and his followers should behave toward one another, run through most Old English poetry either explicitly or implicitly. Alfred takes up the theme although the Latin text demonstrates no concern with the real power of a king. The *De consolatione* makes many references to kings and even kingship, but they are images, not political statements. Anecdotes about kings' actions and their effects on others illustrate the nature of fortune: fortune is as changeable as the whims of Nero or Antoninus, and it is best to isolate oneself from them just as one must escape the tyranny of fortune. Anecdotes about the kings themselves also illustrate the necessity of self-control, showing rulers' lack of restraint and inability to attain the ends they desire. Both kinds of citations of kings employ them as images. Kings themselves are not the real focus. The possible exception is Nero, who, Gerard O'Daly argues, represents Theodoric, whom Boethius could not name for obvious reasons.[85] This veiled allusion lends a personal note to the text, but one instantly transformed into metaphor. Nero may represent Theodoric, but his role as a figure lacking self-control overshadows other meanings.

Alfred and his audience, however, have great interest in the real power of kings. As Bourdieu makes clear, such interest need not be the result of cynical calculation; the habitus one has acquired from experience makes certain thoughts thinkable and others unthinkable.[86] For Alfred, and for many of his readers, a world in which the power of the king does not matter is simply unthinkable. Nor must Alfred's expansion of the material on kings be calculated to support his position as monarch. Indeed, although Alfred's translation makes kings and kingship a new theme, his additions and changes do not simply champion the crown but present a much more complex picture.[87]

A closer translation of the Latin text would leave the audience with the impression that kings use their power for ill and that that power is ultimately ineffective even for the king. Alfred keeps the examples, but sometimes modifies the impression produced by such passages through a few alterations and additions. In one passage Philosophy declares the impotence of rulers:

> O praeclara potentia, quae ne ad conseruationem quidem sui satis efficax inuenitur! Quodsi haec regnorum potestas beatitudinis auctor est, nonne, si qua parte defuerit, felicitatem minuat, miseriam importet? Sed quamuis late humana tendantur imperia, plures necesse est gentes relinqui quibus regnum quisque non imperet. Qua uero parte beatos faciens desinit potestas hac impotentia subintrat, quae miseros facit; hoc igitur modo maiorem regibus inesse necesse est miseriae portionem. (II pr. v. 2–5)
>
> What eminent power, which is indeed found to be not powerful enough to save itself! Even if this power of kings were author of happiness, would it not, if it were lacking in any part, diminish happiness, bring misery? But however far human rule extends, of necessity many peoples are left whom one does not rule. In whatever part the power making people happy fails, impotence enters there, which makes them miserable; in this way therefore by necessity there must be a great portion of misery for all kings.

In Alfred's translation, the sarcastic "O" of the Latin becomes a genuine lament, "Eala ea" (65.15), and he expands on the last two sentences:

> Hwæt, þa cyningas, þeah hi mænig ger þioda wealden, ne wealdað hi þeah ealra þara þe hi wealdan woldan, ac bioð forðæm swiðe earme on hiora mode forðy hi nabbað sume þara þe hi habban wolden; forðæm ic wat þæt se cyning þe gitsere bið, þæt he hæfð maran ermðe þonne anwald. (65.22–7)
>
> Lo, the kings, although they rule peoples for many years, yet they never rule all of those they want to rule, but they are always very wretched in their minds because they do not have some of those that they want to have [under their rule]; therefore I know that the king who is avaricious, that he has more sorrow than power.

This passage, especially the "forðæm" clause, transforms the meaning of what has gone before. The avaricious king who wants more power appears implicitly in opposition to the king who is not so grasping. A little later in the text, Alfred limits a warning against involvement in royal affairs to a warning against entanglement with "leasan cyninge" ("lying kings," 66.22), making it even clearer that there are both bad and good kings.[88]

Alfred does not deny that the power of a king is limited; not only does he translate and expand on the previous passage but, he also repeats the idea soon after (66.11–9), culminating in the rhetorical question, "Hu magon þa cyningas oðsacan oððe forhelan heora unmeahte, þonne hi ne magon nænne weorðscipe forðbrengan buton hiora þegna fultume?" ("How can the kings deny or conceal their lack of power, when they cannot produce any worship without the help of their thanes?" 66.16–9). Alfred clarifies the limits of royal power but does not diminish the king; instead, he transforms the metaphorical kingship in the Latin text, which represents expansive but false power, into a real, and realistically bounded, kingship familiar to Anglo-Saxon audiences.

Just as a world where the power of kings is irrelevant is unthinkable to Alfred, so too Boethius's lack of distinction between good and bad uses of power is unthinkable. After finishing the stories of Nero and Seneca, and Antoninus and Papinianus, by saying that neither could buy their lives, Alfred adds: "forðæm þara cyninga wælhreownes wæs to ðæm heard þæt hiora eaðmetto ne meahton nauht forstandan, ne huru heora ofermetto dydon; swa hwæðer swa hi dydon ne dohte him ða nawðer, þeah hi scoldon þæt feorh ælætan" ("because the cruelty of those kings was so harsh for them that their humility could not withstand it at all, nor indeed did their pride; whatever they did, nothing availed them, but they had to forfeit their lives," 67.7–10). Alfred elaborates on the failings of kings. Where Boethius writes: "detrahat si quis superbis uani tegmina cultus, / iam uidebit intus artas dominos ferre catenas" ("If anyone takes off the covering of vain clothes, then he shall see that inside the lords wear confining chains," IV met. ii. 4–5), Alfred writes:

> Ac gif him mon þonne awint of þa claþas, 7 him oftihð þara þenunga 7 þæs anwealdes, þonne miht þu geseon þæt he bioð swiðe anlic þara his þegna sumum þe hi þar þeniað, buton he forcuðra sie. 7 gif him nu weas gebyreð þæt him wyrð sume hwile þara þenunga oftohen, 7 þara claþa, 7 þas anwealdes, þonne þincð him þæt he sie on carcerne gebroht, oððe on racentum. (111.20–6)
>
> But if any man takes the clothes off him and takes away the retinue and the power, then you might see that he is very like some of those thanes who serve him there, except that he is baser. And if woes beset him now so that for some time fate took away the retinue, and the clothes, and the power, then it would seem to him that he had been brought into a prison, or into chains.

In the process of rationalizing the image and making it more concrete, Alfred invites readers and hearers to imagine a real king deprived of real attendants and power. Moreover, he adds that the king will be found to be *forcuðra*, "perverse" or "infamous"—stronger language than in the Latin, which avoids overt moral judgment here. The Old English judges the king in the image and finds him morally repugnant, perhaps to justify the misery that the unnamed king undergoes. This passage also reflects real anxiety that the good do not always prevail and that the evil do have some power in this world, even if that power ultimately fails.

Alfred keeps all the stories of bad kings that Boethius tells and supplies more.[89] Nero is Boethius's exemplar of the tyrant: he has no self-control and his actions are arbitrary and highly destructive.[90] Alfred not only translates these passages, he also expands them.[91] In an added passage that mentions Nero, 34.15–30, he also names Theodoric as another example of office without virtue. The prologue condemns Theodoric most harshly, as both an Arian heretic and the tyrannical executioner of Boethius (7.6–24), but he is also criticized as "unrihtwisan" twice in a passage (62.2–14) that corresponds to accusations against a contemporary of Boethius, Decoratus, who is omitted from the Old English text.[92] All of these kings are represented as tyrants in the Latin, but the Old English gives specific details of tyranny, glossing each of the stories. This may be due to the audience's unfamiliarity with the figures, but it also serves to particularize the bad kings. They do not represent all rulers but have specific faults that can be avoided.

Two ambiguous kings are also included: Orpheus, in Alfred's portrayal, is an excellent musician and a sympathetic character. Yet he is never shown ruling, and the Old English moral makes clear that he represents the sinner who looks back at his sin and loses the good he had achieved (103.12–21).[93] Ulysses is described favorably at first and avoids falling prey to the metamorphic spell of Circe, but he abandons his responsibilities and his people as he falls for Circe.[94]

Alfred balances his discussion of real limitations on kingship with a sketch of the positive possibilities. He creates a space in the text for good kings where Boethius only sees powerlessness and vice. The mere establishment of a category of kings who are *gitseras* ("graspers") implies the opposite, a group of kings who are not. The possibility of kings who are not motivated by a desire for power, a possibility not imagined in the *De consolatione*, is also invoked when Wisdom tells the narrator: "þonne secge ic eow buton ælcum tweon þæt ge magon þurh [wisdom] becuman to anwealde, þeah ge no þæs anwealdes ne wilnigan" ("Then I say to you without a doubt that you can through wisdom come to power, although you do not want that power," 35.20–1). Philosophy explains that not wealth and power but wisdom makes one worthy of respect: "At si quem sapientia praeditum uideres, num posses eum uel reuerentia uel ea qua est praeditus sapientia non dignum putare?" ("But if you see someone gifted with wisdom, would you not be able to think him worthy either of reverence or of that wisdom itself with which he is endowed?" III pr. iv. 6). Alfred changes the meaning of the passage with one word added near the end: "gif þu nu gesawe sumne swiðe wisne man þe hæfde swiðe gooda oferhyda, 7 wære þeah swiðe earm 7 swiðe ungesælig, hwæder ðu wolde cweðan þæt he wære unwyrðe *anwealdes* 7 weorðscipes?" ("if you now saw a certain very wise man who had very good high-mindedness, and was however very wretched and very unhappy, whether you would say that he was unworthy of *power* and reverence?" 62.14–8, emphasis added). The concept of being worthy of power or rule is simply not in the *De consolatione*, but it is doxa for Anglo-Saxons.[95]

The Old English text, unlike the Latin, tells of good rulers. Alfred adds the epithet *heretoga* for Cicero (43.6–7), Brutus (46.22), and Cato (46.24 and 61.24), who all appear in the Latin but are not described as leaders. One addition does show how good rulers rule: the thirty-line speech Alfred adds on the work of a king (40.5–41.6) addresses the king's responsibilities, including both exercising wisdom (40.25–8) and granting his followers "heora biwist: land to bugianne, 7 gifta, 7 wæpnu, 7 mete, 7 ealo, 7 claþas, 7 gehwæt þæs ðe þa þre geferscipas behofiað" ("their sustenance: land to inhabit, and gifts, and weapons, and food, and ale, and clothes, and whatever of those things are appropriate for the three orders," 40.18–23).

Another passage, although not directly mentioning kings, reflects a concern with justice that properly belongs to a king. The Latin text concludes that malefactors are in more need of help than their victims, adding: "Quo pacto defensorum opera uel tota frigeret uel si prodesse hominibus mallet in accusationis habitum uerteretur" ("In this way the work of defenders would either freeze entirely or, if one preferred to benefit humanity, he would turn his practice to accusation," IV pr. iv. 39). Alfred replaces this with:

> Ne cweðe ic na þæt þæt yfel sie þæt mon helpe þæs unscyldgan 7 him foreþingie; ac ic cweðe þæt hit is betere þæt mon wrege þone scyldgan; 7 ic secge þæt sio forespræc ne dyge nauðer ne þæm scyldgan ne ðæm þe him foreþingað, gif hi þæs wilniað þæt him heora yfel unwrecen sie be ðæs gyltes andefne. (123.15–20)

> Nor do I say that it is evil that men help the innocent and defend him; but I say that it is better that one accuse the guilty; and I say that the defense can neither help the guilty nor defend him, if they want this, that their evil not be avenged according to the amount of guilt.

Alfred retains the basic meaning of the passage, but adds the qualification that defending the innocent is not wrong—a concern that troubles Boethius not at all, but one that the king who promulgated the first extant Anglo-Saxon law code could hardly ignore. Similarly, the passage that describes God as a king with free servants states that for a king to be served by unfree men would be unsuitable ("uncynlicre," 142.6).[96] The implications of this remark are not only theological but also social: a king is served by people who freely choose to serve him; this in turn implies a king whom people would choose to serve, a king who is good and does good for them.

The *Boethius* has many political ideas, but it does not propose a comprehensive political theory; the text is less prescriptive and more speculative than the *Pastoral Care*. It considers kingship more in the way that *Beowulf* does. That poem provides views of many kings and some praise for them, but still leaves readers in some doubt: Is Hrothgar truly a good king? Is Beowulf?[97] Alfred's readers would not necessarily expect an explicit prescription; they would recognize the debate and Alfred's contributions. The *Boethius* does not settle the issue for its readers, but it does provide some guidelines for thinking about kings. Kings should not be avaricious or self-willed; they should be concerned for justice and for the proper use of resources. These unstartling prescriptions would feel familiar to the audience while reinforcing the views proper to the ruling class. Leaders must be prepared to sacrifice, to put their people ahead of themselves in the *Boethius*; in the *De consolatione*, no such selfless rulers exist.

Alfred's changes and additions develop kingship into a theme of the *Boethius*, a familiar Anglo-Saxon concern that would help make the text acceptable to its audience. Other elements of strategy may operate here as well. The translations in Alfred's program seek to inculcate a specific habitus into readers. The model ruler, in his texts, is a man aware of the limitations on leaders and the pitfalls of power. The *Boethius* demonstrates Alfred's own engagement with these problems—and thus his concern for his subjects. It also exhorts readers to engage with these issues, inculcating a sense of responsibility into future men of power and position while framing the terms of the debate and offering a textual reference point. The *Boethius* does not offer any easy solutions, but easy solutions would not help young men make choices as thanes or ealdormen and would also not fit comfortably into the field of Old English literature where more questions about kingship arise than simple directives.

Concern for acceptability affects the *Boethius* at all levels. The use of doublets sometimes represents the Latin text adequately, but more often it fulfills Anglo-Saxon expectations. References to the text as a book remind readers that reading such a book is an achievement and offer the audience a sense of accomplishment. Many of the illustrations in the *Boethius* have been glossed and rationalized in keeping with the tendencies of oral cultures in general and expectations of Anglo-Saxon poetry in particular. The argumentation in the *Boethius*, with its less formal logic and greater anticipation and repetition of points, also reflects oral tendencies. Arguments are framed in more personal terms as the characters become less academic and more familiar figures. Their relationship in turn supports a new theme as friendship, already a positive good in the Latin source text, undergoes a transformation from a classical ideal to an Anglo-Saxon one and a key thread woven into the text. The theme of kingship, which is not really a theme at all in the Latin text but a recurring metaphor, becomes a serious concern throughout the Old English text.

Thus Alfred adapted the *De consolatione* into a text acceptable to an Anglo-Saxon audience largely ignorant of Latin, unfamiliar with late-antique learning and philosophy, and potentially uncomfortable with Boethius's understanding of friendship and particularly kingship. Alfred varied his strategies to meet existing norms in language, literature, and society, displaying a sensitivity to his audience that is, as Bourdieu notes, essential to effective discourse. The translation's acceptability encouraged readers to accept the less familiar elements discussed here and in previous chapters, from the treasure trove of scientific, historical, and mythological information it contains to Boethius's philosophical argumentation. The *Boethius* also enjoined readers to consider their own society, particularly the roles of friendship and kingship—and Alfred set the parameters of the discussion, framing the terminology and the questions for his audience as they considered the roles of subjects and rulers. So far, this study has focused on the ingredients with which Alfred worked: the Latin source text, the Christian tradition, and Anglo-Saxon materials and expectations. The final chapter will explore the blending of these elements.

chapter 4

the translator's cræft

The *Boethius* melds late-antique and Christian Latin discourses with Anglo-Saxon elements. Thus Alfred's translation bridges three cultures, linking the two higher in prestige with the one most familiar to his readers. To succeed as a translation, Alfred's *Boethius* had to be comprehensible to his Anglo-Saxon audience; yet, as Bourdieu notes, to speak or write in purely common language lacks distinction and therefore authority.[1] Alfred gives his text distinctiveness not through grammar or dialect, as in modern French examples, but through this synthesis of cultural references and modes of discourse. Bourdieu writes, "the legitimate language is a semi-artificial language";[2]Alfred's mingling of Christian, philosophical, and Anglo-Saxon norms of speaking and writing provides a language that is somewhat artificial but still quite recognizable to readers. Ultimately, Bourdieu notes, "utterances are not only (save in exceptional circumstances) signs to be understood and deciphered; they are also *signs of wealth*, intended to be evaluated and appreciated, and *signs of authority*, intended to be believed and obeyed."[3] Alfred must balance these signs of wealth and authority with the need to be understood, because "the conditions of reception envisaged are part of the conditions of production" of speech.[4]

Alfred's syncretism helps maintain the authority of the *Boethius* while providing a readers with a text that offers points of familiarity. From the Christian tradition, Alfred borrows the figures of Wisdom and of those who need her most, in Old English the *dysig* ("foolish"), to make Philosophy more welcoming. From differing treatments of worldly goods, Alfred selects the strand best suited to his audience and goals, one that values earthly things as a means to something more precious instead of devaluing them as Boethius does. From Christian iconography he selects three images familiar to his audience—the eye, tracking and hunting, and the woods—to give his audience concrete ideas to anchor themselves in an otherwise highly abstract text. Finally, Alfred unites Boethius's ideas with other patristic work and Anglo-Saxon vocabulary to bring together powerful ideas in a single word: *cræft*. This blending of elements gives the *Boethius* unity, authority, and appeal for Anglo-Saxon readers, in whom the text could then inculcate Alfred's favored model of society. At the same time, the combination replaces some of Boethius's values and emphases with those Alfred has selected.

Perhaps the most thorough Christianizing of the text is in the characterization of *Wisdom*.[5] *Wisdom* corresponds to the figure of Wisdom in the Old Testament (the Latin *sapientia*). She can be found in all the Wisdom Books except the Song of Songs, and she is closely related to God and is often identified with the Second Person of the Trinity.[6] Her presentation in the Old Testament provided Alfred with precedent for several characteristics he would give his own figure; some were derived from the source text, but others seem at odds with it.

Wisdom and Philosophy are first and foremost teachers. They both lecture the prisoner and lead or cajole him into conclusions. Philosophy's depiction as a teacher in *De consolatione* resembles Wisdom's sufficiently to suggest and even authorize Alfred's substitution. The Book of Wisdom, particularly chapter 8, presents Wisdom as a teacher. In Proverbs too Wisdom teaches publicly: "sapientia foris praedicat in plateis dat vocem suam" ("Wisdom preaches outdoors, gives her voice to the plains," 1:20). Yet, as subsequent verses make clear, the people ignore or despise her. Likewise, Boethius's Philosophy has few adherents, as the prisoner notes: "Tum ego: Cum tuas, inquam, rationes considero, nihil dici uerius puto; at si ad hominum iudicia reuertar, quis ille est cui haec non credenda modo sed saltem audienda uideantur?" ("Then I said, 'When I consider your arguments, I think nothing could be said more truly; but if I return to the judgments of men, who is there to whom these things seem worthy not of believing but even hearing?" IV pr. iv. 26).[7] This portrayal of Wisdom also informs the *Pastoral Care*: Wisdom flees those who flee him, and so will not be available when they wish to seek him.[8]

The connection between Philosophy and Wisdom was perhaps more obvious to medieval writers than modern. Pierre Courcelle argues convincingly that Alcuin's *Grammatica* draws heavily on the *De consolatione*, but its prologue too substitutes *sapientia* for *philosophia* as the student's goal.[9] No direct evidence exists for Alfred's knowledge of Alcuin's *Grammatica*, but clearly Alfred's transformation was not unprecedented, whether Alfred was influenced by the *Grammatica* or by the same traditions that inspired Alcuin's usage. Alfred's replacement of the more general *Philosophia* with the Christian *Wisdom* had the effect not only of making the work more Christian, but also more Anglo-Saxon. The word "wisdom" occurs in native poetry, including *Beowulf*, *Precepts*, *The Rune Poem*, and *Maxims*

II; in the translated non-Christian romances *Apollonius of Tyre* and *The Letter of Alexander to Aristotle*; several times in laws, charters, and royal letters; and many times in religious texts, in glosses, and in miscellaneous other texts.[10] *Beowulf* presents it as a crucial quality in a king. In the Corpus of Old English, the adjective *wisa* appears nearly 3,600 times across the full range of genres. Secular rulers as well as religious figures are praised for their wisdom.

By contrast, equivalents for "philosophy" are rare in Old English. *Filos-* only occurs in a few glosses and heavily Latin-influenced texts, including the *Orosius* and Ælfric's Grammar.[11] *Uþwit-* occurs seventy-two times in the Old English Corpus, mostly in Ælfric and in glosses. Alfred does avail himself of "uðwita" to translate the word "philosopher,"[12] and Ælfric uses forms for "philosophy" and "philosophers," but this appears to be an adaptation from the common usage of it for a "*person distinguished for wisdom* or *learning* in general or in a special branch, *a philosopher, scribe, geometrician*, etc."[13] Janet Bately argues that the translator of the *Orosius* uses *philosoph(us)* without the kind of explanation he provides for other technical terms because he expects readers to recognize it.[14] As the likely patron of the *Orosius*, Alfred would probably have known the term, yet he did not himself use it.[15] Instead, he employs the native *uðwita* for specific individuals or groups who practice wisdom or philosophy.[16] For the character of Philosophy herself, he selects a more general word, removing the character from the limitations of a particular office or a specialized study.

The similarities between Old Testament Wisdom and Philosophy may have led Alfred not only to name his character *Wisdom*, but also to give that character some of the other attributes of the Wisdom of the Old Testament. *De consolatione* calls Philosophy a nurse: "nostro quondam lacte nutritus" ("once nursing on our milk," I pr. ii. 2), but the Wisdom Books present Wisdom as a mother. The *Boethius* combines the two to describe Wisdom as a "fostermodor" ("fostermother," 8.27) and the narrator's "agne modor" ("own mother," 9.1) who "tyde 7 lærde" ("raised and taught," 9.2) him. Adoption by Wisdom may have been suggested by the Psalms; the Paris Psalter addresses God: "þu eart fultumiend þara þe nabbað nawðer ne fæder ne modor" ("You are a helper for those who have neither father nor mother," 9.34).[17] Sirach speaks of the "sapientia filiis" ("children of Wisdom," 4:12), and according to Matthew, "iustificata est sapientia a filiis suis" ("Wisdom is justified by her children," 11:19).[18]

Alfred uses details from Latin Christian literary tradition in his construction of Wisdom to make his portrait distinctive, but he selects a familiar Old English word. Although the personification of Wisdom is unique in Old English literature and so engages readers' interest, Alfred's depiction remains comprehensible to Anglo-Saxon readers. The king strikes a balance between more prestigious and more familiar traditions. If he inclines toward Christian prestige, he does not stray so far from Anglo-Saxon understandings and expectations as to alienate readers.

Sometimes this balance swings away from the source text. The Scriptures frequently deplore the fact that Wisdom is needed by all but ignored by most, a concern that fits Alfred's circumstances well. The *De consolatione* acknowledges the existence of people who do not believe or cannot understand the ideas contained in it, but it only mentions them a few times and reveals no particular anxiety about them. Although comprising the majority, these people are inconsequential. Philosophy acknowledges that what she says will be unbelievable to most: "quod incredibile cuiquam forte uideatur" ("What might seem incredible to anyone . . ." IV pr. iv. 3). The prisoner twice says that conclusions he has just accepted would be generally rejected: "Quod quidem cuipiam mirum forte uideatur . . ." ("What indeed would seem marvelous to anyone . . ." IV pr. ii. 33) and "Hoc, inquam, uerum est, tametsi nemo audeat confiteri" ("'This,' I said, 'is true, even if no one would dare confess it,'" IV pr. vii. 16).

Alfred treats these passages differently. Those who do not understand form a more defined group: the foolish, or *dysig*: "þeah his dysige men ne gelefen" ("although foolish men will not believe this," 117.14–5 for IV pr. iv. 3, cited previously); "Ac ic wene nu hwonne þæt dysige men willen wundrian þæs ðe ic ær sæde . . ." ("But I know now that foolish men will wonder at that which I said before . . ." 109.22–4 for IV pr. ii. 33, cited previously). The text betrays real anxiety about this group and their incomprehension: IV pr. vii. 16 (quoted previously) becomes "Ða wearð ic afæred 7 cwæð: Þæt is soð þæt þu sægst; ic nat þeah hwa hit dyrre secgan dysegum monnum, forðæm his ne mæg nan dysi man gelefan" ("Then I became frightened and said: 'That is the truth which you say; I do not know, however, who would dare say it to the foolish people, because no foolish man can believe this,'" 138.13–4). The shift to declamation may possibly result from Alfred's reading of the Latin; perhaps he took *confiteri* as meaning "publicly confess" rather than "accept the belief" and inferred a direct object.[19]

Alfred may have read the source passage this way because of his own interests in the text; the alteration accords with his practice elsewhere in the translation. In the *De consolatione*, Boethius sees ignorance as a tragedy, not a threat: "Eheu, quae miseros tramite deuios / abducit ignorantia!" ("Alas, down what miserable wrong paths ignorance leads!" III met. vii. 1–2). Seth Lerer notes that in both Boethius's tractates and commentaries, "the *vulgi* are treated only with contempt, as a potential readership hostile to the method and goal of Boethius's intellectual pursuits"; the same attitude pervades the *De consolatione*.[20] For Alfred, however, ignorance poses a real danger: he renders this passage, "Eala wa, hu hefig 7 hu frecendlic þæt dysig is þe ða earman men gedwelað 7 alæt of þam rihtan wege" ("Alas, woe, how severe and how dangerous that foolishness is that misleads the wretched men and takes them from the right path," 73.22–4).

In translating the text, Alfred adds a new theme. The adjective and noun *dysig* and the verb *dysegan* occur more than forty times in the work. The Latin text occasionally uses *uulgi, stultus*, and *caecus*, but much less often. In many passages where Alfred uses the word, he narrows a wholesale condemnation of the foolishness of people in general to a criticism of one group of them. At other times, the word occurs in additions to the text. Wisdom even addresses the prisoner himself, "Dysine 7 ungelæredne ic þe underfeng þa þu ærest to monnum become, 7 þa þe getydde 7 gelærde . . ." ("I took charge of you, foolish and untaught, when you first became a man, and then raised and taught you . . ." 17.11–3).[21] The Latin text presents the prisoner's youth in more neutral terms: "Cum te matris utero natura produxit, nudum rebus omnibus inopemque suscepi, meis opibus foui et, quod te nunc impatientem nostri facit, fauore prona indulgentius educaui . . ." ("When nature produced you from the womb of your mother, I took you up naked of all things and helpless, fostered you with my riches and, that which now makes you impatient with me, I raised you indulgently with easy favor . . ." II pr. ii. 4).

The frequency of the word *dysig* and the variety of contexts in which it appears lend it prominence in the *Boethius*. Its use in both historical and mythical anecdotes and in reference to the prisoner's contemporaries show that ignorance has both a long history and long-lived repercussions. Yet Alfred's usage has optimistic implications too. The broad usage of the word for the young prisoner whom Wisdom enlightens in the course of the text, as well as for misguided pagans, Theodoric, and all those who cannot understand the text itself, suggests that ignorance is not invincible. Alfred makes this point explicit later, when he changes a passage in the Latin that indicates that one must accept a conclusion that follows from premises one has accepted to encourage the *dysig* to try to follow the argument. The Latin reads:

> Recte, inquit, aestimas, sed qui conclusioni accedere durum putat aequum est uel falsum aliquid praecessisse demonstret uel collocationem propositionum non esse efficacem necessariae conclusionis ostendat; alioquin concessis praecedentibus nihil prorsus est quod de inlatione causetur. (IV pr. iv. 11)

"You judge rightly," she said, "but he who thinks it hard to accept the conclusion must either show something preceding it to be false or show that the collocation of propositions does not necessarily lead to the conclusion; otherwise, if he has conceded the previous points, there is nothing that can be given as a reason against the conclusion."

The Old English, however, is:

> Ða cwæð he: Ic ne sprece nu no to dysegum monnum, ac sprece to ðam þe wel wilniað wisdom ongitan; forðæm þæt bið tacn wisdomes þæt hine mon welnige geheran 7 ongitan. Ac gif dysegra hwone tweoge æniges þara spella þe we ær ymb spræcon on þisse ilcan bec, ðonne gerecce he gif he mæge oðer twega, oððe þara spella sum leas, oððe ungelic þære spræce þe wit æfterspyriað; oððe þridde wend, ongite 7 gelefe þæt wit on riht spyrigen. Gif he þara nan nyte, þonne nat he hwæt he mænð. (118.9–17)

> Then he said, "I do not speak now to foolish men, but I speak to those who want to understand wisdom well; for that is a sign of wisdom, that one wishes to hear and understand it well. But if any foolish man doubts any of the arguments that we said before in this same book, then let him show if he may one of two things: either one of the statements is false, or one is not related to the speech that we pursue; or he may know a third, he may understand and believe that we follow rightly. If he does not know any of these, then he does not know what he means."

Alfred's Wisdom declares that he does not speak to the *dysig*, but later he offers the possibility that they will see his rectitude and understand. Similarly, the Old Testament's Wisdom sometimes states that she will not speak to these people when they finally do seek her, but in her second address in Proverbs she makes another attempt to get their attention: "intellegite parvuli astutiam et insipientes animadvertite" ("Let the small understand astuteness and the foolish pay attention," 8:5). On the road to Emmaus, Christ calls the pilgrims *stulti* for not recognizing him (Luke 24:25) but then explains the resurrection to them.[22] In the Christian tradition, Wisdom (or Christ) offers the foolish second chances. By contrast, Philosophy has no interest in reaching the vast majority who do not understand her. The *Boethius*'s concern with ignorance, and the hope that it can be vanquished, follows the Wisdom Books rather than the *De consolatione*, and addresses an Anglo-Saxon audience different from the elite readers Boethius envisioned.

The words that the Paris Psalter renders as *dysig* are ususally *insipiens, uanus*, or related forms.[23] *Insipiens* also appears in later Psalms for those with no understanding of the divine:

quam magnificata sunt opera tua Domine nimis profundae factae sunt cogitationes tuae vir insipiens non cognoscit et stultus non intellegit ea (91:6–7) [24]

How magnificent your works are, Lord, and how deeply profound your thoughts! The foolish man does not know them, nor does the stupid understand them.

et dixerunt non uidebit Dominus neque intellegit Deus Iacob intellegite nunc qui insipientes estis in populo et stulti aliquando sapite (93:7–8)

And they say the Lord does not see, nor does the God of Jacob understand; understand now, you among the people who are foolish, and know, anyone who is stupid!

Similar ideas can also be found in the other Alfredian-era works. Criticism of the *dysig* (in Old English) or the *stulti* (in the Latin *Historia ecclesiastica, Dialogi,* and *Regula pastoralis*) appears in each text, but especially the *Pastoral Care,* where it usually stems from Scripture.[25] Augustine shows less concern about the problem of the *dysig,* but the *Soliloquies* uses *dysig* once (71.25) for *impudentia* (I.16). In Caput XVII, *De videndo deo* quotes I Corinthians 2:14–5 about how some do not understand: "Animalis autem homo non percipit quae sunt spiritus Dei: stultitia enim est illi; et non potest scire, quoniam spiritualiter dijudicatur" ("However, the animal man does not perceive those things that are of the spirit of God; for stupidity is theirs; and they are not able to understand, since this is judged spiritually," *PL* 33, cols. 616–7). Most of these passages merely criticize those foolish enough to oppose Christianity, but three of those in the *Bede* address conversion. First Cefi, the pagan high priest, recognizes his own *dysignesse* and amends:

Hwa mæg þa nu eað, þe ic longe mid dysignesse beeode, to bysene oðerra monna gerisenlicor toweorpan, þonne ic seolfa þurh þa snytro, þe ic from þæm soðan Gode onfeng? Ond he ða sona from him awearp þa idlan dysignesse, þe he ær beeode, ond þone cyning bæd þæt he him wæpen sealde 7 stodhors, þæt he meahte on cuman 7 deofolgyld toweorpan. Forðon þam biscope heora halignesse ne wæs alyfed, þæt he moste wæpen wegan, ne elcor buton on myran ridan. (136.27–138.4)[26]

"Now who may then more easily and more appropriately be an example to other men to destroy those [idols] to which I long went in foolishness than I myself, through that wisdom that I have obtained from the true God?" And he at once cast from himself that idle foolishness

> that he followed before, and asked the king that he give him a weapon and a stallion, that he might go and destroy the idol-worship. For the bishop of their religion was not allowed to carry a weapon, nor to ride except on a mare.

In the second passage a people turns aside from "þa aldan dysignesse 7 deofolgild" ("old foolishness and idol-worship," 304.2–3; for the Latin, see IV.23, 374), and in the third a cleric tries to set an example that will cause people to convert from their "dyslecan gewunan" ("foolish custom," 362.9; the Latin is "stultae consuetudinis," IV.27, 432).

The attitude of the *Boethius* (and other Alfredian texts) toward the uneducated or foolish is very much in the interests of Alfred's program. The whole project of vernacular translation and education assumes the educability of those who are not already learned. Boethius, writing in late antiquity, deems those who do not already possess learning unlikely to profit from it, and he dismisses them. The *De consolatione* relies on an "internal reading" by those already initiated into philosophical language; the text excludes everyone who has not learned this language.[27] Alfred's program, on the other hand, offers the first concerted attempt at lay education known in England, and his text addresses an audience comprised of beneficiaries of this program. The needs of the program and the text create tension between criticizing and comforting the *dysig*. The *Boethius* cannot require a purely internal reading but seeks to initiate its audience into Christian learning; its Wisdom is thus more responsive to those who have little or no learning. Readers of the *Boethius* might fear that they (or those close to them) are among the *dysig*, but they need not feel beyond redemption. At the same time, the mere construction of this lesser group establishes the existence of an elite: those who read this text leave the ranks of the *dysig* to become men of learning and status. Unlike Boethius's audience, they are part of a program that seeks to educate more people; the text both presents an appealing sense of superiority to its readers as they leave their *dysignesse* behind and reminds them that others need assistance to overcome *dysignesse*.

Concern for the *dysig*, like the change from Philosophy to Wisdom, derives from a combination of Christian tradition and Anglo-Saxon expectations, but this change departs from the source text. Similarly, Alfred's position that worldly goods, although they should not be desired for themselves, are desirable for what they can do, differs greatly from Boethius's exhortation to move beyond worldly goods.[28] Jerold Frakes convincingly argues that Alfred's presentation of these goods is more positive than Boethius's; in his view, the crucial move Alfred makes to rescue worldly goods from condemnation is to provide them with a different source.[29] In the *Boethius*, Wisdom, not Fortune, grants them in the first place.[30] As a result, Frakes writes, the goods become positive and "themselves assume a primary role in the argument."[31]

This role of Wisdom as benefactor derived from Christian tradition but fitted neatly into Anglo-Saxon expectations. Wisdom bestows both temporal goods and intellectual and spiritual ones. The narrator of the Book of Wisdom declares:

venerunt autem mihi omnia bona pariter cum illa
et innumerabilis honestas per manus illius
et laetatus sum in omnibus
quoniam antecedebat ista sapientia
et ignorabam quoniam horum omnium mater est
quam sine fictione didici et sine invidia communico
et honestatem illius non abscondo
infinitus enim thesaurus est hominibus
quod qui usi sunt participes facti sunt amicitiae Dei
propter disciplinae dona commendati (7:11–4)

All good things came to me together with her, and uncountable honors through her hands, and I rejoice in all those things since Wisdom preceded them, even though I did not yet know that she was the mother of them all. What I learned I will communicate without lying and without jealousy, and I will not hide her wealth; for her treasury is infinite to men, because those who use it become participants in the friendship of God, they are rewarded according to the gifts of learning.

A later passage lists different gifts:

haec cogitans apud me et commemorans in corde meo
quoniam inmortalitas est in cogitatione sapientiae
et in amicitia illius delectatio bona
et in operibus manuum illius honestas sine defectione
et in certamine loquellae illius sapientia
et praeclaritas in communicatione sermonum ipsius
circuibam quaerens ut mihi illam adsumerem. (8:17–8)

Thinking these things over with myself and recalling in my heart that immortality is in the meditation of wisdom, and in her friendship a good delight, and in the works of her hand honor without defect, and in her contest of speech wisdom, and great distinction in the imparting of her words, I went around seeking her so that I might acquire her for myself.

Also in the Book of Wisdom, Wisdom is described as the giver not only of virtue and *sapientia*, but also of riches and fame (7:12–4, 8:18–21). Psalms praises God as a provider to his people of "geniht hwætes and wines and eles and ealra goda" ("abundance of wheat and wine and oil and all goods," 4.8).[32] Otten notes that in Proverbs 3:15–9 and 8:14–9, Wisdom is the giver of goods.[33]

Alfred does not make these changes arbitrarily but finds authorization in a tradition strong enough to justify altering a classic text. He draws on Christian tradition to tell his readers who they are and what they must be:

> The authorized spokesperson is the one whom it behooves and on whom it is incumbent to speak on behalf of the collectivity. It is both his privilege and his duty, his proper function, in a word, his competence (in the legal sense of the term). Social essence is the set of those social attributes and attributions produced by the act of institution as a solemn act of categorization which tends to produce what it designates.[34]

In the Latin text, worldly goods are simply incomplete, and the complete good must be sought. Temporal goods are not evil, but they are a distraction from the true good that one must seek, and so they are left behind on the journey. For Alfred and his readers, the situation is more complex. The Boethian journey to the good is an individual one that recognizes no responsibilities toward others, but the Gregorian ruler must be constantly concerned with the spiritual well-being of his subjects and must engage with the world to understand his fellows and the temptations they face.[35] Alfred adopts these Gregorian values for inculcation into current and future rulers. By speaking in a familiar language that draws on both native Anglo-Saxon vocabulary and church concepts and terms, the king assumes the role of the authorized speaker and gives voice to tradition—or the strand of available traditions that best suits his "practical sense," to use Bourdieu's term, of how society must operate. For tradition is not static or monolithic; tradition is always, as Craig Calhoun explains, something handed on or handed down, modified by both individual holders and groups to fit their own interests and habitus.[36] Alfred reads the *De consolatione* in terms of Gregory and hands it on thus to his readers.

In the *Boethius*, temporal goods are not to be ignored but properly used.[37] Alfred alters some of Boethius's references to all worldly goods as useless, specifying instead that only some of them are. As early as the first book, the Old English softens the Latin text's rejection of earthly emotion. Boethius writes:

> gaudia pelle,
> pelle timorem

spemque fugato
nec dolor adsit. (I met. vii. 25–8)

banish joy, banish fear and put hope to flight, nor will sadness remain.

Alfred renders, "afyr fram þe ða yfelan sælþa 7 þa unnettan, & eac ða unnettan ungesælþa 7 þone yflan ege þisse worulde" ("banish from you the evil goods and the useless, and also the useless misfortunes and the evil fear of this world," 14.19–21). Wisdom specifies the evil and useless goods, implying that some goods are positive and useful. Alfred also specifies things as good when they are to Boethius at best neutral: where the latter has "aurum" ("gold," II pr. v. 4), the former adds "hit nu god sie 7 diore" ("now it is good and precious," 27.29). Boethius ultimately denies that partial goods exist as such: "et dum rei quae partibus caret partem conatur adipisci, nec portionem, quae nulla est, nec ipsam, quam minime affectat, assequitur" ("and when [human perversity] seeks a part of a thing that lacks parts, it finds neither the portion, which is nothing, nor the thing itself, which it does not seek," III pr. ix. 16). Alfred instead writes: "Forðy ne fint ælc mon þæt he secð forðy he hit on riht ne secð. Ge secað þæt ge findan ne magon, þonne ge secað eal good on anum goode" ("Therefore each man does not find what he seeks because he does not seek it rightly. You seek that which you may not find when you seek all good in one good," 76.21–3). Alfred does not deny that partial goods are goods, just that they are the one good.[38]

Most important, Alfred makes several additions to the text that assert the necessity of temporal goods, not as ends in themselves, but as a means to fulfilling one's duty in this world: "Gif þu þonne þæt gemet habban wille, 7 þa nydþearfe witan wille, þonne is þæt mete and drync 7 claðas 7 tol to swelcum cræfte swelce þu cunne þæt þe is gecynde 7 þæt þe is riht to habbenne" ("If you then want to have that measure, and want to know what is needful, then is it food and drink and clothes and tools for such craft as you know that are natural for you and right for you to have," 30.7–10). *Tol* is a key word in this context: in Alfred's view, all temporal goods are instruments for carrying out one's responsibilities. Such a position has some precedent in the source text. The prisoner attempts to justify himself in the Latin: "Scis, inquam, ipsa minimum nobis ambitionem mortalium rerum fuisse dominatam; sed materiam gerendis rebus optauimus, quo ne uirtus tacita consenesceret" ("'You know,' I said, 'that ambition for mortal things has dominated me very little; but I wished for material for accomplishing things, lest virtue, silent, decay,'" II pr. vii. 1). Philosophy responds that in fact the desire for fame was the one temptation such a noble mind could not resist; she attacks him on the question of his ambition, but she keeps silence on the issue of tools. Alfred takes this opportunity to turn the prisoner's three-line sentence into a thirty-line speech on the necessity of tools for pursuing one's *cræft*, particularly if one is a king (40.5–41.6). Thus Alfred allows for the necessity of using earthly goods and so redeems them, although they always remain means, never ends.[39]

In so doing he departs from Platonic tradition to adhere to a strand of Christian tradition that does not require total denial of the world, merely the rejection of the world as an end in itself and the embrace of God as the true goal of life. This strand appears prominently in the Wisdom Books. In the Book of Job, Job emphasizes in his own defense that he has governed the people under him justly and shared the goods he has been given (29:12–20, 31.1–40); Elihu reiterates these points as general principles (36:16–9).[40] Job includes in the list of his goods harvests, tents, children, honor and favor, and justice. The Psalms are largely concerned with earthly needs and victories. Proverbs offers much practical advice. Both the Pauline epistles and the *Regula pastoralis* emphasize good stewardship; they are primarily concerned with the care of souls, but the justice and good works they recommend must be carried out in this world, through this world's goods. Alfred's Christian influences authorized the redemption of these goods and reassigned their distribution from Fortune to Wisdom—bringing the text into conformity with Anglo-Saxon expectations.

One of the most problematic rehabilitations in Alfred's *Boethius* is that of fame or honor, which the source text specifically lists as the most dangerous temptation for virtuous minds (II pr. vii. 2). The shift in the presentation of fame in the Old English text was partly occasioned by the well-known value Anglo-Saxons placed on it. Alfred could also find authoritative precedent for a positive presentation of it in the Old Testament and the *Regula pastoralis.* Proverbs 22.1 says, "melius est nomen bonum quam divitiae multae super argentum et aurum gratia bona" ("Better is a good name than great wealth, good favor than silver and gold"). Gregory cautions against pride and desire to win the people's approval as motivations.[41] Yet Gregory also recognizes the legitimacy of worldly honor in the Christian era: "Ac forðonðe nu eall se weorðscipe ðisse worolde is gecierred, Gode ðonc, to weorðscipe ðæm æwfæstam, ðæt ða sindon nu weorðoste ðe æwfæstoste sindon…" ("But now all the worship of this world is turned, thank God, to the worship of the righteous, so that now the most honored are the most righteous…" *Pastoral Care* 27.2–4).[42] Although worldly honor presents a real danger and should not be desired as an end in itself, it is useful and desirable because it helps to draw people to the love of God (*Pastoral Care* 147.5–15).[43] Thus Alfred introduces a more positive view of fame into his *Boethius.*[44]

Just as Alfred condemns only false or useless goods, he condemns only false or unearned fame (in a passage cited previously, 41.8–16). Where

Boethius points out the foolishness of attempting to spread fame throughout a little corner of such a large universe (II pr. vii. 6), Alfred cautions only against excessive fame: "Is þæt þonne fordyslic geswinc þæt ge winnað eowre woruld to ðon þæt ge wilniað eowerne hlisan *ungemetlice* to brædanne ofer swelcne cauertun" ("That is then foolish labor, that you struggle in your world for that, that you want to spread your fame *out of measure* over such an enclosure," 42.10–2, emphasis added).[45] He similarly changes the "gloriam" of II met. vii. 2 to "þone *idelan* hlisan 7 þone *unnyttan* gilp" ("the *idle* fame and the *useless* boasting," 46.3, emphasis added). A later criticism of honors (III pr. iv. 1) now criticizes only the *dysig* (61.1–4).[46] The glory won by a good death seems to be neutral or even positive; he translates "saeculis nomen gloriosae" ("name of temporal glory," IV pr. vi. 42) as "weorðlicne hlisan þisses andweardan lifes" ("worthy fame in this present life," 133.29). Fame or renown here is less a gift of fortune and more a corollary of virtue or worth than in the Latin.

Of course, Alfred's rehabilitation of earthly goods is not unproblematic. Christian tradition has strong precedents for rejection of the world, containing a powerful ascetic strand from the outset. The New Testament repeatedly admonishes readers to forget the world. Matthew 6:25–34 exhorts readers not to worry about even the necessities of life; a similar passage occurs in Luke (12:22–32). Luke's version of the Beatitudes concludes with curses for the rich (6:24–6), and Christ later says, "Sic ergo omnis ex vobis qui non renuntiat omnibus quae possidet non potest meus esse discipulus" ("So therefore every one of you who does not renounce all that you possess cannot be my disciple," Luke 14:33). This strain is also reflected in Gregory's stern cautions that honor and other worldly goods are to be used *only* for higher purposes, never for oneself. Augustine's *Soliloquia* are more dualistic and go further than Gregory in rejecting *divitias, honores*, and *uxor* ("riches," "honors," and "wife," I.17; all are translated literally in the Old English *Sol* 72.11–73.8).

The austerity of that strand might not fare well with an Anglo-Saxon audience for whom riches and honors were very important; note Asser's repeated assertions both of Alfred's importance and his wealth.[47] Fortunately for Alfred, Christian tradition did not limit him to strict denial. Even Augustine would accept worldly goods such as riches or honors if they led to wisdom or could lead others to them (*Soliloquia* I.17).[48] The New Testament also shows some practical acceptance of the world. The stories of the talents (Matthew 25:14–30 and Luke 19:12–26) and the good steward (Luke 12:42–3) are exhortations to use one's gifts well in this world, and these gifts can be read either as talents and skills or as the worldly goods that one has. Acts presents stories of communal life and Christians' charitable giving to others from the goods they have (for example, 6:1–6)—not pure renunciation but managing and sharing temporal goods wisely. In I Corinthians 5:10, Paul specifically says that he does *not* ask Christians to cut themselves off from the world entirely. This emphasis on the instrumental nature of worldly goods allows Alfred to balance Christian austerity with the Anglo-Saxon love for material riches and beauty, evident in glittering descriptions from that of Beowulf's winnings in *Beowulf* (2163–2199) to the booty of the victorious Israelites in *Exodus* (580–90). Alfred drew on Paul to authorize his changes to the source text, but Paul did not compel the alterations; the king selected the most advantageous of the available strategies for dealing with earthly goods because "anticipation of the sanctions of the market helps to determine the production of the discourse."[49] Boethius's dismissal of riches, honor, and other earthly goods in the *De consolatione* would collide with the value placed on them in much Anglo-Saxon literature, particularly poetry; Alfred's translation reduces the tensions to make the translation acceptable to his audience.

Alfred's recuperation of earthly goods also moves the text from the abstract to the practical plane. That attention to the practical finds parallels in his elaboration of the *De consolatione*'s imagery. Alfred used the *De consolatione* and other Christian texts to create concrete images that would be familiar to his audience, further developing the imagery of the eye and of hunting from the source text and adding the image of the forest.

Alfred consistently elaborates the image of the mind's eye. Sometimes he simply develops Boethius's imagery of eyes and seeing, which occurs in several passages; for example, "Haec dixit oculosque meos fletibus undantes contracta in rugam ueste siccauit" ("She spoke and, gathering her dress into a fold, she dried my eyes, which were flowing with tears," I pr. ii. 7) becomes "se Wisdom ... adrigde þa mines modes eagan" ("Wisdom ... then dried my mind's eye," 8.24–6). Literal eyes in the source text become figurative eyes in the target text. Alfred also makes eyes that are implicitly figurative in the source explicitly so: the tale of the man who has forgotten how to see (IV pr. iv. 31) becomes that of the child who, after becoming blind, forgets that his eyes and mind's eye could see (122.1–16). Alfred even introduces the image where the source text simply has "mind": a reference to *mentes* in III met. x. 13 is translated into *modes eagan* not once but three times in Alfred's rendition (89.14, .16, and .21). Finally, Alfred introduces the image in passages that in Latin contain no mention of the eye or the mind. One criticism of the worldly minded elaborates on Boethius's nonmetaphorical treatment, becoming "lociað mid bæm eagum on þas eorðlican ðincg ... ge on þæs modes eagum ge on þæs lichoman" ("look with both eyes on earthly things ... both the mind's eye and the body's," 121.27–9). He adds a similar idea at 129.30. In an addition near the end, Wisdom tells the prisoner, "Þu me ahsast micles 7 earfoðes to ongitanne; gif þu hit witan wilt, ðu scealt habban ær þines modes eagan clæne 7 hlutor" ("You ask me something great and difficult to understand; if you want to know it, you shall first have your mind's eyes clean and bright," 147.23–5).

Boethius himself writes in several places of eyes that are clearly not literal, but Alfred gives the image more emphasis both by developing some of the passages in which it appears and introducing it into others.[50] The impetus to repeat and elaborate the image of the eye could easily have come from any of several Christian texts, most obviously Augustine's *De videndo deo*, which uses the image throughout. Similar imagery can be found in the *Soliloquia*.[51] The Psalms also refer to the eyes and seeing, and Alfred makes the same alteration in translating them as he does in translating the *Boethius*: he repeatedly translates "eye" as "mind's eye," as in a passage, reminiscent of 121.27–9 cited earlier, where he renders "praeceptum Domini lucidum inluminans oculos" ("the precept of the Lord lighting the eyes," Psalm 18.9): "Godes bebod is swiðe leoht: hit onliht þa eagan ægþer ge modes ge lichaman" ("God's command is very light; it lights the eyes, both the mind's and the body's," 18.8).[52] Images of light and eye are pervasive in the New Testament.

Gregory had the greatest influence on Alfred's use of this image. Not only does he use eye imagery repeatedly in both the *Dialogi* and the *Regula pastoralis*, he sometimes invokes the *mentis oculorum*.[53] This usage occurs in the first book of the *Regula pastoralis* at 9.18, where Alfred translates it faithfully as "modes eagan" (57.11). Another passage that refers to the eyes does not call them explicitly *mentis oculorum* but does refer to the "ueri luminis claritatem intellectus nostri" ("the brightness of the true light of our intellect," 11.70), making clear reference to the mind's eye. Gregory also uses the phrase "incorporeum oculum mentis" once in the *Dialogi* (IV.27.5–6, translated as "þæt unlichamlice eage þæs modes," 297.2–3, "the incorporeal eye of the mind" in both languages) and forms of *mentis oculorum* twice (IV.5.53/270.3, IV.7.4–5/272.2–4).[54]

Thus Christian texts offered ample precedent for Alfred's elaboration of eye imagery. He makes the metaphorical dimension more explicit for an audience perhaps already struggling with the text, but keeps the image one that any reader could quickly and easily understand. As in modern English, Old English *seon* can mean to understand, and it forms compounds such as *oferseon* ("observe" or "despise") and *forseon* ("despise" or "look down upon"), which describe perceptions and attitudes rather than the physical act of seeing.[55] Alfred adapted the text to his audience's interests and experiences by developing elements already present in the source text and in Christian literary tradition.

Many scholars have noted that Alfred makes hunting imagery pervasive in the *Boethius*, developing a few brief references to it into several longer images. In two passages, Boethius uses a hunting image to describe the mental pursuit of a question or an idea.[56] "In his igitur quae singula quaedam expetendorum praestare creduntur beatitudo nullo modo uestiganda est" ("Happiness is therefore in no way to be tracked in these things that are believed to bestow individually those things that are sought," III pr. ix. 23). Alfred preserves the image while changing the import: "Ne þearf nan mon on ðys andweardan life spyrian æfter þæm soðum gesælðum, ne þæs wenan ðæt he ær mæge good genog findan" ("Nor must a man track after the true good in this present life, nor believe that he may find enough good in it," 77.31–78.1). Boethius uses the image again at the start of III met. xi: "Quisquis profunda mente uestigat uerum..." ("Who would track the truth with a profound mind..."). Alfred translates, "Swa hwa swa wille dioplice spirigan mid inneweardan mode æfter ryhte" ("Whoever would track the truth deeply with inward mind..." 94.27–8). Both the source and target texts employ verbs that quite clearly mean "to track" and contain the roots "track," "trace," or "footprint."

In two other places Boethius uses images related to hunting. III met. viii says, "non altis laqueos montibus abditis / ut pisce ditetis dapes" ("you do not hide nets on high mountains so that you may enrich your feast with fish," III met. viii. 5–6). Alfred elaborates:

> Hwæðer ge nu settan eower nett on þa hehstan dune, þonne ge fiscian willað? Ic wat þeah þæt ge hit þær ne settað. Hwæðer ge nu settan eower hundas 7 eower net ut on þa sæ lædon, þonne ge huntian willað? Ic wene þeah þæt ge hi þonne setton up on dunum 7 innon wudum. (73.27–31)
>
> Now do you set your net on the highest mountain, when you want to fish? I think, however, that you do not set it there. Now do you set your hounds and lead your nets out on the sea, when you want to hunt? I think, however, that you set them on mountains and in woods.

Later the image of death as an assailant occurs in the Latin text:

> Si mortem petitis, propinquat ipsa
> sponte sua uolucres nec remoratur equos.
> Quos serpens, leo, tigris, ursus, aper
> dente petunt idem se tamen ense petunt. (IV met. iv. 3–6)
>
> If you seek death, she draws her vultures near willingly and does not delay her horses. Those whom the serpent, the lion, the tiger, the bear, the boar seek with their teeth seek themselves, however, with the sword.

The use of the verb *peto* and the comparison of death with both the jaws of animals and the sword make it an image as much of war and attack as of the hunt.[57] Alfred substitutes an image that intersects with Boethius's but becomes explicitly a hunting image:

> oððe hwy ne magon ge gebidan gecyndelices deaðes, nu he eow ælce dæg toweardes onet? Hwi ne magon ge gesion þæt he spyrað ælce dæg æfter fuglum 7 æfter diorum 7 æfter monnum, 7 ne forlæt nan swæð ær he gefehð þæt þæt he æfterspyreð. (124.5–9)

> Or why can you not await your natural death, now that he hastens towards you each day? Why can you not see that he hunts each day after birds and after beasts and after men, and does not abandon any track before he takes that which he tracks?

Alfred does not simply draw on Boethius's limited hunting imagery for his translation and other texts; he elaborates on it several times with the characters' references to their own dialogue and mental processes. The prisoner's acceptance of an argument, "Ita est, inquam" ("'It is so,' I said," III pr. iii. 13), becomes: "Genoh ryhte þu spyrast; swa hit is swa þu segst" ("Rightly enough you track; so it is as you say," 59.27–8). "Quonam modo?" ("In what way?" III pr. xi. 10) reads, "Sege me þæt sweotolor; ne mæg ic fullice ongitan æfter hwa þu spyrast" ("Say that more clearly to me; I cannot fully understand what you are tracking," 90.25–7). Alfred shifts eight other references to the argument itself into the realm of hunting as well.[58]

Alfred also translates a few other passages in terms of hunting although they were not originally set in that context, such as when Wisdom exhorts the prisoner to track God at 147.12–7 (V pr. vi. 1).[59] Some of his references, such as "spyrian æfter cræftum 7 æfter wisdome" ("follow after virtue and after wisdom," 109.3) are completely added to the text.[60] Thus Alfred takes a source text with four brief references to hunting or fighting and produces a text with more than a score of hunting images, some of which are relatively long and developed. Seth Lerer suggests the hunting imagery arises from a desire to project a manly persona; T. A. Shippey argues for the role of Alfred's own love of hunting.[61] The confluence of personal taste with Anglo-Saxon norms and Christian tradition provides an even more likely explanation. Alfred's debt to Scriptural and patristic sources lends a literary and religious status greater than mere personal experience.

The Wisdom Books of the Old Testament provide the strongest authorization for Alfred's hunting imagery. Proverbs makes several references to bird snares and nets (for example, 1:17, 6:5, and 7:23). Fish snares appear in Ecclesiastes (9:12). Snares are not Alfred's favorite hunting image, however;

as in the source text, his most frequent image is that of tracking, and Sirach offers these images of tracking wisdom:

> in omni animo tuo accede ad [sapientiam]
> et in omni virtute tua serva vias eius
> investiga illam et manifestabitur tibi
> et continens factus ne derelinqueris eam (6:27–8)[62]

> in all your soul approach [Wisdom] and in all your virtue serve her ways; track her and she will be shown to you, and, when you hold her, you shall not let her go.

Job contains three references to following footprints (11:7, 13:27, 23:11). Romans speaks of following the *vestigia* of Abraham (4:12), whereas II Cor 12:18 and I Peter 2:21 speak of following the footprints of Christ. Similar images can be found in Gregory's *Dialogues* (I.9.68–9/60.24–6) and an untranslated passage in the *Regula pastoralis* (64.2–6).[63] Alfred had plenty of Christian literary precedent for hunting and tracking imagery, particularly from Scripture. Perhaps even more important, the image resonated with people's experience.[64]

Alfred's replacement of the labyrinth with the wood may likewise have been suggested by the king's reading. In the Latin, the prisoner complains: "Ludisne, inquam, me inextricabilem labyrinthum rationibus textens, quae nunc quidem quae egrediaris introeas, nunc uero quo introieris egrediare, an mirabilem quendam diuinae simplicitatis orbem complicas?" ("'Are you playing with me,' I said, 'weaving me inextricably into a labyrinth with your arguments, where now indeed you go in where you went out, but now to come out where you went in, or do you enfold a marvelous orb with divine simplicity?'" III pr. xii. 30). In the Old English, Alfred describes not a labyrinth but a forest:

> Ða cwæð ic: Me þincð þæt ðu me dwelle 7 dydre, swa mon cild deð; lædst me hidres 7 ðidres on swa þicne wudu ðæt ic ne mæg ut aredian. Forðæm ðu a ymb sticce fehst eft on ða ilcan spræce þe þu ær spræce, 7 forlætst eft ða ær ðu hi geendod hæbbe, 7 fehst on uncuðe; þu ic nat nu hwæt þu wilt. Me þincð ðæt ðu hwerfe ymbeutan sume wundorlice 7 seldcuþe spræce ymbe ða anfealdnesse þære godcundnesse. (100.4–11)

> Then I said, "It seems to me that you mislead and deceive me, as a man does a child; you lead me hither and thither in such a thick wood that I may never go out. For after a while you take up again the same speech you spoke before, and leave it again before you finish it, and take on an uncertain matter; I do not know what you want. It seems to me that

> you are turning about some wonderful and little-known speech concerning the simplicity of divinity."

Janet Bately compares the image to Alfred's image of building from a wood at the start of the *Soliloquies*, but the latter image is one of clarity and careful selection, not confusion.[65] A closer parallel can be found in a portion of the *Soliloquia* that Alfred did not translate but probably read: "Quaerebamus enim, quid sit veritas, quod ne nunc quidem in hac silva rerum omnibus paene callibus oberratis video nos investigare potuisse" ("For we sought what the truth was, but I still do not see that we have been able to find it in this wood, although we have wandered almost all the roads," II.26). This passage more closely resembles the passage in the *Boethius* and may have inspired Alfred to change the image from a labyrinth, which would require explanation for his audience, to the more familiar forest.

The images of the eye, the hunt, and the forest show influence from Scripture and patristic literature. Recognizing the contribution of Christian literature in Alfred's imagery denies neither his accomplishment in the treatment of individual passages, which contain original details, nor the role of his personal experience. Rather, the parallels demonstrate that Alfred constructed a self-consciously literary work in which he consistently selected and developed images that fit both into Christian tradition and Anglo-Saxon habitus. His blend of elements anticipates the text's market even as it supports his chosen values.

Perhaps the best example of Alfred's syncretism, however, lies in a single word. Although Alfred's unusual usage of *cræft* has been noted, its thematic import has not been fully explored.[66] His usage of the word reveals both connections and divergences between his philosophy and Boethius's, and it illuminates how he conceived of his program of translation and education. It also both reflected and reinforced certain values. In choosing the words for his translation, Alfred chose the terms in which certain debates could be framed. Bourdieu writes:

> Official language, particularly the system of concepts by means of which the members of a given group provide themselves with a representation of their social relations (e.g., the lineage model or the vocabulary of honour), sanctions and imposes what it states, tacitly laying down the dividing line between the thinkable and the unthinkable, thereby contributing towards the maintenance of the symbolic order from which it draws its authority.[67]

Alfred uses the word *cræft* with its standard meanings: power, physical skill and craftsmanship, and mental ability. He also uses it for *virtus*, meaning strength and virtue, a translation unique in Old English. Both this shift and his pervasive use of *cræft* in the *Boethius* call attention to the word and to each of the meanings it bears in the text. Bourdieu finds such linguistic play common in later philosophy.[68] The king's use of the same word for ideas that were normally expressed by different words encouraged his audience to reconsider the categories they constructed to describe life. Alfred's linguistic linkage of power with virtue makes the relationship between the two not only thinkable but even necessary for his audience.

Alfred's adaptation of *cræft* relies on its generally accepted senses. The *Dictionary of Old English* defines *cræft*:

> The most frequent Latin equivalent of *cræft* is *ars*, yet neither "craft" nor "art" adequately conveys the wide range of meanings of *cræft*. "Skill" may be the single most useful translation for *cræft*, but the senses of the word reach out to "strength," "resources," "virtue" and other meanings in such a way that it is often not possible to assign an occurrence to one sense in ModE without arbitrariness and the attendant loss of semantic richness.[69]

The *Dictionary* then gives six main definitions:

1. strength, power, might (either physical or due to the possession of resources);
2. skill, ability, dexterity, facility (physical);
3. strength, merit, excellence, power (mental or spiritual);
4. skill, ability, faculty, talent (mental or spiritual);
5. art, an organized body of knowledge, discipline, one of seven liberal arts; and
6. idea, concept.[70]

Cræft appears more than 700 times in the extant Old English Corpus in poetry, prose, and glosses.[71] The primary definitions 1–4 are in common use throughout the Anglo-Saxon period; meaning 5 is somewhat restricted; and definition 6 seems to have been used only by Ælfric, and even then only rarely.

The first and broadest definition the *Dictionary* gives, "power," appears about 120 times in 30 texts. This sense figures in both poetry and prose as here, in Ælfric's *Lives of Saints*:

> Efne ðæs on mergen him com swa mycel mennisc to
> þæt nan mann ne mihte ða meniu geriman.
> and begunnon to feohtenne fæstlice mid *cræfte*.
> and nyston þæt machabeus mid þam mannum wæs. (Maccabees 417–20)[72]

On that same morning so many men came to him that no one could count the host, and they began to fight resolutely with strength, and they did not know that Maccabeus was with those men.

This usage spans both genres and periods; it was already available to Alfred and his near-contemporaries and remains in use through the works of Ælfric and the Laws of Cnut.[73] "Power" is the broadest meaning and was certainly one of the primary senses of the word during and after Alfred's time, so any occurrence of the word would most likely carry connotations of power.

The second and fourth definitions, physical and mental skill, were probably distinguished weakly if at all in the Anglo-Saxon period.[74] The *Dictionary*'s use of *Liber scintillarum* is exemplary. For sense 2.a (livelihood), it quotes from the text: "*nulla ars absque magistro discitur* nan *cræft* butan lareowe byþ geleornud" ("No art is learned without a master," 77.9; *Dictionary* 841);[75] for meaning 4.a (teaching), it quotes: "*caput est artis docere quod facias* heafud ys *cræftis* læran þæt þu do" ("The chief thing (head) is to teach of the art that you do," 32.42; *Dictionary*, 844.). Yet the usages in these passages differ little, reflecting the *Dictionary's* caution that "it is often not possible to assign an occurrence to one sense in ModE without arbitrariness" (837). *The Gifts of Men* and other texts also refer to gifts as *cræftas* without specifying particular talents or dividing dexterity from mental ability. Nearly 300 occurrences in four dozen texts, primarily prose, use the word to refer to physical and mental skills.

More important, the most common usage of the word *cræft* in prose was for the more specific sense of "skills" or "livelihood," as here, in Ælfric's *Catholic Homilies*: "Hwæt forlet Petrus? He wæs fiscere, and mid ðam *cræfte* his teolode" ("What did Peter relinquish? He was a fisherman, and with that craft he made his living," I, 27 394.1–2).[76] This meaning is attested over a broad range of time and genres, from Cynewulf's *Elene* and his portion of *Christ* to all the Alfredian-era translations and the Old English *Martyrology* to Ælfric, Wulfstan, and the translators and glossators of the Benedictine Rule. The use of *cræft* for skills or occupations, whether mental or physical, was well established, and this sense would come to mind as easily as "power" or "strength." Indeed, all these meanings are intimately connected; through a talent, skill, craft, or livelihood one exhibits one's physical powers and turns them into a more abstract sort of power or resources. The word appears in New Testament glosses for the Latin *talenta*, illustrating the overlap in these categories nicely.

The third sense, "spiritual or mental merit," is easier to distinguish, although still closely related to the others. This usage occurs just in excess of 100 times, but in only seventeen texts.[77] Alfred is the only writer to use the word as a translation for *virtus*; all four examples given in the

Dictionary are from the *Boethius* or the *Regula pastoralis.*[78] The various spiritual senses are clear in Alfredian and later texts such as Ælfric's works and the Benedictine Rule, but Wærferth's translation of Gregory's *Dialogi* is the only other work of that era that was not done by the king himself to use *cræft* in any spiritual sense. Alfred may have popularized the usage of the word *cræft* for spiritual abilities, but it never became established as a translation for *virtus.*

The opposite sense of *cræft,* "3.c. in a negative sense: vice" (837), is usually marked by a negative adjective to make its meaning clear: "mid þæm *cræfte* þe þa scondlicost wæs" ("with the trick that was the most shameful," *Or* 51.20–1). Related usages include "4.e. in a negative sense: cunning, guile" and "4.f a trick; stratagem, wile" (838). Together these negative senses account for nearly eighty occurrences in thirty texts.[79] This meaning does appear in Alfredian-era works, particularly the *Orosius* and the *Bede,* and so would probably would have been familiar to readers, but Alfred rarely uses it, and it is notably absent from the *Boethius.*[80]

Other meanings are less common. *The Dictionary* gives "God's skill in creating and maintaining the world" as a subdivision (4.d) of mental skill as well (837). It occurs thirteen times in eight texts. Although this unusual usage appears mainly in prose, it is not merely idiosyncratic.[81] *Cræft* as God's ability occurs three times in Alfred's works (twice in the *Boethius,* once in the *Soliloquies*) and several times in Ælfric with scattered occurrences in glosses. *The Dictionary*'s fifth sense, discipline or liberal art, occurs not surprisingly almost exclusively in prose, and fewer than four dozen occurrences are found in thirteen texts.[82] Alfred uses this sense only twice in the *Soliloquies* and once in the *Boethius.*[83] Other senses are so restricted as to bear little relevance to Alfred's texts; Alfred and his audience may not have known them at all, and they were certainly not among the connotations foremost in their minds.

The meanings available to Alfred and his audience, and the ones that could operate in the context of the translation of the *De consolatione,* would then be *The Dictionary*'s primary senses 1–4 (and 4.d): skill, talent, and occupation, both physical and mental; power, strength, and resources; spiritual or mental merit; and God's skill in creating the world. Meaning 3.b, virtue, appears only in Alfred's own works. Other meanings occur in so few works or so late that Alfred and his audience may well not have known them. In any event, he did not avail himself of them.

Alfred uses the word *cræft* sixty-seven times in the *Boethius,* from the fourth page of the printed text until a few lines from the end. His usage covers a broad range; each of the major senses mentioned previously appears at least twice, some several times.[84] By far the most frequent usage in the *Boethius,* however, involves a shift from the accepted meanings. Alfred not only uses it in the sense of spiritual or mental excellence more than any other extant writer, he also uses it specifically to mean virtue.[85]

Using *cræft* for *virtus* was unprecedented, and Alfred could hardly expect his audience to compare the translation with the source and notice that *cræft* had replaced *virtus*. He made the shifted sense clear in multiple ways. First, he had established it in his previous work, a translation of the *Regula pastoralis*. There too he uses the word with various meanings, but most often for spiritual excellence, and virtue in particular. At *Pastoral Care* 59.11–4 the word occurs in a biblical context: "Se ðonne se ðe ðeonde bið on swelcum *cræftum* & geearnungum, swelce we ær spræcon, & ðonne to swiðe wiðsceorað ðæm ealdordome, healde hine ðæt he ne cnytte ðæt underfongne feoh on ðæm swatline ðe Xrist ymbe spræc on his godspelle" ("Then he who is prospering in each virtue and merit, as we said before, and then too strongly refuses authority, let him guard himself lest he knit up that property he has received in the napkin about which Christ spoke in his gospel"). He uses it as an antonym of *unðeaw*, the established word for vice: "forðæm simle ða *cræftas* winnað wið ðæm unðeawum" ("because always the virtues struggle against the vices," *Pastoral Care* 463.8–9). He lists specific *cræftas* that could only be virtues, not mere skills or talents: "ðone *cræft* ðære monnðwærnesse" ("the virtue of mercy," *Pastoral Care* 291.10–1; and compare 359.23–4). Alfred was probably not deliberately preparing for the *Boethius* as much as working out his own translation solutions in the earlier work where he is less consistent.[86] He uses *mægen* for *virtus* much more often in the *Pastoral Care* than in the *Boethius*.[87] Although Alfred had not yet established his personal usage, he already favored *cræft*. (The word *virtus* occurs with monotonous frequency in the Latin *Regula pastoralis*, and Alfred may have used two different words for it to add variety to his own text.)

The *Boethius* is much more consistent than the *Pastoral Care* in its usage of *mægen* and *cræft*. In the *Boethius*, *mægen* appears only once for *virtus*, but *cræft* appears for *virtus* 15 times.[88] *Cræft* is added to the text more than three dozen times, *mægen* never. Alfred also repeats the same techniques he used earlier. He establishes the word in a context of virtue by associating it with wisdom and true good: "Ða mine þeowas sindon wisdomas 7 *cræftas* 7 soðe welan" ("My customs are wisdom and virtues and true wealth," 18.5–6). He uses it repeatedly in the context of judgment and wisdom: "forðæm se wer is domes 7 *cræfta* full, 7 genog orsorg . . ." ("for that man is full of judgment and virtue, and prudent enough," 22.9) and "hwy nyllað hy spyrian æfter *cræftum* 7 æfter wisdome . . ." ("why they do not want to follow after virtues and after wisdom?" 109.3). As the whole text connects wisdom to God and the highest good, the senses of mental skill and divine gift become linked; Clemoes calls *cræft* in the *Boethius* "the organizing principle of the individual's capacity to follow a moral and mental life."[89]

Alfred also uses synonyms and antonyms effectively to convey his meaning. He pairs *cræft* with *þeaw*, meaning both good custom and virtue: "þæt he wolde þara betstena sumes þeawas 7 his *cræftas* gefon" (69.14–5).[90] He uses it as an antonym for *unþeaw*, vice (61.7–9), and for *unrihtwisnes* (104.6–9). He further establishes *cræft* as a word for virtue by listing specific virtues and calling them *cræftas*: "Swa swa wisdom is se hehsta *cræft*, 7 se hæfð on him feower oðre *cræftas*; ðara is an wærscipe, oðer gemetgung, ðridde is ellen, feorðe rihtwisnes" ("Just so wisdom is the highest virtue, and has in it four other virtues: one is reverence, another moderation, the third is zeal, the fourth, righteousness," 62.24–6; see also 87.7–9).

Significantly, other Anglo-Saxon writers do not employ the word *cræft* for virtue or *virtus*. *Þeaw* could mean virtue, as Alfred knew. *Mægen* and *miht* were the usual translations of *virtus*.[91] In Psalter and New Testament translations and glosses, and a few other Old English glosses on Latin texts, *mægen* is the overwhelming choice for *virtus*, occurring more than 600 times. Although many of these readings occur in glosses that cannot be dated with certainty earlier than the tenth century, the Psalter Glosses in Cotton Vespasian A. i date to the ninth century.[92]

Yet Alfred does not use *þeaw, mægen,* or *miht* often for *virtus* in the *Boethius*. He uses *mægen* seven times in the *Boethius*, but generally in the broader sense of strength.[93] *Mægen* occurs with great frequency for *virtus* in the *Bede* and the *Dialogi*, suggesting that this was the usual translation solution in Alfred's time.[94] Alfred uses a word his audience knows and a meaning not far different from the senses that receive regular use, but his usage does not quite follow Anglo-Saxon norms. The difference between common usage and Alfred's gives his language distinction, bestowing symbolic capital on Alfred and his text by calling attention to Alfred's learning and his precise use of language while not increasing the difficulty of the text for readers.[95] At the same time, Alfred defamiliarizes both *cræft* and *virtus* by equating the two terms despite their normal separation. The text rethinks the relationship between power, skill, and virtue—and requires the audience to do the same.

The importance of *cræft* and its usage in the *Boethius* lies precisely in this rethinking. Clemoes writes of "the synthesizing power of the word *cræft* in Alfred's understanding of... spiritual, moral and material elements in a God-devoted wisdom...."[96] Susan Hitch writes of the *Soliloquies*:

> Any *cræft* may... reasonably be spoken of in terms of any other, and... the two *cræfts* compared cannot, by definition, be fully different. Both images are in fact metonymic of a moral structure expressed in the practice of any *cræft*, and centered on the most important of *cræftas*, the pursuit of knowledge of God, with which Alfred's *Soliloquies* begin....[97]

Physical, mental, and moral *cræftas* are all intimately connected in the works of Alfred, particularly the *Boethius*. The idea of a mental movement toward God underlies both the Latin and Old English texts. In the Latin the journey is guided by *Philosophia*, in Old English by *Wisdom*. In both, the mental and the spiritual are inseparably linked, shaping the way Alfred's audience thinks about these aspects of their lives and their society.

Yet the connection of mental and even spiritual skills with physical skill is forged at both literal and metaphorical levels. Virtue has a physical aspect in the Christian tradition of asceticism: all monastic rules limited clothes, food, and sleep, and even the laity might adopt ascetic practices temporarily to atone for sin.[98] Clemoes argues that a link between physical discipline and spiritual virtue also already appears in the Old English poetry that inspired Alfred: "the poets had already used [*cræft*] to portray in action an innate, distinctively human, personal faculty of progressively organizing mental and physical activity to moral ends."[99] The poetry does not have as refined a moral sense for *cræft*, but the seeds of Alfred's usage may well have been planted by Old English verse.[100]

The physical aspect of virtue appears in the Latin text of *De consolatione* when Boethius links asceticism to innocence, looking back to a Golden Age when people sought nothing beyond sufficiency:

> Felix nimium prior aetas
> contenta fidelibus aruis
> nec inerti perdita luxu,
> facili quae sera solebat
> ieiunia soluere glande. (II met. v. 1–5)

> How happy was the former age, content with faithful fields, not lazy with degenerate luxuries, which was accustomed to late meals of easily-won nuts.

Alfred's added interjection increases the nostalgia: "Eala, hu gesælig seo forme eld was þises midangeardes, ða ælcum men þuhte genog on þære eorþan wæstmum" ("Alas, how happy was that former age of the earth, when the produce of the earth seemed enough for each," 33.21–3). Both writers repeatedly emphasize that power does not bring virtue with it; Alfred writes: "Forþam hit bið þætte nan man for his rice ne cymð to *cræftum* 7 to medemnesse..." ("For no man comes to virtues and excellence because of his kingdom..." 35.13–4). Yet Alfred's usage also connects one's occupation with mental and spiritual qualities, especially when Mod asserts the necessity of tools and helpers for the pursuit of *cræft* in an extended addition (40–1). Although Alfred's usage of *cræft* is unique to his own translation, all three contexts in which he works—the familiar but honored Christian Latin culture, the more familiar but less distinguished Old English literature, and the unfamiliar but prestigious Latin source text—bring together physical and moral strength at some moments. Alfred's insistence on combining senses of *cræft* synthesizes elements of all three traditions.

The first, most general definition of *cræft* also takes its place in this fusion. In fact, uniting the concepts of power and virtue is a central theme in both the Latin and Old English works, although Boethius does not generally link the two in one word.[101] Where the Latin text says, "Primum igitur, inquit [Philosophia], bonis semper adesse potentiam, malos cunctis uiribus esse desertos agnoscas licebit, quorum quidem alterum demonstratur ex altero" ("'First therefore,' said Philosophy, 'it is fitting that you know that the good always have power and the evil are always deserted by every strength, of which indeed the one shall be demonstrated by the other,'" IV pr. ii. 2), Alfred renders, "Đa cwæð he: Þu scealt ærest ongitan þæt ða goodan habbað symle anweald, 7 þa yfelan næfre nanne, ne nænne *cræft*. . . " ("Then he said: 'You shall first understand that the good always have power, and the evil never have any, nor any *cræft*,'" 106.1–3).[102] In Latin the words are different: *bonis, potentiam, uires.* In Old English, the crucial concepts are linked in one word: *cræft.* If the evil merely lacked power, Alfred could have used either "næfre nanne" (referring to *anweald*) or *cræft.* The evil lack not just power but something more; senses of *cræft* established earlier must be brought into play here to explain why Alfred makes this distinction.[103] Alfred unites the concepts of power, skill, and virtue in one word, thus underscoring one of the main themes of the text linguistically.

The unity of all goods, another major theme of the text, finds linguistic support when the text embraces all these goods in one word. The Latin explains:

> Atqui illud quoque per eadem necessarium est, sufficientiae, potentiae, claritudinis, reuerentiae, iucunditatis nomina quidem esse diuersa, nullo modo uero discrepare substantiam.—Necesse est, inquam.—Hoc igitur quod est unum simplexque natura prauitas humana dispertit. . . . (III pr. ix. 15–6)

> "But for the same reason this must follow: sufficiency, power, fame, reverence and happiness, indeed are diverse in name, but in no way can one distinguish their substance." "It must be," I said. "Therefore human depravity has dispersed what is one simple nature. . . . "

Alfred translates:

> Swaþeah is to geþencanne þæt ða fif þing þe we ær ymb spræcon, þeah hi tonemde sien mid wordum, þæt hit is eall an þing, þonne hi

gegaderede bioð; þæt is anwald 7 genyht 7 foremærnes 7 weorðscipe 7 blis. Þa fif ðing, þonne hi ealle gegaderade bioð, þonne bið þæt God.... 7 he bið anfeald untodæled, þeah he ær on mænig tonemned wære. Ða andsworede ic 7 cwæð: þisses ic eom ealles geþafa. (76.1–5, 9–11)

"Therefore we must conclude that the five things about which we spoke before, although they are named with different words, that is all one thing, when they are gathered; that is, power and sufficiency and fame and worship and happiness. These five things, when they are all gathered, then that is God... and he is one, undivided, although he was named before as many." Then I answered and said: "I agree with all of this."

Moreover, in the emphasis on naming that Alfred adds to the passage, he acknowledges the importance of words. Where Boethius writes in Latin that man has dispersed the unified good, Alfred writes that man has "divided it by naming": "tonemde... mid wordum"; "on mænig tonemned wære." The division of speech resulted from sin, Alfred notes in a largely original passage on the building of the tower of Babel and the punishment of those involved (99.8–20).[104] If words can divide, surely they can unite or reunite. Alfred applies the same word throughout the text to the most important goods: virtue, mental abilities, honest work, the fulfillment of one's duties and even power. He never uses *cræft* itself in this text in a negative sense, for vice or wile, although he certainly knew it because he uses it in the sense of the devil's tricks or wiles in the *Pastoral Care* (227.5).[105]

Alfred's use of the word *cræft* in relation to God also highlights the central theme of the work. The Latin text centers on the approach to God. The main point of the argument through Book III is the unity of all goods in God, the self-sufficient One, and the approach to the One as the only means of escape from Fortune available to human beings. This explanation leads into a discussion of free will that ultimately offers not only a proof of human freedom but also a discourse on the relationship between that freedom and reaching God (see V pr. vi. 44–8). The *De consolatione* ends with a prayer; although the text is not explicitly theological, God is the goal toward which it is directed. Alfred translates the end of that passage:

Hatiað yfel 7 fleoð swa ge swiðost mægen; lufiað cræftas, 7 folgiað þæm. Ge habbað micle nedðearfe þæt ge symle wel don, forðæm ge symle beforan þam ecan 7 þæm ælmihtgan Gode doð eall þæt þæt ge doð; eall he hit gesihð, 7 eall he hit forgilt. (149.5–9)

Hate evil and flee it as much as you can; love virtues, and follow them. You have great need that you always act well, for you always do all that you do before the eternal and the almighty God; and he sees it all, and he rewards it all.

The journey to God is a central theme in Alfred's version too, and it becomes inseparable from the pursuit of *cræft*, which now links spiritual, mental and practical values.

Both texts claim that people can become like God, or become gods themselves, if they achieve the highest good.[106] This linkage between human beings and God, and the possibility of people becoming like or participating in God, is also strengthened by Alfred's usage of *cræft*. He uses it twice in relation to God, once near the start (30.22–3): "Se wyrhta is God; þæs *cræft* ic þær herige on" ("The workman is God; here I praise his craft"), and later, about halfway through: "Wundorlice *cræfte* þu hit hæfst gesceapen þæt þæt fyr ne forbærnð þæt wæter 7 þa eorþan . . ." ("With wonderful craft you have designed it so that the fire does not burn up the water and the earth..." 80.22–3). These passages unite the senses of power and artisanship. Using the same word for God and for people also helps further the connection between man and God, and between human efforts and divine, an essential parallel in both the Latin and Old English texts. As Clemoes writes, "*Cræft* 'virtue' was the operative word in the creative relationship between the soul and God."[107] *Cræft* bridges the gap between this world and the next.

Here Alfred uses different means to attain similar ends to the source text's. He could have followed the Latin more closely, keeping the distinctions between Latin words for learning and for virtue by employing different Old English words. In uniting the different concepts his usage of *cræft* evokes, Alfred goes beyond Boethius. Moreover, the positive value the Old English text puts on physical skill is unthinkable in the Latin text, but not valuing physical skill was unthinkable to Anglo-Saxons. Alfred can use imagery drawn from occupations because he treats such labor as comparable to spiritual strivings: both fulfill the responsibilities given one by God. For Boethius, anything other than philosophy is a distraction. He does not address earning a living or helping others. In a lengthy speech in I pr. iv, the prisoner tries to defend his worldly interests as serving others and philosophy, and he laments his misfortune in being both punished and thwarted in his good intentions; Philosophy responds in I pr. v by taking his emotional monologue as evidence of his mental disturbance. Later, when the prisoner protests that all he wanted was to serve, Philosophy leads him to see that even this desire is not truly selfless or perfect (II pr. vii. 1–3, discussed earlier in this chapter).[108] Alfred greatly expands this section until Mod defends himself on the grounds that he was serving, and the prisoner's original two-and-a-half–line speech becomes a nearly thirty-line monologue that includes observations on the *cræft* of a king (40.5–41.6). Wisdom's response is also expanded and changed, limiting the criticism to "þonne wilnung *leases* gilpes 7 *unryhtes* anwealdes 7 *ungemetlices* hlisan godra weorca" ("the desire for *false* glory and *wrongful* power and *immoderate* reputation for good works," 41.12–3, emphasis added). Physical skill does not merit consideration in the Latin text, but to the Anglo-Saxon habitus, all kinds of skills are essential.

Although Alfred takes care not to overload the *Boethius* with logical or philosophical terms, and he largely avoids loan-words and calques, his use of *cræft* transforms both word and text. Bourdieu says of later philosophical language:

> All the potential resources of ordinary language are used to create the impression that there exists a necessary link between all signifiers and that the relationship between signifiers and signifieds is established solely through the mediation of the system of philosophical concepts, "technical" words which are ennobled forms of ordinary words... traditional notions... neologisms....[109]

Alfred's language does not stray as far from ordinary usage as a modern philosopher's, but he too mobilizes the vernacular to give new meaning to a word—and to make the newly forged connections appear natural and necessary.

In modern philosophy, words thus removed from their ordinary meaning "assume a distorted meaning," and:

> the incorporation of a word into the system of philosophical language... brings about the *negation* of its primary meaning, that is the meaning which the tabooed word assumes with reference to the system of ordinary language and which, although officially banished from the overt system, continues to lead a clandestine existence. This negation is the source of the duplicity authorized by the dual message registered in each element of discourse, always defined by belonging simultaneously to two systems, the overt system of the philosophical ideolect and the latent system of ordinary language.[110]

Alfred again does not take this process as far as more recent philosophers, for he never denies most of the common meanings. Yet the tension inherent in a transformed usage does appear in one surprising passage. After concluding that power and fame are not real goods because the wicked can attain them, Wisdom comments: "Þæs ilcan is to wenanne to eallum ðæm gesælþum þe seo wyrd brengð þisses andweardan lifes ge on *cræftum* ge on æhtum; forþæmþe hi hwilum becumað to þam forcuðestum" ("The same can be rightly judged of all the goods of this present life that *wyrd* brings both in *talents* and in possessions, for they sometimes come to the most depraved,"

37.30–38.2, emphasis added), implying that *cræft* is not a real good but a gift of fortune. The Latin explicitly refers to gifts of fortune: "Quod quidem de cunctis fortunae muneribus dignius existimari potest, quae ad improbissimum quemque uberiora perueniunt" ("Which indeed can be said of all the goods of fortune, which come more richly to the most wicked," II pr. vi. 15).[111] This sense of *cræft* conflicts with the usage throughout the rest of the text, here reflecting the more common and less positive Old English usage of the term for *craft* or *skill.* The passage reveals lingering tensions between more established meanings of *cræft* and Alfred's shifted, philosophical usage—an inevitable tension, according to Bourdieu. Although he avoids negative usages, Alfred can never entirely dismiss the sense of *cræft* as a skill that might be morally neutral or could be misused (as a "wile"). Nor should he; Bourdieu agrees that such tension "allows for a doubling of profits: the profit of saying and the profit of denying what is said by the way of saying it."[112] The very negation demonstrates the shift in language, the elevation to a new level that sets reader and writer apart from those not equipped to read the text. Those readers who follow the *Boethius* carefully will see the connections between the different aspects of *cræft*, rewarding their investment of time.

Alfred's synthesis results in a unique philosophy that fuses the *De consolatione* with other Christian and Anglo-Saxon elements, a text that goes beyond the source text. Alfred's usage of the fourth sense in particular, mental talent, sometimes disagrees with the philosophy of the Latin text. For Boethius, even some kinds of intellectual pursuit do not belong to the realm of philosophy. Gerard O'Daly reads the first two meters as examples of the kind of poetry that has no place in the work. The first meter, by the prisoner, is too emotional and leads only to despair. The second, however, raises and discards the possibility of traditional didactic poetry; this poetry is not bad in itself, but it has no place in philosophy.[113] Just as certain kinds of intellectual activity do not belong in the poetry of the *De consolatione*, they do not belong in the prose either. Some intellectual activities that Anglo-Saxons associated with *cræft*, from varieties of book learning to knowledge of medicine (a sense Alfred uses at 132.10–13), would not find a place in the Latin work. Yet they are valued in the Old English work.

So too is power, particularly royal power. The Latin text views earthly power as an incomplete good with no ultimate value; the Old English, as a tool necessary to fulfill one's role in life. As Hitch explains, God gives *cræft* so that people may perform the tasks he has assigned them.[114] This kind of *cræft* did not belong to Boethius's conception of the world, but it did belong to the Anglo-Saxon mindset, or at least to Alfred's, once he had been influenced Gregory the Great's efforts to balance the active life and the contemplative.

The *De consolatione* presumes familiarity with Neoplatonic thought that Alfred's audience lacked. Without the original context, the text could make sense only in a Christian tradition of scorning fortune, contemplating higher things, and trying to reach God. This was a Latin tradition as well, and Alfred and his audience may never have understood that this was not the primary tradition to which Boethius appealed. The disjunction Boethius sees between those intellectual fields that are inappropriate to his work, and those intellectual and spiritual pursuits that are his subject, does not pose the same difficulty for the figure who loomed largest for Alfred: Gregory.[115] Neither was this split apparent in the Scriptures, the very foundation for the thought of these Church fathers, nor for their self-conscious successors among the Carolingians.

The Biblical tradition includes some rejection of pagan intellectualism, particularly in the New Testament, but the Old Testament Wisdom books are notable in this context both for justifying earthly wisdom as a support for spiritual wisdom and for admonishing rulers to take up wisdom. Gregory's influence is also plain. Alfred's conception of *cræft* as embracing all kinds of skills, gifts, and powers accords perfectly with Gregory's *Regula pastoralis*, which Alfred knew intimately when he translated the *Boethius*. No division between mental and spiritual gifts exists because both are needed to reach God; learning helps one to worship properly and to guide one's flock. Hence Alfred can translate, "se cræft ðæs lareowdomes bið cræft ealra cræfta" ("The art of the teacher is the art of all arts," *Pastoral Care* 25.17–8).[116] Talents are given to be shared: "Ac monige siendun mid miclum giefum monegra cræfta & mægene geweorðode, forðonðe hie hie scoldon monegum tæcan, & for oðerra monna ðearfe onfoð ðylicca giefa" ("But there are many who are honored with many gifts of virtues [Latin: *uirtutum*] and strengths, so that they should teach many, and for other men's needs they receive such gifts," *Pastoral Care* 41.11–3; 5.3–5 in the Latin). Indeed, to refuse to use one's gifts for others, even to withdraw for religious contemplation, would be a rejection of God and the duties he has given with his gifts: "Gif ðonne seo feding ðara sceapa bið ðære lufan tacen, hwi forcwið ðonne se ðe him God suelce cræftas giefð ðæt he ne fede his heorde, buton he cueðan wielle ðæt he ne lufige ðone Hlaford & ðone hean Hierde eallra gesceafta?" ("If then the feeding of the sheep is a sign of love, why then would anyone whom God has given such virtues [Latin: *uirtutibus*] refuse to feed his herd, unless he wants to say that he does not love the Lord and the high Shepherd of all creation?" *Pastoral Care* 43.5–8; 5.19–22 in the Latin). Service to the community has its place as well in Gregory's *Dialogi*, whose translation Alfred commissioned. Gregory's sense of responsibility to use all one's talents for one's fellow Christians, rather than Boethius's emphasis on single-minded pursuit of the highest good, has informed Alfred's vision of *cræft*.[117]

One further influence lay in the Carolingian Renaissance. Alfred could not help but be aware of this great achievement of an earlier Christian king.[118] Alfred's contacts through family and clerical helpers made the Carolingian Renaissance a prominent model for Alfred.[119] Although Alfred did not simply imitate the Carolingian program, one fundamental tenet of Charlemagne's program was also central to Alfred's: the idea that spiritual progress requires learning of all kinds, not just religious. The *Admonitio generalis* of 789 mentions reading as one of the responsibilities of the religious, and section 78 of the *Admonitio* explains the importance of correct, canonical learning to preserve faith from error.[120] The *Encyclica de litteris colendis*, which Alcuin probably drafted for Charlemagne, similarly directs religious leaders to educate their charges so that knowledge can be preserved and put to the service of God.[121] Insufficient learning leads to errors that corrupt not only the letter, but also the sense of the text. Even basic grammar matters when one copies the Bible, commentaries and liturgical works, and the copying itself requires painstaking effort. Further training is then necessary to understand the Scriptures properly.[122] All talents—physical, mental, and spiritual—work together for the attainment of spiritual ends. Alfred might not have known these specific documents, but he surely knew the ideas behind them from Asser or one of his Continental helpers. If this precedent did not sow the seeds for Alfred's notion of *cræft*, it watered them. Thus Alfred's conception of *cræft* formed not only around the source text, but also native Anglo-Saxon and Christian notions.

Alfred's unique fusion of ideas from different traditions to form his usage of *cræft* had specific thematic ramifications. His language also had broader effects within the text and implications beyond it. The repeated use of the word *cræft* in various contexts helps make the text more concrete, furthering a tendency toward realistic imagery discussed earlier. His use of the word *cræft* connects more abstract intellectual and spiritual pursuits such as wisdom and virtue to more earthly notions of skill and labor. The word occurs repeatedly in the most important of Alfred's additional images, that of the king with his responsibilities, assistants, and tools. This image is foreshadowed at 30.7–10: "Gif þu þonne þæt gemet habban wille, 7 þa nydþearfe witan wille, þonne is þæt mete and drync 7 claðas 7 tol to swelcum cræfte swelce þu cunne þæt þe is gecynde 7 þæt þe is riht to habbenne" ("If you then want to have that measure, and want to know what you must have, then is it food and drink and clothes and tools to such craft as you know that are natural for you and right for you to have"). The text develops the image at length and with specific reference to the king in Mod's speech on 40–1. The image of the king working with tools and material, although very concrete, never loses its more abstract implications; at the end of the passage, *wisdom* is associated with *cræft* (40.25–8).

Alfred thus deploys the word *cræft* throughout the text to ground it in a reality that the Latin text seems to leave behind. The source text advocates abandoning ordinary life; the translation makes abandonment unthinkable, urging transformation instead. Familiar elements would still be present in the new life held out by the Old English text, but they would have new meaning: the mind's eye (*modes eagan*) would focus more on God, and *cræft* would no longer be just a means to a living or even intellectual entertainment, but a complex of skills and virtues that both help one in this life and make this life a path to the next. Alfred synthesizes three contexts—Boethian, Christian, and Anglo-Saxon—to create new meaning for the word.

Alfred's notion of *cræft* befits his goals, most obviously as his program appears in his *Preface* to his translation of the *Regula pastoralis.* He outlines a plan to encourage the spiritual growth of his subjects, primarily through translations of appropriate works. Such an idea could not have been easy to promote. In one sense it was more radical than the Carolingian Renaissance because Alfred wanted the laity to be educated as well as the clergy. This notion must have seemed foreign to the Anglo-Saxon laity, who would never have heard anything like it. It must also have seemed alien to clerics whose monopoly over Latin and Latin texts had never before been challenged. Under these conditions, that Alfred worked to make his text relevant is no surprise. Alfred established a legitimate language that was close enough to current usage for his people to recognize easily what he meant, yet distinctive enough (and close enough to Latin usage) to carry prestige. His language represented his own understanding of how society should work, replacing Boethius's understanding, which centered around the individual. By uniting concepts of mental and spiritual pursuits to those of physical labor and skill in the word *cræft,* Alfred forged a subtle strategy to make his whole program more acceptable to contemporary Anglo-Saxon society. His use of the same word for the king's work and the people's made him appear more like them and his goals for them more realistic.

His attempts to draw parallels between himself and his people had more than literary implications. The *Boethius* presents the ideal king as a hard-working man who struggles to do the best he can for his equally hard-working subjects. The audience was encouraged to identify with the friends of this good king, who appears in the image on *Boethius* 40–1 striving to use his *cræft* and his *andweorc* as best he can. Moreover, as Hitch writes, assumptions about society as a whole underlie Alfred's concept of *cræft*:

> A man's moral being consists in the performance of his proper function. The practice of this function is his *cræft.* A man is equipped by

> the grace of God with the personal qualities necessary, but he nonetheless needs to learn it, and tools, animate—helpers, teachers, servants—and inanimate are also necessary to him. For his supply of these he is dependent on a properly ordered society... in which every man performs his proper function.[123]

Alfred's notion of *cræft* not only depends on the assumption of this structure in society but also reinforces it by presenting it as natural. He never explains it because it is understood and unquestioned. Bourdieu describes, "The power of suggestion which is exerted through things and persons and which, instead of telling the child what he must do, tells him what he is, and thus leads him to become durably what he has to be."[124] The notion of *cræft* tells young men what they are and will be, facilitating social order in the kingdom as a whole.

This social order was, of course, headed by Alfred himself, and what supported it supported his own role in it. His succession as sole ruler may have been a surprise; he was not only the youngest son but was sickly throughout life. His brother left sons who thought they should not have been excluded from the succession (and after Alfred's death, one of his nephews rebelled against Alfred's son).[125] By presenting the good king as a man concerned about the welfare of his own people, not about his own interests, wealth, or power, Alfred encouraged his people to rely on his judgment and care, and thus his text supported his position.

Yet both the Latin and the Old English texts point out that men may become king regardless of their virtue, and that office confers no virtue, although Alfred adds the idea that a man may become king because he is virtuous. Alfred presents the image of the good king as an alternative but never contradicts the Boethian idea that some men achieve office without virtue and then remain bereft of it. The image of the good king and his *cræft* helps to counteract the negative presentation of monarchs in the text. When tyrants are a real possibility, a conscientious king, even if his succession came as a surprise, must be honored and obeyed. Alfred takes real risks in acknowledging the possibility of bad kings, but even greater risks in his investment of time in translations, which offer his own religious and social vision for England.

Thus the implications of Alfred's notion of *cræft* are quite far-reaching. His idea not only has the literary effect of making the text more concrete, but also advances his own political goals, both his program of translation and education and his desire to keep the kingdom (and his place at its head) secure. Alfred's strategic deployment of the word *cræft* combines the common senses of power, physical or mental skill, and God's skill in creation with a rarer usage, spiritual merit, and his own usage, virtue. He makes the meaning clear by the contexts in which he places the word, the synonyms and antonyms he uses, and his list of specific *cræftas*. That Alfred's usage of *cræft* for *virtus* was never imitated in any extant texts is surprising. Perhaps the usage of *mægen* or *miht* for *virtus* was so established by Alfred's time that writers automatically used one of those terms instead of *cræft*; or perhaps Alfred's translations were viewed as unique works whose usages could not be transferred to different contexts.

The use of a single word helps Alfred strengthen and add connections between ideas. He forges a connection between power, talent, and virtue, and between man and God. He uses the word to underscore the themes of unity and creation within the Latin work. His conception of *cræft* as uniting all occupations would be more acceptable to the king's Anglo-Saxon audience than to Boethius or his late-antique audience, and the model he presents of work, responsibility, wisdom, and virtue belongs more to Christian patristic tradition than Latin philosophical tradition. The implications are not merely abstract and literary but immediate and practical; the usage of *cræft* in the *Boethius* works to inculcate Alfred's understanding of gifts and responsibilities into the upcoming generation of readers. The text both advocates a specific way of life (in the world but not directed toward it) and a political and social system. The word *cræft* is indeed a powerful word in Alfred's *Boethius*.

Perhaps only Alfred could attempt such risky strategies from the level of individual words to the conception of his whole program. The combination of Alfred's power as king, and the sense of insecurity ingrained by watching his brothers die one by one and his kingdom suffer repeated Viking attacks, made him uniquely well placed to take risks simultaneously literary, religious, and social. Bourdieu explains, "All forms of social consecration or statutory assignment—whether conferred by an elevated social origin, a major scholastic success or, for writers, the recognition of peers—have the effect of increasing... *assurance*, of increasing the subjective capacity to realize [possibilities] in practical terms." He adds:

> The propensity to orient oneself towards the most risky positions, and especially the capacity to hold on to them in the absence of any economic profit in the short term, seems to depend in large part on the possession of significant economic and symbolic capital.
>
> But above all, the conditions of existence associated with high birth favour dispositions like audacity and indifference to material profit, or a sense of social orientation and the art of foreseeing new hierarchies, which incline a person to head for the most exposed outposts of the avant-garde and towards investments which are the riskiest....[126]

At the same time, those at the top of the social hierarchy often have a vested interest in the status quo. Alfred did not grow up expecting to be sole king of a greater Wessex, and so perhaps as a youth did not develop as great an investment in the status quo as his older brothers might have.

Thus Alfred transformed the *De consolatione* with the help of Christian tradition, but his choices of when to invoke that tradition, and which particular strands of it to invoke, were conditioned by Anglo-Saxon norms and his own interests and strategies. Alfred selected the personification of Wisdom and her relationship with the foolish from Scripture and emphasized the strand of Christian tradition that valued good stewardship rather than rejecting earthly goods entirely. He employed images that combined Christian textual parallels and everyday experiences. His transformation of the word *cræft* also drew on all three contexts in which the king worked. The translation offered a distinctive mode of discourse comprehensible to an Anglo-Saxon audience not well versed in late-antique literature, but not unacquainted with patristic imagery and language. Alfred's *Boethius* gathered learning from multiple sources into a hoard accessible and acceptable to his audience while quietly reshaping it into something new and unique. Even while Alfred shared this cultural capital, he accrued symbolic capital for himself; even while his treasure appealed to readers, the king's translation inculcated particular values. Wealth indeed brought wisdom—those gems of wisdom that Alfred deemed most necessary.

CONCLUSION

Alfred the Great crafted an array of strategies to join competing traditions into one coherent work, the *Boethius.* His translation retained much of the content of the source text but simultaneously appealed to the expectations and abilities of his audience. That appeal in turn helped Alfred to profit in symbolic capital while inculcating certain philosophical, religious, and political ideas into a select group of readers, who in turn profited in cultural capital.

The *Boethius*'s adequacy to the *De consolatione philosophiae* helped authorize the translation. The few readers possessing some acquaintance with this particular Latin text, or some sense of how a late-antique text should sound, would recognize elements of the source text in the original. Even those who lacked any familiarity with late antiquity would catch a glimpse of the foreignness of the text. Boethius's own prestige was thus translated to Alfred and his text, helping to authorize Alfred's program of translation and education as well as this particular text. Alfred gained symbolic capital as the elite Anglo-Saxon laity and clergy, and perhaps some abroad, recognized his accomplishments and his investment of effort. At the same time, Alfred shared some of his knowledge, endowing his readers with cultural capital. He made the text a treasure trove of mythological, historical, and scientific material, glossing all these elements of the late-antique text to make them accessible to readers with no Latin as well as useful for teaching. Alfred also retained less practical elements, including the structure of the dialogue and much of the argumentation. Readers who successfully negotiated the *Boethius* thus gained experience with unfamiliar styles of writing and thinking—a grounding in the liberal arts never before available to those who could read only the vernacular. Such readers would be better prepared for Latin texts and Christian theology if they were among the few for whom Alfred prescribed: "lære mon siððan furður on Lædengeðiode ða ðe mon furðor læran wille & to hieran hade don wille" ("afterwards teach a man further in the Latin language as much as you want to teach him and to promote him to higher office," Preface to the *Pastoral Care*, 7.13–5). Most readers would not go further, but his audience of Latin-poor clerics and lay noblemen would receive an unprecedented education.

Yet even readers who had some exposure to Latin texts or their translations might have found the *De consolatione*, with its Neoplatonic bent, implicit Christianity, and rigorous logic, unfamiliar and even distasteful. Alfred's introduction of explicitly Christian material into the text made the *Boethius* more familiar to readers without sacrificing the higher status of Latin culture. Alfred had Christian precedent for his program, both in the Old Testament Wisdom books and in the recent Carolingian Renaissance. His accommodation of the *De consolatione* with Christian language was facilitated by the fact that Boethius's major themes are in fact Christian themes. God as unity, highest good, and ultimate goal of humanity; the rejection of the world as an end in itself; the soul's need to recollect its own good; reassurance that the evil ultimately do not win over the good; and the genre of consolation itself can all be found both in Scripture and in patristic writings. Alfred revised the text to embrace a Gregorian sense of duty toward others, although this sense of responsibility directly conflicted with the source text's emphasis on personal responsibility and turning away from the world. Alfred incorporated many specifically Christian ideas and references and reinterpreted Neoplatonic language in Christian terms, explicated poetry and pagan myth in Christian modes, and invoked authority over logic at times in accord with common patristic practice. Thus Alfred produced a translation that readers could understand and credit with spiritual authority even while it told them how they must respond to their own leaders and exercise authority over others.

Moreover, Alfred adapted the *Boethius* to native norms derived from poetry and common experience, producing a text acceptable to Anglo-Saxon audiences. Aside from his retention of proper nouns, Alfred's vocabulary and syntax carry little trace of Latin, keeping the text comprehensible at its most basic level. His use of doublets and antitheses drew on Anglo-Saxon poetics. The *Boethius*'s self-consciousness of its own textual status reminded Anglo-Saxon audiences of their accomplishment in reading it and set them apart from all those without access to such a text. The shift toward more concrete images and narrative passages, the anticipation and repetition of argument, and the reduction of technical language and difficult logical forms all made the text easier to follow, especially for an audience attuned to oral presentation. Alfred developed a more dynamic and familiar relationship between the narrator and his interlocutor, characterizations more engaging for Alfred's audience than the Latin portraits would be. Finally, the development of the themes of friendship and kingship emphasized topics that native poetry often treated and issues crucial to a king.

Some of the most exciting moments in the *Boethius* come when Alfred melds these elements. Boethian Neoplatonism becomes more explicitly Christian, while Christianity simultaneously frequently takes on an Anglo-Saxon flavor. The *Boethius* takes up the Old Testament's treatment of the foolish, transforming it into a concern that they not be left behind entirely—a concern highly appropriate to an audience aware of its own status as new readers, and of the status of many relations and friends as wholly uninitiated. The tension between rejection of the world and good stewardship of its gifts is resolved in favor of the latter, making the text more palatable to Anglo-Saxons who highly valued wealth, honor, and position. Alfred also introduces images found in Christian literature but that resonate with everyday experience. Finally, his use of the word *cræft* unites the source text's sense of the relationship between virtue and power with the Christian understanding of one's responsibility for others in a common Anglo-Saxon word.

Thus Alfred stood to gain symbolic capital from his translation of the *De consolatione philosophiae*. The *Boethius* displays a marvelous range of knowledge, from the Old Testament to Roman mythology to late-antique science. Alfred already has political status as king, but his work in this translation elevates him above both predecessors and contemporaries in intellectual and spiritual authority. At the same time, Alfred condescends to share some of this heaping treasure trove of learning with a portion of the nobility. He offers them cultural capital otherwise unavailable to the vast majority. His varied and sophisticated strategies would appeal to well-born Anglo-Saxon readers and hearers while teaching them difficult, foreign material and inculcating a mixture of native and Latin Christian ideas and values. West Saxon achieves status as a literary and religious language, and presents itself as *the* language of the English.

The cultural capital that the *Boethius* offers does carry a price, however. Most obviously, it requires a sizeable investment of time and energy. A reader (or hearer) must learn to read (or find someone to read aloud), obtain or share a copy, and set aside the time to study a lengthy and complex work. Less obviously, making this investment opens the reader to inculcation by the *Boethius*. The reader who labored over the text would already have accepted the value of education before making such an investment in it, and he would then find the *Boethius* mirroring and reinforcing his own values. He would also read repeatedly of Alfred's conception of the rights and responsibilities of leadership as well as the necessity for endurance and trust in God. The *Boethius* anticipates an audience who will assume leadership positions, and it tells them what those in such positions must do and be. Who could argue against a self-definition that flattered readers, suggesting that they fit the model of the good ruler even as it told them how a good ruler must behave?

This study has examined the *Boethius* in detail to understand its strategies and their possible effects. Alfred employed similar strategies in his other translations as well, varying the blend but producing comparable effects: the enhancement of his own symbolic capital, the communication of cultural capital to his chosen audience, and the inculcation of specific notions of rulership. The Psalms and the *Pastoral Care* might well have seemed less foreign to Alfred's readers than the *De consolatione* because they did not call on unfamiliar disciplines or employ classical allusions and imagery. For these texts, Alfred could focus less on achieving acceptability and more on adequacy, and he did not have to labor to make them clearly Christian.[1] Only the *Soliloquies* might be as foreign as the *Boethius* because it too contains Neoplatonic philosophy and difficult arguments. Thus for the *Soliloquies* Alfred had to work especially hard to ensure acceptability, and he uses some of the strategies we see in the *Boethius*: he maintains native language usage, retains but glosses some difficult references, tends to use more concrete and familiar imagery, and shifts the balance from logic toward authority.[2] In all these texts, Alfred maintains adequacy even at the cost of some unfamiliarity. He does not remove all foreign or controversial content. Each of his texts emphasizes the afterlife over this world's honor and riches, although the latter are clearly a major concern in much Anglo-Saxon poetry. His insistence on religious as well as secular responsibilities for the laity and on education are otherwise unparalleled in his own time. The translations together work to inculcate many of the same ideals of secular conduct that the *Boethius* offers.

Further work is needed to assess Alfred's use of strategies in his other translations. This study of the *Boethius* offers a foundation; Alfred did not begin anew in each translation, and so the question is more one of proportion than of different strategies. How Alfred dealt with the challenges of each source text provides a fascinating field for study that can still yield a wealth of insight. How much and in what ways did Alfred modify the ascetic strains in Gregory and Augustine when he translated their works? Which literary allusions or pieces of scientific information did Alfred find valuable for his people and why? Does a Scriptural text require different treatment than a patristic one? Answering such questions will give a fuller picture of Alfred's goals and achievements.

Those achievements remain another question. The translations each have their own fascinations and merits; as works themselves they deserve attention and intensive study. Although this study asked what kinds of effects these texts might produce and what ideas they might inculcate, it could not determine the historical and literary impact the *Boethius* or the other translations actually had. To what extent did Alfred's program make an impression on the ruling elite of his time? Can any effects be found in Anglo-Saxon politics or education? How much did the program and its particular translations spawn admirers or imitators?

Some answers can be suggested. Whereas Robert Stanton writes, "In fact, Alfred's cultural achievements had a limited effect beyond his own generation," the impact of his work can be seen long after his death.[3] Alfred's influence on Ælfric, a century later, is well known.[4] Many of the historical and mythological figures Alfred retains from Boethius appear in later texts in Old English, indicating that later writers possessed and valued the knowledge. References to figures who appear in the *Boethius* occur not only in Ælfric, but in anonymous homilies and saints' lives, Byrthferth's *Manual*, and a number of anonymous glosses.[5] Alfred's work still mattered to Geoffrey of Monmouth; his account of Alfred's accomplishments may not be correct in all details, but he wanted to give full credit to Alfred for the intellectual work the king did for his people. Even the fact that Geoffrey thought Alfred's literary work deserving of note shows the king's accomplishment: "the discourse of celebration," Bourdieu writes, constructs an artist as "worthy of a historical account."[6] David Pratt argues that the translator of the *Disticha Catonis* into Old English knew Alfred's *Boethius*.[7] Its use by Nicholas Trevet in his thirteenth-century commentary on the *De consolatione* has been established as well.[8]

Yet we do not see strong evidence for a transformation of the upper reaches of lay society along the lines Alfred's Preface to the *Pastoral Care* sketches. Bourdieu's work may suggest why the effects were less dramatic than the Preface envisions. Alfred's program attempts to create a cultural market. Some market already exists, especially for clerical learning, and it is in this arena where we see most evidence for the program's effects. Outside the religious markets, effects appear very limited. Bourdieu writes of social ideas that they "can succeed only if they converge with the (sometimes unconscious) strategies of groups outside the field."[9] Alfred's ideas perhaps converged only with the strategies and interests of narrow groups—his own circle, some other clergy, a fraction of the nobility. Bourdieu also notes of the later "society of artists" that "One of its major functions, and yet one always overlooked, is to be its own market."[10] Unfortunately for Alfred, his program sought more than just a few readers and copyists. At the same time, these few would keep the *Boethius* and some of his other translations alive at least into the twelfth century and possibly as late as Chaucer's time.[11]

Yet David Dumville suggests that Alfred laid the groundwork for the tenth-century monastic revival.[12] Roy Liuzza writes of the Old English Gospels finding their context in the monastic revival and "more broadly, in the tradition of vernacular education fostered by Alfred the Great and his successors."[13] When Helmut Gneuss writes:

> I feel we should not ignore the Old English Benedictine achievement: nowhere else in Western Europe in the tenth and eleventh centuries would one have found—quite apart from England's early poetry and the vernacular law codes—a collection of competent translations and adaptations of standard Latin texts, or the provision of continuous glosses, in all the country's leading libraries....

and provides a list of texts that include the Alfredian translations, we can again see Alfred's shadow stretching over the Benedictine Reform.[14] Kathleen Davis concludes her study of Alfred's Preface and its work of inventing the nation by noting the dominance of English square minuscule by the tenth century, after its beginnings at the end of the ninth. The use of one script for both Latin and vernacular texts unified writing throughout the various regions of England and made Latin and English visually equivalent, thereby enacting the ideas of the Preface and the ideals of the program.[15] Janet Nelson offers a broader argument for the effects of Alfred's policies, including his work on education and translation:

> Through the tenth century and beyond, law-making went on, and so did the rhetoric of public service. Ealdormen and thegns looked to the king and attended his assemblies. Muscular christianity [*sic*] persisted. Saxon songs were copied and composed. Wessex was never again dismembered. *Engla lond* survived even the vicious internal and external wars, and the treachery of ealdormen, unleashed in Æthelred II's reign. The royal courts, even of kings who were no scholars and lacked Alfred's charisma, maintained their centripetal pull. Winchester and London throve. The books most necessary for all men to know survived, and they continued to be read by ealdormen and thegns.[16]

Although separating the afterlife of Alfred's program from other social, political, and literary developments in later Anglo-Saxon England may be difficult, clearly the king's work and his texts had lasting effects. This conclusion can only hint at what further study may develop.

The questions and methods of this study can be extended to other translations and educational efforts throughout the Middle Ages as well. Translation Studies helps us to recognize the various goals and components of translation without focusing on only one or degrading some, allowing scholarship to extricate itself from modern notions of fidelity to the text to recover the strategies of particular eras, movements, or translators. To what extent did they seek adequacy and how did they achieve it? What techniques lent translations acceptability? Were they primarily linguistic, enacted at the level of the word and sentence, or did they operate upon higher order concerns such as textual structure, imagery, characterization, and themes? These questions can illuminate medieval translations from the *Roman d'Eneas* to Chaucer's *Boece* to Wycliffite Bible fragments. Pierre Bourdieu's ideas also allow for further exploration of translations. The notions of symbolic and cultural capital, and their importance within society and speech, provide a valuable framework in which to consider why, for whom, and how certain texts were translated. Bourdieu's recognition of the power of language and its ability to inculcate even bodily practices can help us reconsider tensions between languages and cultures and the reasons for and against translating Scripture, learned texts, and more popular texts. Bourdieu's ideas of strategy and habitus allow scholars the freedom to consider a translator's "practical sense" or "feel for the game"—to understand how and why that translator might produce certain effects without reducing the choices to specifically conscious or unconscious calculations. His notion of field helps us to recognize and interpret different stakes and different games. Finally, some of the particular strategies Bourdieu highlights in speech and writing in later eras prove useful for the Middle Ages. A strategy of condescension occurs not just when the mayor of Béarn speaks the provincial dialect in modern France; medieval translators constantly demonstrate their superior knowledge and abilities while assisting less able readers and hearers.[17] The idea of an internal reading not only explains why and how nineteenth- and twentieth-century philosophical texts demand readers who have already been initiated into their specialized language, but it also helps us understand how and why some Latin texts and even their translations shut out the uninitiated, and how some medieval translators compensated for the difficulties of their texts. Bourdieu does not himself treat the question of how a writer authorizes himself or herself in the absence of an official language; medieval studies can in turn inform anthropology and sociology. Bourdieu's work on nineteenth-century artists can also be nuanced with an understanding of the status of earlier art and artists.

Using Translation Studies and Bourdieu's work with medieval literature enables productive readings. Alfred's translations, and many other such medieval works, have been studied seriously for well over a century. Yet only relatively recently have scholars regularly tried to understand them on their own terms, not as failed attempts to render a sacrosanct original, or as the graspings of unsophisticated minds at ideas too deep for them, but as texts that both engage with a foreign culture and carry a value and meaning of their own. Alfred's *Boethius* and many other medieval translations deserve neither our censure for their differences from the source text nor our praise for "getting it right" in the midst of difficulties. They deserve our attention as the art of another era. We, like the translators, must both find ourselves in these texts and make room for these texts in ourselves, mediating between old and new, between language and language, between text and gloss.

APPENDIX: THE COMMENTARY PROBLEM

One of the thorniest issues the *Boethius* raises involves commentaries. Medieval manuscripts of the *De consolatione philosophiae* often contained marginal and interlinear glosses to explain difficult references and offer interpretive guidance. Alfred's translation incorporates a multitude of glosslike comments and explanations. Did Alfred create his own glosses as he translated, or did he simply incorporate remarks he or his assistants found in a Latin manuscript? Georg Schepss suggested more than a century ago that Alfred used Latin glosses to aid his translation.[1] Other scholars traced possible borrowings in more detail: Diane K. Bolton studied the mythological glosses of fourteen manuscripts concerning III met. xii, IV met. iii, and IV met. vii, and Kurt Otten studied several manuscripts in conjunction with the full text of the *Boethius* to suggest numerous possible borrowings.[2]

In a landmark study, Joseph S. Wittig scrutinized forty-eight manuscripts to see if they could explain Alfred's additions to the Orpheus meter (III met. xii).[3] He not only found that a number of glosses had small pieces of information that matched Alfred's additions, but also that all this information was readily available elsewhere, that most of the glosses did not match Alfred's work, and that much of Alfred's elaboration of the meter bore no connection to the glosses, even contradicting them in a few places. Furthermore, Wittig makes the important point that although numerous Alfredian additions parallel glosses, those glosses were not all found in one commentary but spread over several. Alfred and his helpers most likely worked with one or two manuscripts, not an array. Unless Alfred had access to a composite gloss tradition that has since disappeared, even those elements that look as though they derived from the commentaries would not all be available to him. Wittig's article did not, however, offer a final solution to the problem. Others have continued to review glosses and have generally reached the same two conclusions as earlier scholars: that Alfred used a commentary or commentaries, but only very selectively; or that Alfred need not have used a commentary at all but could garner the same information elsewhere.[4]

Wittig's most recent work on glosses on the *De consolatio* reveals the glossing traditions to be much more complex than previously thought.[5] He argues that the "Remigian glosses" are not in fact by Remigius, although some specific notes may result from Remigius's work, and he demonstrates that the "St. Gall" type of commentary comprises at least two separate versions, while the "Remigian" commentary can be broken into four separate families, some with subfamilies of their own. He concludes that both grew by evolution, as scholars edited more and more glosses, adding a note here, modifying one there, rejecting an idea there. Wittig also places the dates for the seeds of these commentaries before Alfred's time; some of the specific glosses may have been available at Alfred's court, and certainly the idea of glossing was well-known to students of the *De consolatione.* Scholarly consensus now leans toward the idea that Alfred used glosses selectively, but the exact form of the commentaries to which he would have had access has not been determined.

My work on commentaries cannot settle the issue conclusively either, but it does add to the conviction that Alfred used commentary material, but very selectively. I focused on two manuscripts, Cambridge, Trinity College O.3.7 (T), and Cambridge, University Library Kk.3.21 (Kk.). Although these postdate Alfred, they may well trace earlier English commentary traditions. I selected fifty-three passages of varying lengths in which Alfred added information to Boethius's text, then examined the glosses on those passages. In nineteen of these places, neither manuscript had any gloss. In the other thirty-four, at least one manuscript had a gloss, but at best only nine of those in Trinity and fourteen in Kk. were relevant to Alfred's additions. (Six of these glosses occurred, with some minor variation, in both of the manuscripts.)

Some of these glosses carry information that was perhaps not uncommon, but that was neatly assembled by the commentary tradition. In the best example, the Old English adds many pieces of information to III met. xii, including two that parallel glosses. T says of Tantalus "per hunc autem avaritia significatur is enim rex" ("through this king, indeed, avarice is signified," 31r) where the Latin *De consolatione* has only the name and punishment (III met. xii. 37), but Alfred has "Tantulus se cyning ðe on ðisse worulde ungemetlice gifre wæs" ("Tantalus the king, who in this world was immoderately greedy. . . . " 102.31–2). Kk. offers more tidbits, including "hoc carmen fabulosum" ("this fabulous song," 61r), which Alfred may pick up in his "ealdum leasum spellum" ("old false spell," 101.22), but that is an obvious comment. Kk.'s "tergeminus . . . Cerberus" ("threefold Cerberus," 61r) gives explicitly a name found in the Old English (102.14), but not the Latin (see III met. xii. 29). Similarly, "rex laphitarum" ("king of the Lapiths," 61r) and "habuit uxorem euridicem" ("had a wife, Eurydice," 61r) supply details found explicitly in the Old English (102.30 and 101.26), but assumed by the Latin source text. Another such passage is IV met. i. 11 (105.12), where Alfred correctly supplies "þe we hatað Saturnes steorra" ("which we call Saturn's star") for "gelidi senis" ("frozen old man"); he may or may not have needed such comments as T's "id est saturni" ("that is Saturn," 31v) or Kk.'s "Senex saturnus depingitur..." ("The old man Saturn is depicted," 63r) to make the identification.

Most of these glosses offered information available elsewhere: over "Regulus" in the Latin manuscript (II pr. vi. 11), Trinity has "romanorum consul" ("consul of the Romans"), and over "poenorum" ("of the Carthaginians"), Trinity has "affricorum" ("of the Africans," 15r); the *Boethius* offers "Regulus, se foremæra heretoga, þa he feaht wið Africanas" ("Regulus, the very famous consul, when he fought against the Africans..." 37.5–6) here. Where Alfred expands the name M. Tullius (II pr. vii. 8), Kk. explains: "marcus hoc est eius pronomen tullius proprium nomen cicero uocatur" ("Marcus is this man's first name, Tullius his proper name, but he was customarily called Cicero," 31r), and the *Boethius* reads "on Marcuses dagum... se wæs on oðre naman haten Tullius, 7 þriddan Cicero" ("In the days of Marcus... who as his second name was called Tullius, and his third Cicero," 43.6–7).[6] II met. vii. 15–6 contains glosses on Brutus, "primus consul romanorum" ("first consul of the Romans," T 16v and Kk. 33r) and Cato, "philosophus" ("philosopher," Kk. 33r); Alfred describes Brutus as "se foremære 7 se aræda Romwara heretoga" ("The very famous and bold Roman consul," 46.21–2) and Cato as "se wisa 7 fæstræda" ("the wise and steadfast," 46.23). In the Odysseus meter (IV met. iii), Trinity and Kk. comment "fabula cyrce solis filiae" ("the fable of Cyrce, daughter of the sun," T 35r and Kk. 69v, where the name is spelled "circae"). Kk. both suggests the fabulous nature of the story (*Boethius* 115.12: "ealdum leasum spellum") and the identification of Cyrce as Apollo's daughter (116.2–3), a point implicit in the Latin. In each case the information can be found elsewhere, and the content does not always match well.[7]

A few glosses seem more significant. At the end of II pr. iv, Philosophy speaks of those who endured suffering and death for the sake of good; both T and Kk. comment, "hic sanctos martires uult intellegi" ("Here the holy martyrs are to be understood," T 12v and Kk. 24r). Alfred elaborates on the Latin to explain that these people sought "þæm ecan life; þæt wæron ealle þa halgan martiras" ("eternal life; those were all the holy martyrs," 26.20–1). At 26.23–7.13, the meter concerning houses built on sand, rock, and mountains, Alfred adds comments connecting the mountain to pride ("ofermetta," 26.25)—as do two glosses in Kk. (24r) and one in T (12v). In

II met. vi, Nero's burning of Rome is glossed in both Cambridge manuscripts "uolens uidere quantum incendium fuerit Troiae" ("wanting to see how the fire proceeded at Troy," T 15v and Kk. 30r), and Alfred similarly adds, "æfter þære bisene þe gio Trogiaburg barn. Hine lyste eac geseon hu seo burne, hu lange, 7 hu leohte be þære oðerre" ("after the example that once burned at Troy. He wanted also to see how it burned, and how long, and how brightly, by [the example of] that other," 39.20–1). When the Latin briefly mentions Seneca's death, "Nero Senecam familiarem praeceptoremque suum ad eligendae mortis coegit arbitrium" ("Nero forced Seneca, his servant and master, to choose the means of this death," III pr. v. 10), Alfred adds, "Ða he þa þæt ongeat, þa geceas he hi þone deað ðæt hine mon oflete blodes on ðæm earme; 7 ða dyde mon swa" ("Then, when he understood that, he chose a death caused by a man bleeding him from the arm; and so they did," 66.27–9), perhaps influenced by remarks such as Kk.'s "mandauit ut sibi genus mortis eligeret et uenam utriusque brachii incidi fecit" ("he ordered that he choose the manner of his death, and he made an incision in the vein of either arm," 43r). 89.22–3, which says that the eyes of man's mind is to the brightness of the heavenly light as the light of sun is "to metanne wið ða ecan birhtu Godes" ("compared with the eternal brightness of God") seems to pick up Kk.'s remark "ad comparationem uerc lucis solem esse candidem" ("compare the brightness of the true light to the sun," 54v).

Several glosses, then, have parallels among Alfred's additions or changes. Alfred could have gleaned all this information from various other sources, although he could more easily have obtained it if it were collected it in one or two places, whether separate commentaries or glosses in the Latin manuscript that he used as a basis for his own translation. Still, the great majority of his additions and changes have no parallel in the commentaries I examined. In most of these passages, either no glosses exist on the points Alfred expands or the glosses have no relevance to Alfred's changes. In some places Alfred does not use glosses that would seem very apposite; for instance, Kk.'s extensive glosses to III met. ix (49v–50r) include comments on angels and men, the three capacities of the human mind, and the elements, all topics that interest Alfred. Yet Alfred does not use either of the first two at all, and his remarks on the elements differ in order and content from the glosses. The majority of Alfred's work cannot at this time be traced back to existing commentaries.

Glosses did have some impact on Alfred's translation, at least as a practice of reading and writing. At a minimum, Alfred must have been familiar with the practice of glossing, and so he frequently glosses his Latin source. Alfred almost certainly also had a glossed manuscript of the *De consolatione* before him and his assistants as he worked; he might occasionally have drawn on glosses that he found useful. However, either the manuscript had minimal glosses, or, more likely, Alfred and his team passed over in silence the vast majority of glosses as irrelevant to their work. Quite possibly Alfred used a commentary that has been lost; that more connections will be discovered between his work and the commentary tradition remains possible.

In any case, as this study demonstrates, Alfred molds his material strategically. Few if any readers would recognize specific borrowings from the commentary tradition, although many of Alfred's other materials—the Latin source text, patristic models, and vernacular repertoires—would be recognizable to some contemporaries, who would also recognize the distinction and the connotations of those materials. Alfred's Latin borrowings provided prestige to his translation and added to his people's store of learning while establishing firmly the king's own symbolic capital. His use of vernacular elements from vocabulary to imagery and allusion asserted his ability to bridge the gap between cultures and invited his audience to continue reading the *Boethius* despite its difficulty and often foreign nature. Alfred's use of commentary material could add to the cultural capital of his people and again support his own symbolic capital, but, unlike many of the other materials he used, imagining that Alfred expected any recognition of the sources of these glosses, or that they offered any specific strategic value, is difficult. A strong possibility remains that Alfred made very limited use of a commentary, but without more certain knowledge of the particular commentary or tradition, that usage does not have as much to teach us about Alfred's techniques and strategies of translation as his other sources and methods do.

ABBREVIATIONS

ASE: Anglo-Saxon England
ASPR: *The Anglo-Saxon Poetic Records*
Asser: *Asser's Life of King Alfred together with the Annals of Saint Neots*
Bede: The Old English Version of Bede's Ecclesiastical History of the English People
Bo or *Boethius: King Alfred's Old English Version of Boethius De Consolatione Philosophiae*
Bosworth-Toller: Bosworth, *An Anglo-Saxon Dictionary*
Chronicle: *The Anglo-Saxon Chronicle: A Collaborative Edition*
Corpus: Dictionary of Old English Corpus online
De cons or *De consolatione: Anicii Manlii Severini Boethii Philosophiae Consolatio*, ed. Bieler
Dialogi: Gregory the Great, *Dialogues*
Dialogues or *GD: Bischof Wærferths von Worcester Übersetzung der Dialoge Gregors des Grossen*
DOE: Dictionary of Old English
EETS: Early English Text Society
Fontes*: Fontes Anglo-Saxonici: World Wide Web Register*
HE or *Historia ecclesiastica: Bede's Ecclesiastical History of the English People*
MGH: Monumenta Germaniae historica
Or or *Orosius: The Old English Orosius*
PC or *Pastoral Care: King Alfred's West-Saxon Version of Gregory's Pastoral Care*
PL: Patrologia latina
Prose Psalms: *King Alfred's Old English Prose Translation of the First Fifty Psalms*
Psalms: *Le psautier romain et les autres anciens psautiers latins*, ed. Robert Weber
RP or *Regula pastoralis:* Gregory the Great, *Règle Pastorale*

Sol or *Soliloquies: King Alfred's Version of St. Augustine's Soliloquies*, ed. Thomas A. Carnicelli

Soliloquia: Augustine, *Soliloquies and Immortality of the Soul*

Supplement: T. Northcote Toller, *Supplement to An Anglo-Saxon Dictionary*

TRHS: Transactions of the Royal Historical Society

NOTES

Introduction

1. The order in which they are listed here is the most likely order of translation. The time of the translation of the Psalms is highly uncertain, however, and evidence exists that work on the *Soliloquies* overlapped some of the work on the *Boethius*, although most of it was done later. Frank G. Hubbard lists numerous passages in the translations in which one translation seemed to reflect the other translation rather than its own source text; in each case but one, the *Sol* borrowed from the *Bo* or the *De cons*; see "The Relation of the 'Blooms of King Alfred' to the Anglo-Saxon Translation of Boethius," *Modern Language Notes* 9 (1894): 161–71. Dorothy Whitelock indicates one other borrowing in the *Bo* from the *Sol*; see "The Prose of Alfred's Reign," *Continuations and Beginnings: Studies in Old English Literature*, ed. Eric Gerald Stanley (London: Nelson, 1966), 67–103, at 95. Both suggest that Alfred knew but had not yet translated the *Soliloquia* when he translated the *Boethius*, or that he began his translation of the former only when the latter was nearly complete. Furthermore, "Alfred" the translator is to some extent a construction. In his Preface to the OE *Pastoral Care*, the king thanks his helpers, Plegmund, Asser, Grimbold, and John. To what degree they helped, edited, or even wrote his texts is still debated. Most recently, Wilhelm G. Busse doubts that a king would have time to devote to such work (176–9) and thinks the king's authorship a mere topos (180–1); see "Die 'karolingische' Reform König Alfreds," in *Karl der Große und das Erbe der Kulturen*, ed. Franz-Reiner Erkens (Berlin: Akademie Verlag, 2001), 169–84. His arguments are purely circumstantial, lacking any positive evidence. The problem is not unique to Alfred; as Gideon Toury notes, "As long as it is only pairs of target vs. source texts that are available for study, there is no way of knowing how many different persons were actually involved in the establishment of a translation . . ." or what their roles were; *Descriptive Translation Studies and Beyond* (Philadelphia: John Benjamins, 1995), 183. Yet the role that Alfred's own prefaces, contemporary accounts, and later histories ascribe to him cannot simply be dismissed. The king himself assembled the scholars, chose the texts, and worked on the translations that bore his name (even if he was not solely responsible). Moreover, the *Bo* is not a patchwork of techniques but the product of a fairly consistent set of strategies;

whether one man, one man with some assistance, or a committee led by the king put it together, one voice can be found that tradition labels "Alfred." See also Janet M. Bately, "Lexical Evidence for the Authorship of the Prose Psalms in the Paris Psalter," *ASE* 10 (1982): 69–95, especially 94–5, and David Pratt, "Persuasion and Invention at the Court of King Alfred the Great," in *Court Culture in the Early Middle Ages: The Proceedings of the First Alcuin Conference,* ed. Catherine Cubitt (Turnhout: Brepols, 2003), 189–221, which argues for a dominant voice, consistent style, and coherent plan for Alfred's translations and a group of artifacts including the Fuller Brooch and the Alfred Jewel. Because of the very different nature of the Laws, I have not dealt with them here, but Alfred's Laws are indeed part of his program. For the Laws, see especially David Robert Pratt, "The Political Thought of Alfred the Great" (Ph.D. diss., University of Cambridge, UK, 1999; forthcoming in the series Cambridge Studies in Medieval Life and Thought, Cambridge: Cambridge University Press, 2004) and Patrick Wormald, *The Making of English Law: King Alfred to the Twelfth Century* Vol. 1: *Legislation and its Limits* (Oxford, UK: Blackwell, 1999).

2. For the Alfredian canon, see Bately, "Lexical Evidence," her "Those Books that Are Most Necessary for All Men to Know: The Classics and Late Ninth-Century England, A Reappraisal," in *The Classics in the Middle Ages: Papers of the 20th Annual Conference of the Center for Medieval and Early Renaissance Studies,* ed. Aldo S. Bernardo and Saul Levin (Binghamton, NY: Center for Medieval and Early Renaissance Studies, 1990), 50–65, and "The Alfredian Canon Revisited: One Hundred Years On," in *Alfred the Great: Papers from the Eleventh-Centenary Conferences,* ed. Timothy Reuter, Studies in Early Medieval Britain 3 (Aldershot, UK: Ashgate, 2003), 107-120. The OE *Martyrology* may have been part of his program or otherwise associated with scholars from his circle; see Bately, "Old English Prose before and during the Reign of Alfred," *ASE* 17 (1988): 93–138, at 103–4. If Alfred's circle did not produce the *Martyrology,* they may have known it.

3. For recent work and references on Alfred's assertion of political authority, see Janet L. Nelson, "Power and Authority at the Court of Alfred," in *Essays on Anglo-Saxon and Related Themes in Memory of Lynne Grundy,* ed. Jane Roberts and Janet Nelson (London: Centre for Late Antique and Medieval Studies, King's College, 2000), 311–37; Anton Scharer, *Herrschaft und Repräsentation: Studien zur Hofkultur König Alfreds des Großen* (Munich: R. Oldenbourg Verlag, 2000), esp. chap. 5, "Das Vermächtnis Gregors des Großen: Einheitsbewußtsein und Zusammenhörigkeitsgeful," 118–33; and Pratt, "The Political Thought of Alfred," which discusses both policy and texts. For the status of literacy and Alfred's use of the authority of writing, see Simon Keynes, "The Power of the Written Word: Alfredian England 871–899," in *Alfred the Great: Papers from the Eleventh-Centenary Conferences,* ed. Timothy Reuter, Studies in Early Medieval Britain 3 (Aldershot, UK: Ashgate, 2003), 175–97.

4. See Bourdieu's "The Social Space and the Genesis of Groups," *Social Science Information* 24.2 (1984): 195–220, and Bourdieu and L. J. D. Wacquant, *An Invitation to Reflexive Sociology* (Chicago: University Chicago Press, 1992), 96–109, for an excellent introduction to Bourdieu's concept of fields and his thinking in general. For critiques of Bourdieu's work, see *Bourdieu: Critical Perspectives,* ed. Craig Calhoun, Edward LiPuma, and Moishe Postone (Cambridge, UK: Polity Press,

1993), especially Craig Calhoun, "Habitus, Field, and Capital: The Question of Historical Specificity," 61–88. Most criticisms regard specifically modern phenomena, but the most serious recurring charge against Bourdieu is that he fails to treat social change. His account of change is incomplete, but he certainly treats it, especially in later work such as *The Field of Cultural Production*, ed. Randal Johnson (New York: Columbia University Press, 1993), and *The Rules of Art: Genesis and Structure of the Literary Field*, trans. Susan Emanuel (Stanford, CA: Stanford University Press, 1996), as Robert Holton explores in "Bourdieu and Common Sense," *SubStance* 26 (1997): 38–52. This study engages some of his understandings of how social change both works and fails. Loïc J. D. Wacquant, "Bourdieu in America: Notes on the Transatlantic Importation of Social Theory," 235–62, and also John Guillory, "Bourdieu's Refusal," *Modern Language Quarterly* 58 (1997): 367–98, recount Bourdieu's reception in the United States; they acknowledge certain weaknesses but also defend his ideas against reductive readings.

5. Unless otherwise specified, all citations of the *Chronicle* are from *The Anglo-Saxon Chronicle: A Collaborative Edition*; see my list of abbreviations and bibliography. I generally follow the A text, ed. Janet Bately (vol. 3, 1986), noting others only in case of significant variation.

6. MGH *Epistolae Karolini Aevi*, V, 71–2. See also Janet L. Nelson, "'A King across the Sea': Alfred in Continental Perspective," *TRHS*, 5th series 36 (1986): 45–68, at 46, and Richard Abels, *Alfred the Great: War, Kingship and Culture in Anglo-Saxon England* (New York: Longman, 1999), 244–5, for brief discussions of this letter and other clerical complaints against Alfred.

7. "The Franks and English in the Ninth Century Reconsidered," in *The Preservation and Transmission of Anglo-Saxon Culture*, ed. J. Rosenthal and P. Szarmach (Kalamazoo: Medieval Institute Publications, Western Michigan University, 1997), 141–58, esp. 145–6.

8. Nelson, "Power and Authority," at 311, and see 311–26 on the difficulties both of gaining and keeping power and of maintaining Wessex as a kingdom. See also Michael J. Enright, "Disease, Royal Unction, and Propaganda: An Interpretation of Alfred's Journeys to Rome, 853 and 855 A.D." *Continuity* 3 (1982): 1–16, esp. 6–7, on Alfred's need for propaganda to secure his rule.

9. "The Performance of Translation Theory in King Alfred's National Literary Program," in *Manuscript, Narrative, Lexicon: Essays on Literary and Cultural Transmission in Honor of Whitney F. Bolton*, ed. Robert Boenig and Kathleen Davis (Lewisburg, PA: Bucknell University Press, 2000), 149–70, at 149.

10. On becoming an authorized speaker, see Pierre Bourdieu, *Language and Symbolic Power*, ed. John B. Thomson and trans. Gino Raymond and Matthew Adamson (Cambridge, MA: Harvard University Press, 1991), 107–111. For Alfred as "eloquent ruler," see Robert Stanton, *The Culture of Translation in Anglo-Saxon England* (Cambridge, UK: Brewer, 2002), esp. 91–100.

11. Citations for major primary texts will be given in the main text by page and line number; refer to the list of standard editions.

12. I discuss the multivalent *sped*, meaning both intellectual ability and financial means, in "Wealth and Wisdom: Symbolic Capital and the Ruler in the Translational Program of Alfred the Great," *Exemplaria* 13 (2001): 433–67, at 451–3.

This essay also treats the question of audience in depth, and I have not included all its points here. Nelson too sees "privileged youths" (329) as the primary audience for Alfred's translations, see "Power and Authority," 327–30. Similarly, see Pratt, "The Political Thought," especially the sections "Alfred's Office-holders in Asser's *Life*" (50–60) and "The *Consolatio* as a Court Text" (262–72), for a lay court audience.

13. Alfred's audience differs from the audience for the OE Gospels envisioned by Roy Michael Liuzza, "Who Read the Gospels in Old English?" in *Words and Works: Studies in Medieval English Language and Literature in Honour of Fred C. Robinson*, ed. Peter S. Baker and Nicholas Howe (Toronto, ON: University of Toronto Press, 1998), 3–24. Liuzza concludes that these Gospels addressed clerics with insufficient Latin—nearly all clerics, he argues (6–7)—and would reach lay audiences, at best, via homilies that readers of the vernacular Gospels crafted. The anxiety about lay access to the Scriptures, however, would not be an issue with most of the Alfredian translations, and this Ælfrician anxiety never appears overtly in Alfred's work. I use the term *reader* loosely for both readers and hearers throughout this study; because of the cost of books, and because so few actually learned to read themselves, many of those who encountered the *Bo* would have done so by hearing others read.

14. *Language and Symbolic Power*, 68–9.

15. *Language and Symbolic Power*, 48, emphasis in original.

16. "Introduction: Proust's Grandmother and the Thousand and One Nights," in *Translation, History and Culture*, ed. Susan Bassnett and André Lefevere (London: Pinter Publishers, 1990), 1–13, at 3.

17. See Sarah Foot, "The Making of *Angelcynn*: English Identity before the Norman Conquest," *TRHS* 6th ser. 6 (1996): 25–49; Kathleen Davis, "National Writing in the Ninth Century: A Reminder for Postcolonial Thinking about the Nation," *Journal of Medieval and Early Modern Studies* 28 (1998): 611–37; the work of Janet L. Nelson, especially "Power and Authority" and "Wealth and Wisdom: The Politics of Alfred the Great," in *Kings and Kingship*, ed. J. Rosenthal, Center for Medieval and Early Renaissance Studies, State University of New York, Acta 11 (Albany: State University of New York Press, 1984), 31–52; and Stanton, *The Culture of Translation*, esp. 55–6 and 63–73. For detailed consideration of Alfred's policies and translations, see also Pratt, "The Political Thought."

18. See Helmut Gneuss, "The Origin of Standard Old English and Æthelwold's School at Winchester," *ASE* 1 (1972): 63–83.

19. "National Writing," 615.

20. See especially *Rules*, 223–4.

21. "The (M)other Tongue: Translation Theory and Old English," in *Translation Theory and Practice in the Middle Ages*, ed. Jeanette Beer, Studies in Medieval Culture 38 (Kalamazoo: Medieval Institute Publications, Western Michigan University, 1997), 33–46, at 33–4. See also his *Culture of Translation*, esp. 78–100.

22. "Rhetoric and Translation in Ælfric's Prefaces," *Translation and Literature* 6 (1997): 135–48, at 136. See also his discussion of the developments between Alfred and Ælfric's times, *The Culture of Translation*, 144, and of Ælfric's anxiety about the status of English, 156.

23. *The Culture of Translation*, 84.

24. Bourdieu, *The Field of Cultural Production*, ed. Randal Johnson (New York: Columbia University Press, 1993), 58. On theorizing change, see also Robert Holton, "Bourdieu and Common Sense," *SubStance* 26 (1997): 38–52.

25. For positions most likely to encourage risk-taking, see *Rules*, esp. 261–2.

26. See *Outline of a Theory of Practice*, trans. Richard Nice (Cambridge, UK: Cambridge University Press, 1977), chap. 2, "Structures and the Habitus," 72–95. For linguistic habitus in particular, see *Language and Symbolic Power*, 37–8. In *Rules*, Bourdieu argues that habitus is a disposition more creative than mere "habit" but one socially inculcated, especially at a young age; "Questions of Method" 179–208, esp. 179–80.

27. "National Writing," 618; she critiques Foot's "Making of *Angelcynn*" here.

28. See especially Nelson, "Power and Authority," and Pratt, "The Political Thought," for Alfred's uses of and differences from Carolingian models.

29. See *The Field of Cultural Production*, where Bourdieu concludes there is "no simple answer" to questions about conscious calculation (72) and briefly deals with how a writer can treat the conditions of his or her own writing (72–3). See also *Invitation* 131 and *Rules* 272–7. Other writers have pursued this question, including Brigid Rooney, "Writers Behaving Badly: Stead, Bourdieu and Australian Literary Culture," *Australian Literary Studies* 20 (2001): 76–8, and Guillory, who writes, "Human beings are complex enough, Bourdieu is saying, both to believe in the game they are playing and to entertain a sense of its artificiality and fungibility," "Bourdieu's Refusal," *Modern Language Quarterly* 58 (1997), 367–98, at 396.

30. *Language and Symbolic Power*, 81.

31. *Practical Reason*, 6; emphasis in original. To use the terminology of capital is not to project a modern economic practice into the past; instead, capitalism provides a useful model for understanding both similarities and differences in precapitalist societies. John Guillory explains Bourdieu's economic models in "Bourdieu's Refusal."

32. For a detailed description, see *King Alfred's Old English Version of Boethius De Consolatione Philosophiae*, ed. Walter John Sedgefield (Oxford, UK: Clarendon, 1899), xi, and N. R. Ker, *Catalogue of Manuscripts Containing Anglo-Saxon*, reprint with supplement (Oxford, UK: Oxford University Press, 1990), item 167. The best-preserved leaves measure about 180 by 110 mm; the *Bo* itself has 129 vellum leaves and is bound with a Latin life of Edward the Confessor. The first six leaves of the *Bo* are now lost, as are one after f. 11, two after 79, and two after 127.

33. Sedgefield, *Boethius*, xii.

34. See Sedgefield, *Boethius*, xii, and Ker, *Catalogue*, item 167.

35. The 94 vellum leaves measure about 210 by 150 mm. In this study, I have not treated either the table of contents, which is likely scribal, nor the prayer. The prayer seems clearly written in a later hand (despite Ker's comment that is written "more roughly and with a finer pen, but is probably in the main hand," *Catalogue*, item 305) and does not occur in manuscript C. Because of the difference in hand, its absence from C, and some usages in the prayer itself, I have not considered it part of the Alfredian text. Janet M. Bately finds at least one usage in the prayer that is otherwise unprecedented in Alfred's work, "Lexical Evidence," 79, footnote 65. Although some doublets and antitheses in this brief prayer resemble Alfred's (see chap. 2), the

closing phrase, "nu 7 a a a" ("now and forever, forever, forever," 149.25) does not match any of Alfred's usages elsewhere, and the improper declension of the Latin title "sanctus" for Mary and Michael deviates from Alfred's usual handling of Latin (see chap. 1).

36. Ker, *Catalogue*, item 167.

37. Ker, *Catalogue*, item 337, and Sedgefield xv–xvi. Napier edited the fragment in "Bruchstück einer altenglischen Boethiushandschrift," *Zeitschrift fur deutsches Altertum und deutsche Literatur* 31 (1887): 52–4.

38. Malcolm R. Godden believes that Leofric's gift is in fact the Bodleian text: "King Alfred's Boethius," *Boethius: His Life, Thought, and Influence*, ed. Margaret Gibson (Oxford, UK: Basil Blackwell, 1981), 419–24, at 420.

39. Sedgefield's examples include "mihte" for "meahte" and "ðam" for "ðæm," xviii.

40. Parts of words that are legible in C are used and the words completed from B or J, as indicated in the footnotes, and all deviations from C are indicated by italics and brackets of different kinds. Sedgefield gives a full explanation of his system on xviii. I have not reproduced all the italics and brackets because the difficulty of reading and writing such a system outweighs its value here. Readers interested in the exact source of each word should consult the edition. Where I think there may be a significant question about the manuscript I discuss it in an endnote. Sedgefield does not generally expand contractions and prints the "7" ("and") symbol as it occurs in the text; I have silently expanded the contractions but left "7" as it is.

41. "Editing Old English and the Problem of Alfred's *Boethius*," in *The Editing of Old English: Papers from the 1990 Manchester Conference*, ed. Donald G. Scragg and Paul E. Szarmach with Helene Scheck and Holly Holbrook (Cambridge, UK: Brewer, 1994), 163-76, at 163.

42. "Editing Old English," 166.

43. Christopher Rawlinson published a version in 1698 that relied on the Junius transcript, apparently with no corrections (Sedgefield xxi); Cardale's 1829 edition uses the B manuscript exclusively. Samuel Fox published an 1835 edition containing only the Meters and a complete edition in 1864, but he relies on Rawlinson and Cardale (Sedgefield xxii). Other editions of the Meters have been done, but because this study treats only the prose translation, those will not be discussed here. The best edition of the Meters remains *The Paris Psalter and the Meters of Boethius*, ASPR V.

44. For more on the print edition that Malcolm R. Godden and his team are preparing, please see the Introduction to the Boethius Project, http: users.ox.ac-uk/ -pemb0138/boethiusproject.html, and the page for the Boethius Project itself, http://www.english.ox.ac.uk/boethius/index.html (which also features links to some of the papers given at the annual Boethius Project Symposia). For Kevin Kiernan's work on the CD-ROM with images and many useful tools for studying the manuscript, see http://beowulf.engl.uky.edu/~kieman/eBoethius/mainpage.html.

45. *Anicii Manlii Severini Boethii Philosophiae Consolatio*, ed. Ludwig Bieler (Turnhout, BEL: Brepols, 1957). All citations from it are given in the text in this form (book.prose.boldface number or book.meter.line number), for example, III pr. ii. 6;

IV met. i. 10. This indicates that the first citation is from Book III, prose 2, boldface number 6 in Bieler's text; the second is from Book IV, metrum 1, line 10. I cite the boldface numbers because they are shared by other editions, whereas line numbers apply to Bieler's edition alone.

46. For full details, see my "Sources of King Alfred's Old English Version of Boethius's *De consolatione philosophiae* (Cameron B.9.3)," 2001, *Fontes.*

47. Helmut Gneuss believes the manuscript was produced in Wales, Cornwall, or southwestern England. *Handlist of Anglo-Saxon Manuscripts: A List of Manuscripts and Manuscript Fragments Written or Owned in England up to 1100* (Tempe, AZ: Arizona Center for Medieval and Renaissance Studies, 2001), item 908. For descriptions of Boethian manuscripts in the British Isles, see *Codices Boethiani: A Conspectus of Manuscripts of the Works of Boethius*, vol. I, Great Britain and the Republic of Ireland, ed. M. T. Gibson and Lesley Smith with Joseph Ziegler, Warburg Institute Surveys and Texts 25 (London: Warburg Institute, University of London, 1995); see especially items 9 (Cambridge, University Library, Kk. 3. 21), 51 (Cambridge, UK, Trinity College, O. 3. 7), 107 (London BL, Egerton 267), 163 (Oxford, UK, Bodleian Library, Auct. F. 1. 15), and 179 (Oxford, UK, Bodleian Library, Digby 174, fol. iii). 101 (London, BL, Arundel 514), 119 (London, BL, Harley 2685), and 124 (London, BL, Harley 3095) have Continental provenances and came to England after the Middle Ages. The Latin glosses in Vat. Lat. 3363 appear to be Welsh and from the late ninth century; Fabio Troncarelli suggests that these glosses were written by Asser, *Traditione Perduti,* Medioevo e umanismo 42 (Padua, IT: Antenore, 1981), 137–9. Janet M. Bately disagrees in "The Literary Prose of King Alfred's Reign: Translation or Transformation?" Inaugural Lecture in the Chair of English Language and Medieval Literature delivered at University of London King's College on March 4, 1980 (reprint *Old English Newsletter Subsidia*, vol. 10, 1984), 16. Malcolm Godden suggests that, at the least, Asser might have introduced Alfred to the glosses, "King Alfred's Boethius," 419. Malcolm Godden's recent discovery that one word of the glosses in Val. Lat. 3363 is actually in the Welsh language strongly supports the belief that the manuscript is Welsh, though it cannot support or deny Asser's involvement (presented at the second Boethius Symposium, July 21, 2004, Oxford, UK.) For more details on the manuscript without an ascription of the glosses, see M. B. Parkes, "A Note on MS Vatican, Bibl. Apost., lat 3363," *Boethius: His Life, Thought, and Influence*, ed. Margaret Gibson (Oxford, UK: Basil Blackwell, 1981), 425–7. See my appendix for Alfred's possible use of commentaries.

48. Experts generally agree that the Meters derive from the OE prose and not the Latin verse. See, for example, K. A. Martin Hartmann, "Ist König Alfred der Verfasser der alliterierended Übertragung der Metra des Boetius?" *Anglia: Zeitschrift für englische Philologie* 5 (1882): 411–50, and more recently Daniel Donoghue, "Word Order and Poetic Style: Auxiliary and Verbal in *Metres of Boethius*," *ASE* 15 (1986): 167–96. But see note 52 following for Szarmach and Kiernan's questioning of the conventional wisdom.

49. ASPR V, xxxv–lv, at xlv.

50. ASPR V, xlvii. Kenneth Sisam's "The Authorship of the Verse Translation of Boethius' Metra," in *Studies in the History of Old English Literature*

(Oxford, UK: Clarendon, 1953), 293–7, settled the issue for most critics in favor of Alfred. Yet some doubt still remains; Allan A. Metcalf's "On the Authorship and Originality of the *Meters of Boethius*," *Neophilologische Mitteilungen* 71 (1970): 185–7, points out flaws in arguments on both sides while refusing to adjudicate between them. See Sisam and Metcalf for detailed bibliography.

51. "The Political Thought," 314, emphasis added.

52. Paul Szarmach's provocative proposal that Otho A. vi, with its Meters, may be the "high art" version for which Bodley 180 is the pedagogical text raises significant issues, but ones that deserve their own study; see "*Meter 20*: Context Bereft," *ANQ* 15.2 (2002): 28–34. Relevant questions include to what extent Alfred and his circle would have distinguished art and pedagogy. Bourdieu argues in *Rules* (esp. 315–21) that "art for art's sake" is a purely modern formulation and that earlier art was closer to craft: part of the life of the community, it partook of and reproduced common values. See also Bridget Fowler, *Pierre Bourdieu and Cultural Theory: Critical Investigations* (London: Sage, 1997), 62 and 90. Szarmach also poses the question of whether the prose really preceded the verse; could the prose instead be a simplification of the verse (31–32)? Kevin Kiernan earlier suggested that the prose version of the Meters is in fact a back-translation from the authentically Alfredian Meters; see "Alfred the Great's Burnt *Boethius*," in *The Iconic Page in Manuscript, Print, and Digital Culture*, ed. George Bornstein and Theresa Tinkle (Ann Arbor: University of Michigan Press, 1998), 7–32 at 26. Although the preponderance of evidence so far has seemed to indicate the priority of the prose, this question too deserves separate study. Most of my evidence relies on prose translations of prose passages from the Latin. I have found the prose renderings of the Latin meters consistent with the strategies of the prose-to-prose translations and have used that evidence in places.

53. This study must of necessity fall short of Bourdieu's "task . . . of constructing the space of positions and the space of the position-takings [*prises de position*] in which they are expressed" (*The Field of Cultural Production* 30; see also *Rules* 71). Bourdieu argues, "It would be quite unjust and futile to reject this demand for complete reconstitution on the ground (which is undeniable) that it is difficult to perform in practice and in some cases impossible. . . ." Toril Moi notes the difficulties of using Bourdieu's approach to study a particular figure in a much more thoroughly documented era in "The Challenge of the Particular Case: Bourdieu's Sociology of Culture and Literary Criticism," *Modern Language Quarterly* 58 (1997): 497–508, esp. 505–6. My study can only attain a very partial reconstitution, for the Anglo-Saxon era is surely one of those cases in which full reconstitution is impossible. Although this study can never meet Bourdieu's goals, Bourdieu has too much to offer scholars of the Anglo-Saxon era to be abandoned—and the Anglo-Saxon era has too much to offer modern-day theorists to be ignored. Medievalists have drawn on his work fruitfully for later periods, but not for the Anglo-Saxon era; see, for instance, Mark Addison Amos, "'For Manners Make Man': Bourdieu, de Certeau, and the Common Appropriation of Noble Manners in the *Book of Courtesy*," in *Medieval Conduct*, ed. Kathleen Ashley and Robert L. A. Clark, Medieval Cultures 29 (Minneapolis: University of Minnesota Press, 2001), 23–48.

Chapter 1

1. See *Language and Symbolic Power*, ed. John B. Thompson and trans. Gino Raymond and Matthew Adamson (Cambridge, MA: Harvard University Press, 1991), especially chap. 1: "The Production and Reproduction of Legitimate Language," 43–65.

2. The standardization of OE did not occur until later; see Helmut Gneuss, "The Origin of Standard Old English and Æthelwold's School at Winchester," *ASE* 1 (1972): 63–83.

3. See, for instance, his *Admonitio generalis*, section 78, MGH, *Legum Sectio II: Capitularia Regum Francorum*, Tomus I, ed. A. Boretius (Hanover, GER: Supersis Bibliopolii Hahniani 1883), p. 58. For recent work on Carolingian influence on Alfred's program, see David Robert Pratt, "The Political Thought of Alfred the Great" (Ph.D. diss., University of Cambridge, 1999), and Janet L. Nelson, "Power and Authority at the Court of Alfred," *Essays on Anglo-Saxon and Related Themes in Memory of Lynne Grundy*, ed. Jane Roberts and Janet Nelson (London: London, Centre for Late Antique and Medieval Studies, King's College 2000), 311–37.

4. Roy Michael Liuzza, "Who Read the Gospels in Old English?" writes that virtually no Anglo-Saxons had any knowledge of Latin and adds, "translations, particularly of the major liturgical or monastic texts, are concessions, not accomplishments," *Words and Works: Studies in Medieval English Language and Literature in Honour of Fred C. Robinson*, ed. Peter S. Baker and Nicholas Howe (Toronto, ON: University of Toronto Press, 1998), 3–24, at 6. This judgment overstates the case and ignores the accomplishments of translators, who, together with their less-Latinate audiences, were not native speakers of a Latinate language. The Franks spoke vulgar Latin.

5. Bourdieu deals frequently with questions of credentials; see especially his treatment of competing academies and rejections of credentials in *The Rules of Art: Genesis and Structure of the Literary Field*, trans. Susan Emanuel (Stanford, CA: Stanford University Press, 1996). John Guillory writes, "Cultural capital is certainly a species of symbolic capital generally, but it is a form of symbolic capital certifiable by objective mechanisms" in "Bourdieu's Refusal," *Modern Language Quarterly* 58 (1997): 367–98 at 381; although this holds true for modern societies as Bourdieu's work demonstrates, the early Middle Ages did not have the rigid "objective mechanisms" that the later universities would offer.

6. Pierre Bourdieu, *The Field of Cultural Production*, ed. Randal Johnson (New York: Columbia University Press, 1993), 33–4, and *Rules*, 306–7.

7. Bourdieu treats the struggle to define the field itself in chap. 1, "The Field of Cultural Production, or: The Economic World Reversed," *The Field of Cultural Production*, 29–73.

8. Bosworth-Toller defines *sped*: "f. Speed, success, means: . . . I. speed, quickness . . . II. speed (as in good speed), success, prosperous issue . . . III. means, substance, abundance, wealth . . . IV. power, faculty . . . V. opportunity, or means of doing anything." (899). "VI. *progeny* (?)," is cancelled in the addenda to Toller's *Supplement to an Anglo-Saxon Dictionary* with enlarged addenda and corrigenda by Alistair Campbell (Oxford, UK: Clarendon, 1972), 56. A simple translation of *sped* as means *or* opportunity would lose some meaning, so I render it as both. For more

details, see my "Wealth and Wisdom: Symbolic Capital and the Ruler in the Translational Program of Alfred the Great," *Exemplaria* 13 (2001): 433–67, at 451–2.

9. The texts in Alfred's program repeatedly confirm and naturalize the identity of the readers; as translated into OE, they address men who will rule in some capacity. The *Pastoral Care*, for instance, offers its advice to the *reccere*, or ruler, although the Latin *Regula pastoralis* aims primarily at the *pastor*, or spiritual leader.

10. *The Field of Cultural Production*, 51.

11. See Asser. I follow the translation of officials' titles from Simon Keynes and Michael Lapidge, trans., *Alfred the Great: Asser's Life of King Alfred and Other Contemporary Sources* (New York: Penguin, 1983), 110. For introductions to the controversy over the life, see Alfred P. Smyth, *King Alfred the Great* (Oxford, UK: Oxford University Press, 1995); Simon Keynes's review of it, "On the Authenticity of Asser's *Life of King Alfred*," *Journal of Ecclesiastical History* 47 (1996): 529–51; and Anton Scharer, *Herrschaft und Repräsentation: Studien zur Hofkultur König Alfreds des Großen* (Munich: R. Oldenbourg Verlag, 2000), especially "III. Hof und Geschichtsschreibung: Asser *De rebus gestis Aelfredi*," 49–108. I am persuaded of the authenticity of Asser's life but do not have the space to rehearse the arguments here.

12. Kurt Otten, *König Alfreds Boethius*, Studien zur englischen Philologie, neue Folge no. 3 (Tübingen, GER: Max Niemeyer Verlag, 1964), 165–86, concludes that Alfred's philosophical terms do not entirely match the Latin. Olga Fischer, "A Comparative Study of the Philosophical Terms in the Alfredian and Chaucerian Boethius," *Neophilologus* 63 (1979): 622–39, argues that they are fairly close. Otten's arguments are more detailed and convincing; he considers multiple senses for each word whereas Fischer concentrates on primary meanings. See also Janet M. Bately, "An Alfredian Legacy? On the Fortunes and Fate of Some Items of Boethian Vocabulary in Old English," in *From Anglo-Saxon to Early Middle English: Studies Presented to E. G. Stanley*, ed. Malcolm Godden, Douglas Gray, and Terry Hoad (Oxford, UK: Clarendon, 1994), 8–32, for detailed analysis of the words available to Alfred. Bately concludes that Alfred and his circle not only used terminology already available but also coined new words, or shifted uses, to develop a vocabulary capable of expressing philosophical ideas accurately. Bately used the Microfiche Concordance to the Corpus of Old English, a resource not available to Fischer.

13. See Roman Jakobson, "On Linguistic Aspects of Translation," *On Translation*, ed. Reuben A. Brower (Cambridge, MA: Harvard University Press, 1959), 232–9; reprinted in *Theories of Translation: An Anthology of Essays from Dryden to Derrida*, ed. Rainer Schulte and John Biguenet (Chicago: University of Chicago Press, 1992), 144–51, at 147.

14. *Cristen*: 7.6, 7.14, 7.22, and 131.10. *Engel*: 57.8, 98.13, 129.4, 140.28 and 140.31, 142.9, 143.31, 144.3, 146.10, 146.13 (twice), 146.16, 146.19, and 146.22, and 148.2. *Papa*: 7.11; *martyr*: 26.21; *arianisc*: 7.7.

15. *Læden*: 1.9; *consul*: 7.11. Forms of *Rome*: 7.1, 7. 3, 7.7, 7.15, 34.31, 35.2, 35.5, 36.17, 39.19, 39.22, 43.6, 43.8, 43.17, 46.22, 46.24, 50.7, 61.20, 61.24, 64.12, 112.21, and 143.7. *Casere*: 7.16, 7.20, 34.24, 39.18, 39.30, 66.31, 115.15, 115.16, 115.17, and 115.19.

16. *Leo*: 57.9, 72.6 and .7, 102.7, 114.30, and 116.16; *tigris*: 72.6 and 72.8; *elpend*: 72.4 and 72.6.

17. *Must*, 12.11; *rosa*, 21.6; *capitula*, 73.15; *magister*, 57.10, 66.23, and 70.30; and *gigant* 98.30, 98.33, and 99.7.

18. 22.20: *æf–* is an equivalent of the Latin deprivative *ab–*, and *weard* comes from *weorðan*, roughly equivalent to *sum, esse*; the word translates the Latin *absentia* (absent) from *absum, abesse*. For *þiofscole*, see 33.10: forms of *scole*, derived from the Latin *schola*, are not uncommon, appearing about sixty-six times in OE, mostly in glosses, translations, homilies, or saints' lives, but also five times in *Christ* and one each in *Genesis, Juliana*, and *Beowulf*. Data on word usage in this chapter come from the online Corpus.

19. See Ludwig Borinski's *Stil König Alfreds: Eine Studie zur Psychologie der Rede* (Leipzig: Bernhard Tauchnitz, 1934) and William Brown's *Syntax of King Alfred's Pastoral Care* (The Hague: Mouton, 1970). Kurt Otten treats style in the *Bo*, 158–263.

20. Derrida touches on the problem of translating proper nouns in his "Des Tours de Babel," *Difference in Translation*, ed. Joseph F. Graham (Ithaca, NY: Cornell University Press, 1985), 231–2. Derrida writes that the crucial element of the original is not the syntax or even the idea, but the individual word. The proper noun is a special case:

> Ce privilège du mot soutient évidemment celui du nom et avec lui la propriété du nom propre, enjeu et possibilité du contrat de traduction. Il ouvre sur le problème *économique* de la traduction, qu'il s'agisse de l'économie comme loi du propre ou de l'économie comme rapport quantitatif (est-ce traduire que transposer un nom propre en plusieurs mots, en une phrase ou en une description, etc?).

> This privilege of the word evidently sustains that of the noun and with it, the property of the proper noun, the stake and possibility of the contract of translation. It raises the *economic* problem of translation, that it concerns the economy as law proper or the economy as quantitative relationship (is it translation to transpose a proper noun in several words, in one phrase or in one description, etc?). [231, emphasis in original].

Yet Alfred's treatment of proper nouns offers assurances to his original audience that he respects the privilege of the word and the name.

21. Latin names in the *Bo* frequently appear in the Latin nominative and belong in the OE nominative, so determining whether Alfred is taking them as indeclinables or simply keeping them in the nominative is difficult. A few have clearly been taken as indeclinables (Ierusalem as a genitive at 11.18; Ptolomeus as a genitive at 41.27; and Sicilia as a dative at 7.4 and as dative or genitive at 34.29). Two Latin modifiers seem to have been misdeclined, giving "in sanctam Marian" and "sanctem Michaeles" for genitive at 149.13 and 149.14 respectively, but these occur in the prayer at the end of MS B only, which is probably a later addition to the text; see my Introduction. In no cases does Alfred decline according to the Latin where the Latin

would be in conflict with the OE. He seems to be interested in adequacy in the names that he uses, but not in their case endings. Peter S. Baker, in his article "The Inflection of Latin Nouns in Old English Texts," in *Words and Works: Studies in Medieval English Language and Literature in Honour of Fred C. Robinson*, ed. Peter S. Baker and Nicholas Howe, Toronto OE Ser. 10 (Toronto: University of Toronto Press, 1998), 187–206, lists as the first of five options available to OE writers using Latin words: "Writers may attempt to match a Latin case to the equivalent Old English one" (198), and as the fifth: "They may use a Latin nom. form for any case" (198). Alfred uses both these strategies. Yet 76 proper nouns from the Latin are omitted from the Old English, although the passages in which they occur are translated; for instance, where I met. v. 9 refers to "Phoebo," Alfred's translation renders the allusion literally as "se mona" ("the moon," 10.5.) 56 of these are mythological names mostly figurative such as Auster (for the south wind), or Musae. Another 59 occurrences of Latin names are in passages not translated into OE; these are mostly in dense mythological passages or in historical passages. (When counting occurrences of proper nouns in either text, I did not count occurrences of the two main characters' names, for the practices of Alfred and Boethius diverge too widely for comparison to be illuminating.)

22. Plato (9.23); Croeses (MS B: Croesos, 18.18); Creca (18.18; for "Lydorum" II pr. ii. 11); Cirus (18.19); Pærsa (18.19); Simachus (22.5); Simaches (22.12); Ætne (34.8); Etne (34.28); Bosiridem (36.29); Erculus (36.33); Regulus (37.5); Africanas (36.7, 37.6; for "Poenorum" II pr. vi. 11); Neron (39.18); Astralogium (41.23; not a proper noun in Latin); Ptolomeus (41.27); Romana (43.6; implied in Latin); Marcuses Tullius Cicero (43.6–7); Romana (43.8); Caucaseas (43.9); Parðum (43.12); romanisc (43.17); Romwara (46.22; implied in Latin); Brutus Cassius (46.22–3); Cato (46.23); Epeccurus (55.8); Catulus (61.17, 61.21, 61.23, 61.24); Nonium (61.18); Neron (64.24, 66.23); Nerone (67.2); Seneca (66.25, 67.1); Papinianus (66.30, 67.2); Antoniose (66.30, 67.2); Indeum (67.31); Tyle (67.32); Euripides (70.30); Alcibiadis (72.30); Aristotelis (MS B: Aristodelis, 73.1); Plato (79.4, 95.20, 95.25); Parmenides (101.3); Platones (101.14); Đracia (101.23); Orfeus (101.25; implied in Latin); Eurudice (101.26; implied in Latin); Ixion (102.29); Tantalus (102.31); Orpheus (103.10; implied in Latin); Platones (110.30); Retie (115.16, an error for Neritii); Boeties (126.8); Ursa (135.29); Aristoteles (140.8); Fisica (140.9); Omerus (141.11, 141.13); Marcus Tullius Cicero (143.5–6).

23. In this count I did not include the names of God, because OE offers a wholly different set of options from the Latin. Boethius's *deus* is not a proper noun but a word both for the one true God and for humans who are becoming gods, leaving only the context to distinguish the usages. Alfred, on the other hand, uses both *Drihten* and *God* (capitalized by Sedgefield but not Alfred) as proper nouns, but only *god*, which is not a proper noun, for false gods or people. Partly because Alfred repeats names much more frequently, but primarily because of his Christianization of the text, the number of occurrences are again so vastly different between the two works that evidence from these occurrences do not offer insight into Alfred's usage. Many of the added names reiterate names the Latin mentions nearby, but forty-four of the names added belong to entirely new passages: Ælfred (1.1); Gotan (7.1); Sciððiu (7.1); Romana (7.1); Rædgota (7.2); Eallerica (7.2); Romane (7.3); Italia (7.3); Sicilia

(7.4); Þeodric (7.5, 7.6, 7.14, 7.23); Amulinga (7.6); Romanum (7.7); Iohannes (7.11); romaniscum (7.15); Constentinopolim (7.20); Þeodrice (34.23); Sicilia (34.29); Noes (34.30); Nilus (37.3); Trogiaburg (39.20); Romana (50.7); Þiodrices (62.8); Ðeodrice (62.12); Iob (98.27); Saturnes (98.27); Nefrod (99.6, 99.7, 99.8); Chuses (99.7); Chus (99.7); Chames (MS B: Chaames, 99.8); Cham (MS B: Chaam, 99.8); Noes (99.8); Nensar (99.9); Deira (99.10); Babilonia (99.11); Ðracia (101.23); Creca (101.24); Romana (112.21); Saturnus (126.9); Romana (143.7). Other names added to the Latin are: Ierusalem (11.18); Agustes (12.7); Crist (27.7); Sicilia (34.9); Nerone (34.24); Liberius (36.17); Egyptum (36.29); Iobes (36.33); Sciððeas (43.10); Welondes (46.17, 46.20); Romana (46.24); Caron (102.17); Leuita (102.30); Troiana (115.14); Agamenon (115.17); Wendelsæ (115.22–3); Apollines (115.23); Iob (115.23); Iobes (115.23, 115.27); Saturnus (115.28); Apollinus (116.1); Apollines (116.2); Erculus (127.11); Iobes (127.11); Crecum (141.11); Firgiles (MS B: Firgies, 141.12); Frigilius (141.12); and Lædenwarum (141.12–3).

24. "The month of August" and "threefold doorkeeper." The nineteen implied names Alfred states are: Agustes (12.7); Romana (34.31); Torcwines (34.31); Romebyrig (35.2); romaniscum (35.5); romanisc (36.17); Romeburg (39.19); Romana (39.22); Romwarum (61.20); Rome (61.24); Romana (64.12); Ceruerus (102.14); Parcas (102.23); Sticces (MS B: T^{y}iccies, 103.1); Saturnes (105.12); Aulixes (115.15, 115.17); Iþacige (115.16); Kirke (116.3); and Aulixes (116.8).

25. Twenty names gloss other names twenty-two times in the text: Sicilia (34.29); romanisc (36.17); Egyptum (36.29); Iobes (36.33); Sciððeas (43.10); Romana (46.24, 50.7); Leuita (102.30); Agamenon (115.17); Wendelsæ (115.22–3); Apollines (115.23); Iob (115.23); Iobes (115.23, 115.27); Saturnus (115.28); Apollinus (116.1); Apollines (116.2): Iobes (127.11); Crecum (141.11); Firgilies (MS B: Firgies, 141.12); Frigilius (141.12); Lædenwarum (141.12–3).

26. Weland appears at 46.17 and 46.20 for Fabricius (II met. vii .15), yet this case is exceptional. The change of Fabricius in II met. vii. 15 to Weland is remarked on frequently and the substitution often considered a misreading of "Fabricius" as "faber" ("artisan"); see W. F. Bolton, "How Boethian is Alfred's *Boethius*?" *Studies in Earlier Old English Prose*, ed. Paul E. Szarmach (Albany: State University of New York Press, 1986), 154. Brian S. Donaghey notes that an addition on the next page in the OE text may come from a quotation attributed to Fabricius by the *Liber de Viris Illustribus Urbis Romae*; "The Sources of King Alfred's Translation of Boethius' *De Consolatione Philosophiae*," *Anglia* 82 (1964): 23–57, at 38. The use of the quotation could indicate that Alfred recognized Fabricius and indeed had him in mind, but decided to replace him with Weland. Otten and Janet Bately also think the change deliberate; see Otten, 238–9, and Bately's "Evidence for Knowledge of Latin Literature in Old English," *Sources of Anglo-Saxon Culture*, ed. Paul E. Szarmach with Virginia Darrow Oggins. Studies in Medieval Culture 20 (Kalamazoo, MI: Medieval Institute Publications, Western Michigan University, 1986), 35–51, at 43, and "Those Books that Are Most Necessary for All Men to Know: The Classics and Late Ninth-Century England, A Reappraisal," in *The Classics in the Middle Ages: Papers of the Twentieth Annual Conference of the Center for Medieval and Early Renaissance Studies*, ed. Aldo S. Bernardo and Saul Levin, Medieval and Renaissance Texts and Studies 69 (Binghamton, NY: Center for Medieval and Early

Renaissance Studies, 1990), 45–78, at 51–2. A similar case is the Latin text's story of the unnamed man who, tortured by a tyrant, bit off and spit out his own tongue (II pr. vi. 8); the tale is expanded in the OE, and the character is given a name, Liberius (36.16–26). The name is usually dismissed as a mistranslation of the Latin, which calls the man "liberum quendam" ("a certain free man"); for instance, see Friedrich Fehlauer, *Die englischen Übersetzungen des Boethius 'De Consolatione Philosophiae," I. Die alt- und mittelenglischen Übersetzungen* (Berlin: Emil Felber, 1909), 19. Bately suggests "miscopying or misreading an abbreviation" changed the Latin "liberum" to "liberium," "Those Books," 50.

27. David Pratt argues that Alfred would have seen himself in Ulysses, a king who becomes little more than animal because of sexual desire, in "The Illnesses of King Alfred the Great," *ASE* 30 (2001): 39–90, at 79–83. I see no good reason, however, for readers to identify Alfred with what is clearly a bad king in the *Bo.* As I will discuss in chap. 4, Alfred's treatment of bad kings does raise the possibility of bad kings, yet his description of good kings makes clear that he knows what kind of king he should be. Moreover, because of lust, Ulysses abandons his attempt to return to his people for several years and does not protect the men with him, who become animals; surely Alfred's contemporaries would balk at equating their king with Ulysses, whom Pratt himself calls "an explicitly evil man immersed in bodily pleasures" (79). Pratt seems also to assume that Alfred's works are read in conjunction with Asser's *Life*, even as he argues that that *Life* targeted a Welsh audience very different from the court audience for Alfred's translations. Asser's specific reading of Alfred's illnesses does not appear explicitly in Alfred's own work and may not have been the sole or dominant model for understanding them in the court. See also Susan Irvine's work on Ulysses as a negative figure, "Ulysses and Circe in King Alfred's *Boethius:* A Classical Myth Transformed," in *Studies in English Language and Literature: 'Doubt wisely': Papers in honour of E.G. Stanley*, ed. M. J. Toswell and E. M. Tyler (London: Routledge, 1996), 387–401; and her exploration of Hercules as a more positive figure whom Alfred associates with himself, "Wrestling with Hercules: King Alfred and the Classical Past," in *Court Culture in the Early Middle Ages: The Proceedings of the First Alcuin Conference*, ed. Catherine Cubitt (Turnhout, BEL: Brepols, 2003), 171–88.

28. *Distinction: A Social Critique of the Judgement of Taste*, trans. Richard Nice (Cambridge, MA: Harvard University Press, 1984), 28.

29. Guillory defines Bourdieu's habitus not as "an unconscious rationality" but "an embodied rationality" ("Refusal," 378). I depart from Bourdieu's emphasis on habitus as bodily practice for two reasons: first, bodily practices of the Anglo-Saxons are in many ways now nearly impossible to recover; second, as James Bohman argues, the emphasis on the physical limits critical thinking about habitus; see his "Reflexivity, Agency and Constraint: The Paradoxes of Bourdieu's Sociology of Knowledge," *Social Epistemology* 11 (1997): 171–86. Although Bourdieu often criticizes what he sees as excessive intellectualization of habitus, he acknowledges that habitus is "a relation of knowledge or *cognitive construction*"; Bourdieu and L. J. D. Wacquant, *An Invitation to Reflexive Sociology* (Chicago: University of Chicago Press, 1992), 127, emphasis in original; see 120–40 for a good introduction to his notion of habitus. For writers and readers, habitus must have a heavily intellectual

component as well as bodily and social elements. As for the possibility of changing one's habitus, Robert Holton writes, "the *habitus* is a historical product: neither complete nor sealed off from further development, it is 'an *open system of dispositions* that is constantly subjected to experiences, and therefore constantly affected by them in a way that either reinforces or modifies its structures. It is durable but not eternal!'" Robert Holton, "Bourdieu and Common Sense," *SubStance* 26 (1997): 38–52, at 46, quoting *Invitation*, 133.

30. The major exceptions are I pr. iii, where Alfred omits the names of philosophical schools and philosophers, and I pr. iv, where Alfred omits all details of Boethius's downfall, including his enemies' names. The substitution of Theodoric for Decoratus at 62.8/III pr. iv. 4 is exceptional but significant. Boethius could not criticize Theodoric directly and probably did so through his attacks on Nero; see Gerard O'Daly, *The Poetry of Boethius* (Chapel Hill: University of North Carolina Press, 1991), 85–6. By substituting criticism of Theodoric for that of Decoratus, Alfred mined a hidden vein of the source text. That Alfred distinguished myth from history seems clear from his references to the falsity of certain mythological stories and his different treatments of these source materials.

31. Similar concerns emerge in Charlemagne's *Admonitio generalis*, which emphasizes correct copying (section 78). MGH, *Legum Sectio II: Capitularia Regum Francorum*, Tomus I, ed. Alfredus Boretius (Hanover, GER: Supersis Bibliopolii Hahniani 1883), 58.

32. Historical figures include Croesus, Cirus (Cyrus), Torcwine (Tarquin), Bosirides (Busiris), Regulus, Neron, Marcus Tullius Cicero, Brutus Cassius [*sic*], Cato, Catulus (the consul and the poet are collapsed into one figure), Nonius, Seneca, Papianus (Papinianus), Antonie (Antonius), and Alcibiadis. Liberius (36.17) is a special case, as noted previously.

33. Several figures from the *Boethius* appear in the *Orosius*: Croesus; Cirus; Tarcuinius (Torcwin); Bosirides; Regulus; Nero; Brutus and Casius; Cato; Antonius. Several also appear elsewhere, often in later texts: Cirus in a number of glosses and a letter from Ælfric to Sigeweard; Nero in *Fates of the Apostles, Juliana*, Ælfrican homilies and lives, anonymous lives, the *Sol*, the *Bede*, some versions of the *Chronicle*, and a number of glosses; Cicero in the *Dialogues*, Byrhtferth's *Manual*, and several glosses; Seneca in Ælfric's *Grammar*, Byrhtferth's *Manual*, and many glosses; Cato in Ælfric's *Grammar* and several glosses; and Catullus in a number of glosses. These names gained at least limited currency, although to what extent Alfred's work helped further the recognition of these figures is difficult to determine. These usages were found with the aid of the online Corpus.

34. Writers and thinkers named in the *Bo* are: Boetius (Boethius) himself, Plato, Ptolomeus, Cicero (also mentioned as a historical figure, as noted previously), Cato (also mentioned as a historical figure, as noted previously), Epeccurus, Catulus (the consul is confused with the poet, as noted previously), Eurupides, Aristoteles, Parmenides, Omerus (Homer), and Frigilius (Virgil, who is actually added to the *Bo*; he is not mentioned in the source text). Mentioned in *Orosius* are: Ptolomeus; Cato; Aristotolese (Aristoteles); and Omarus (Omerus). Plato appears in Ælfric's letter to Sigeweard, the *Sol*, Byrthferth's *Manual*, and a number of glosses; Cicero in the *Dial*, Byrthferth's *Manual*, and several glosses; Aristotle in *Peri Didaxeon* and, of course,

in *Alexander's Letter to Aristotle*, as well as in several glosses; Homer in Byrhtferth's *Manual* and *Leechcraft*; Virgil in Ælfric's *Grammar* and Byrhtferth's *Manual*.

35. Bourdieu describes how "the most innovative works tend, *with time*, to produce their own audience by imposing their own structures, through the effect of familiarization, as categories of perception legitimate for any possible work," *Rules*, 253, emphasis in original. For the pleasures of recognition, see Bourdieu, *Rules*, 319–21. These pleasures have changed little since Alfred's time; they are still enjoyed by everyone from Anglo-Saxonists to fans of Tolkien and *Star Trek*.

36. See 48.22–50.5 (II met. viii); 57.1–58.3 (III met. ii); 79.34–81.13 (III met. ix); 92.16–29 (III met. xi. 25–29); 96.12–98.23 (III pr. xii. 6–8); 131.2–8 (IV pr. vi. 18); and 136.10–4 (IV met. vi. 16–24).

37. For weather and seasons, see: 10.1–13 (I met. v. 1–25); 12.7–11 (I met. vi); 14.9–25 (I met. vii); 17.23–7 (II pr. ii. 8); 18.12–4 (repeats part of II pr. ii. 8); 21.1–9 (II met. iii); 49.18–27 (II met. viii. 5–15); 52.4–7 (III met. i. 7–10); 89.10 (elaboration on III met. x. 5–6); 124.3–4 (elaboration on IV met. iv. 1–2); 125.31–126.24 (IV met. v); and 136.15–21 (IV met. vi. 25–33). Discussion of the heavens overlaps with that of the weather and seasons: 10.1–13 (I met. v. 1–25); 14.9–25 (I met. vii); 17.23–7 (II pr. ii. 8); and 125.31–126.24 (IV met. v) treat both. See also 57.24–8 (III met. ii. 31–3); 69.21–2 (III met. vi. 3–4); 105.5–20 (IV met. i. 1–19); 131.2–8 (IV pr. vi. 18); and 135.24–136.10 (IV met. vi. 1–18). The *Bo* also gives Latin names for a few constellations and planets: Bootes (Boetius, 126.8); Saturn (Saturnus 126.9); Ursa (135.29). Psychology may seem like a strange term for plants (the narrator himself questions the idea, 91.9–11), but the drives of all living creation are discussed: 36.4–16 (II pr. vi. 5–6); 57.8–58.3 (III met. ii. 7–38); 72.5–8 (III pr. viii. 7); 73.1–3 (III pr. viii. 10); 81.13–23 (greatly expanded from III met. ix. 13–4); 91.9–92.15 (III pr. xi. 15–24, with significant elaboration); 92.32–93.9 (largely added to III pr. xi. 30–31); 93.9–19 (III pr. xi. 32–3); 132.6–16 (IV pr. vi. 27–8); 140.27–141.6 (V pr. ii. 7–9), 142.8–20 (an addition elaborating on the previous cited passage); 143.31–144.8 (an addition); and 145.29–146.32 (V pr. iv. 27–39 with many alterations). The citations from 140.27 and following add the psychology of angels.

38. See also John Guillory's treatment of "social emulation" in *Cultural Capital: The Problem of Literary Canon Formation* (Chicago: University of Chicago Press, 1993), 95–6.

39. Two other images may have been retained because they possess a Scriptural resonance appealing to Alfred and his readers. II met. iv/26.23–27.2 compares the house on solid ground with those on sand and windy peaks; the OE offers an overtly Christian reading here. (Payne discusses Alfred's version in *King Alfred and Boethius: An Analysis of the Old English Version of the Consolation of Philosophy* [Madison: University of Wisconsin Press, 1968], 93–4.) The image of the precious and humble vessels that occurs in both texts is already so Christian that Alfred need not make it more explicitly religious (compare IV pr. i. 6 and 104.16–7). See also chap. 2 for more on Scriptural imagery.

40. For more on Alfred's linkage of economic and cultural capital, see my "Wealth and Wisdom."

41. Augustine uses forms of *rheto-* forty-six times, including twelve in his *Confessiones*, seven in *De doctrina christiana*, and once in *De ciuitate Dei*. All usage

counts for Augustine and Gregory in this chapter were obtained through the *CETEDOC Library of Christian Texts* CD-ROM (Turnhout, BEL: Brepols, 1991). How available these texts were in Alfredian England is unclear, however: the first copies Helmut Gneuss finds of these are late eleventh century: for *Confessiones*, items 163, 434, 603, 697; *De doctrina*, 717; and *De civitate dei*, 53, 236, and 587; *Handlist of Anglo-Saxon Manuscripts: A List of Manuscripts and Manuscript Fragments Written or Owned in England up to 1100* (Tempe, AZ: Arizona Center for Medieval and Renaissance Studies, 2001). See also discussions of *De doctrina* later in this chapter.

42. *Language and Symbolic Power*, 75–6, 109–16.

43. Alfred also shifts some individual images. Janet Bately points out the eagle simile given to Wisdom early in the text (18.11–4) and suggests that recalls a similar passage in IV met. i (which Alfred also translates there, 105.4–12), "Boethius and King Alfred," *Platonism and the English Imagination*, ed. Anna Baldwin and Sarah Hutton (Cambridge, UK: Cambridge University Press, 1994), 38–44, at 41. Where the Latin text speaks of changing fortune without imagery, Alfred adds the metaphor of the wheel to illustrate (18.26–8), transferred from II met. i on Fortune's wheel, which he did not translate. II met. viii. 16–21 contains the metaphor of reins by which God controls the world, translated in the appropriate place (49.27–33). Yet in the OE, the same metaphor is also used a little earlier (49.2–5). Roy Ray Moye, Jr., notes that a fishing image from III met. viii is translated in the appropriate place (73.27), but also added at 43.3; see also his comments on this technique in the *PC*, "Alfred's Method of Translation in the Old English 'Pastoral Care'" (Ph.D. diss., University of North Carolina at Chapel Hill, 1993), 88–93.

44. Alfred does not use the image of doctor and illness everywhere that Boethius does; as Otten notes (121), it is omitted around 14.2, which otherwise corresponds to I pr. vi. Yet Alfred compensates for this loss by reintroducing the image at 51.1–2, and he keeps the image of the doctor when it occurs later in the text (at 107.27–31/IV pr. ii. 25, 123.32–124.1/IV pr. iv. 42, 127.23–4/IV pr. vi. 5, and 132.6–15/IV pr. vi. 27–9).

45. The image of the spiritual doctor occurs in some vernacular sources as well and so might not be wholly unfamiliar. CETEDOC turned up 142 uses by Gregory of *medic–*, including 49 in *Moralia in Iob*, 21 in *Regula pastoralis*, and 14 in *Dialogi*. Gneuss, *Handlist*, lists for *Moralia* one eighth-century copy, "S Mercia or Germany?" (946.5); one ix^{2} or ix$^{3/4}$ but "perh. E. France, prov. England before 1100 possible," item 564; and one seventh- and two eighth-century Northumbrian copies (865.5, fragmentary; 840.5; and 858, fragmentary). Augustine uses forms of the word 1,277 times, including 19 in the *Confessiones* and 5 in the *Soliloquia*.

46. The *PC* uses forms of *læce, læcedom*, or *læcan* forty times and *Sol*, three times. The *Dial* uses such terms thirty-two times. Sometimes they express miraculous healing, but healing in that text is never *simply* literal; it always expresses the spiritual healing power of God, usually through His saints.

47. See 13.32–14.1/I pr. vi. 20 for the first occurrence of this image. This image too does not always occur in the same place in both texts. At III pr. ix. 3 the Latin text refers to a glimmer through a slightly opened door; the OE expresses the same sentiment but without the simile (74.26–7). Later, however, the OE uses the image (97.13–8) where the Latin does not (III pr. xii. 15). The little light reappears in

both texts twice more (99.24–5/III pr. xii. 25 and 123.21/IV pr. iv. 40). The same image is also found once in the *Pastoral Care* (87.3) and once in the *Dialogues* (276.21). Alfred is indebted to the Latin tradition here; *spearca* is not a common word in vernacular texts, and where it appears, it does so in a literal sense (see the online Corpus).

48. See especially chap. 74 on Alfred's illnesses and 104 on the candles.

49. Seth Lerer comments on the source text, "The language of the *Consolation*'s prose, as well as its poetry, is remarkably figurative, and... the dialogue's progress often works through structures of imagery as well as argument," *Boethius and Dialogue: Literary Method in The Consolation of Philosophy* (Princeton, NJ: Princeton University Press, 1985), 9.

50. This does not count the addition of exchanges in which each character has a turn. The narrator loses a line of agreement at 89.1/III pr. x. 43, an objection at 137.14–9/IV pr. vii. 6, and a request for clarification at V pr. i. 7/140.2. There is arguably one more lost turn, at IV pr. iv. 36–7 (around 123.6) where the narrator has a response in Bieler's text but not in the OE: "Apparet, inquam" ("'So it seems,' I said"). Yet Bieler supplied this response because he thinks one has been lost in the text. Whether a response was originally here in the Latin text, Alfred's exemplar, like Bieler's manuscripts, probably lacked it. At 29.11–5/II pr. v. 11–2 part of what is Philosophy's monologue in the Latin text is given to Mod; her rhetorical question becomes his real one. See also 52.22–8/III pr. ii. 3. In a later passage, Philosophy asks rhetorically whether being the king's favorite is worth anything (III pr. v. 1); in the OE text, the narrator answers (65.5–8). Similarly, responses are added at 87.16–7, 96.29, 145.1–5, and 147.22–7. These, like the two previous examples, include questions and challenges; they more than compensate for the lost turns, which had less content.

51. Similarly, see 76.23–4/III pr. ix. 17 and 87.16—21/III pr. x. 32.

52. Other responses of "mimine" are similarly expanded at 62.18–21/III pr. iv. 6 and 77.29–31/III pr. ix. 23; more enthusiastic agreement appears at 59.20/II pr. iii. 12 and 59.27/III pr. iii. 13.

53. In other passages, brief answers are expanded. The best example is 62.18–21/III pr. iv. 6, where one word in Latin becomes thirty-two in OE, but similar alterations occur elsewhere, including 93.28–30/III pr. x. 35 and 98.18–20/III pr. xii. 21.

54. The shortened response in the *Bo* leaves the OE with no explicit conclusion to the argument that led up to this point; readers must supply it themselves. It also means that Wisdom's praise of the narrator for anticipating his conclusion (107.27–31), which comes directly from the Latin (IV pr. ii. 25), does not really make sense. Perhaps a copyist dropped a line in the OE.

55. Exchanges from III pr. iii. 10 and III pr. xi. 37 do not appear in the OE, and three full exchanges are omitted at IV pr. ii. 17–20. Exchanges are added at 90.27–8 and 119.26–8. One passage, 119.8–26/IV pr. iv. 17–8, is reordered; at first glance the narrator appears to have lost two turns, but the points covered in the argument have shifted and his responses therefore come later. These alterations are fairly minor and do not disrupt the structure of the dialogue.

56. For rhetorical questions that are answered, see 29.18, 30.24, 36.27–8, 39.30–1, 48.15–7, 63.18–9, 73.24–31, and 131.31.

57. The OE has no rhetorical question here (113.12–5). See also III pr. viii. 7 with its series of rhetorical questions, some of which are answered; the OE (71.9–73.20) sometimes follows this pattern and sometimes employs simple statements.

58. Alfred changes rhetorical questions into statements at 31.24–30/II pr. v. 24–5; 34.3–6/II met. v. 19–23; 34.10–3/II met. v. 27–30; 36.14–6/II pr. vi. 7; 45.28–31/II pr. vii. 23; 64.11–6/III pr. iv. 15; 113.12–5/IV pr. iii. 8; 134.26–135.1/IV pr. vi. 49; and 137.22–3/IV pr. vii. 9. Yet the text compensates for these; he changes one statement into three rhetorical questions at 37.14–9/II pr. vi. 13, and single statements into rhetorical questions at 46.9–10/II met. vii. 9–14; 73.24–31/III met. viii. 2–8; 83.12–5/III pr. x. 6; 85.2/III pr. x. 16; 85.12–5/III pr. x. 18; 85.27–31/III pr. x. 23–4 (two Latin statements become three rhetorical questions); 95.25–6/III pr. xii. 1; 117.31–2/IV pr. iv. 8; and 145.5–7/V pr. iv. 24.

59. In contrast, both the Latin *Soliloquia* and the OE *Sol* use rhetorical questions quite sparingly and do not answer them. The device is frequently found in the Psalms, Gregory's *Regula pastoralis*, and Alfred's translations of each.

60. Payne, 136.

61. Payne, 136–8.

62. Otten, 37–41.

63. Otten, 188–91.

64. For full details, see my "Sources of King Alfred's Old English Version of Boethius's *De consolatione philosophiae* (Cameron B.9.3)," 2001, *Fontes.*

65. Added prefatory material includes the Proem (1); a biography of Boethius (7–8.5); and chapter headings (3–6), probably scribal. I will not treat the Proem as I do not believe it to be Alfred's work; I suggested that Alfred did not himself write the Prose Proem in "Alfred the Poet and the Proems to the *Boethius,*" MLA, New York, December, 2002. See also Janet M. Bately, "The Alfredian Canon Revisited: One Hundred Years On," in *Alfred the Great: Papers from the Eleventh-Centenary Conferences*, ed. Timothy Reuter, Studies in Early Medieval Britain 3 (Aldershot, UK: Ashgate, 2003), 107–120, and Allen J. Frantzen, "The Form and Function of the Preface in the Poetry and Prose of Alfred's Reign," in *Alfred the Great: Papers from the Eleventh-Centenary Conferences*, ed. Timothy Reuter. Studies in Early Medieval Britain 3 (Aldershot, UK: Ashgate, 2003), 121–136, esp. 133–4. At 19.11–26, Wisdom, acting as the personification of earthly goods, accuses the narrator of misusing goods by not employing them according to the Creator's will. 30.4–10 and 40.10–41.6 both stress that men, especially rulers, need tools. Wisdom also asserts that those who learn wisdom will come to power, even if they do not want it (35.13–24), and he later declares that wisdom is the highest *cræft*, comprising worship, moderation, courage, and righteousness (62.22–31); another addition claims that the abilities of all the animals together do not approach the *cræft* of man (72.4–15). Wisdom argues that as heaven is better than all but man, so man's body is better than all possessions, and his soul is better than his body (72.19–28). The narrative of Nefrod and the Tower of Babel (99.4–20) elaborates the source text's story of the giants. A series of additions interspersed with the Latin emphasize the baseness of an undiscerning mind, particularly a mind ruled by the desires of the flesh (109.2–6, 109.8–12, and 109.17–27). Wisdom offers reassurance that when a good work cannot be completed, the will counts for the work (110.23–111.4). The last additions are

explicitly religious. One settles the question of whether people have free will through a comparison: a great king would not have slaves as subjects, nor would God, as the greatest of all kings (141.28–142.25). Soon after this, Wisdom adds that after death God rewards those who use their freedom well and punish those who use it badly, although he tries to correct people while they are still alive (143.12–144.32). All creation serves only him, except for angels and men. God provides for all that will happen but does not change it. The translation constructs a hierarchy of intelligences at 146.3–25 that partly reflects the source text's concerns but shows a strong religious sensibility. The close of MS B, Sedgfield 149.11–26, invokes God and the saints but is probably a later addition; see my Introduction. Most of these additions will be treated later in this book.

66. For details, see Malcolm R. Godden's "Sources of King Alfred's Old English Version of Augustine's *Soliloquia* (Cameron B.9.4)," 2001, *Fontes*.

67. Dorothy Whitelock's "Old English Bede," *Proceedings of the British Academy* 48 (1962): 57–90, remains fundamental. Sarah Foot discusses the *Bede* as part of Alfred's program in some detail in "The Making of Angelcynn: English Identity before the Norman Conquest," *TRHS* 6 ser. 6 (1996): 25–49, esp. 38–41. See also my "Old English *Bede* and the Construction of Anglo-Saxon Authority," *ASE* 31 (2002): 69–80, for the deletion of documentation.

68. For Alfred's treatment of Boethius's life, see my "Unauthorized Biographies of Anicius Manlius Severinus Boethius," *The Alfredian Boethius Project*, ed. Malcolm R. Godden and Rohini Jayatilaka, 9 Dec. 2003, http://www.english.ox.ac.uk/boethius/Symposium2003.html. The omissions from Book I are: the nature imagery of I met. ii; references to Epicureans and Stoics (I pr. iii. 7–8); a brief passage where Philosophy says that although she is outnumbered, her side is superior, and she can look down and laugh at her foes (I pr. iii. 12–4); and the particulars of the narrator's problems and his defense (I pr. iv. 10–45).

69. Three meters have been eliminated: V met. i, showing that rivers follow laws in their confluence; met. iii, which asks what force binds the warring elements and how the mind could find it; and met. iv, which rejects an idea most Anglo-Saxons would never have encountered, the Stoic notion of the mind as *tabula rasa*. The conflict between prescience and free will, the subject of V met. iii. 4–29, is replaced by a passage in the OE (141.28–142.25) that demonstrates free will through very different arguments. Related material in V met. iv. 4–24 is simply omitted because the OE has already solved the problem. V pr. iv. 26–33 and V pr. v. 5–12, both on different kinds of knowing, are gone, although a much briefer passage on the hierarchy of intelligences appears at 146.3–25. Finally, V pr. vi. 9–43 is replaced by a different presentation of the problems of time and eternity (147.18–148.32).

70. I disagree with Payne, who presents Alfred's work as ultimately unsuccessful because of the awkward marriage of Alfred's new ideas to Boethius's framework; see especially her chap. V: "Conclusion: The Relation of Thought and Style," 135–47.

71. *Early Germanic Kingship in England and on the Continent* (Oxford, UK: Clarendon, 1971), 147.

72. *The Fate of Fortune in the Early Middle Ages: The Boethian Tradition* (New York: Brill, 1988), 166.

73. Payne, 18.

74. 21; she also claims a Boethian "inescapable determinism" (36) that Alfred rejects, 32 and 36.

75. Otten, 78.

76. "King Alfred's 'Consolation of Philosophy,' *Neuphilologische Mitteilungen* 74 (1973): 635–48, at 640.

77. "How Boethian?" 162.

78. Robinson adds that it is only through the "Cædmonization of the vocabulary that 'ece dryhten' assumes the unvarying sense of 'eternal Lord,'" *Beowulf and the Appositive Style* (Knoxville: University of Tennessee Press, 1985), 51.

79. See also 23.9, 26.18, 27.4–8, 27.8–11, 47.1–2, 51.25–6, 113.19–20, 113.21–2, 118.5, 120.9–11, 120.13, 120.17, 137.25–7, 138.22–5, 139.16, and 143.25.

80. Alfred translates: "Gif þu nu getelest þa hwila þisses andweardan lifes 7 þisses hwilendlican wið þæs ungeendodan lifes hwila, hwæt bið hit þonne?" (44.12–3: "If you count the time of this present and temporary life against the time of unending life, what is it then?") A less clear example occurs when Boethius writes of an eternal law: "Constat aeterna positumque lege est, / ut constet genitum nihil" ("It is established in eternal law that nothing created remains still," II met. iii. 17–8). One could argue that the law is the Creator or essentially connected to Him, and therefore is coeternal, but this is more likely a loose usage.

81. Alfred translates: "ða yrmða bioð endelease þe ece bioð" (118.5: "the miseries are endless that are *ece*"). (*Ece* is from MS B; MS C's *eac*, "also", seems to be an error, because it makes no sense.)

82. No OE equivalent exists for this line.

83. This difference is partly due to the fact that Alfred tends to repeat nouns where Boethius uses pronouns or implies words; *ece* appears eight times where no equivalent Latin word appears (9.12/I met. ii. 2; 26.18/II pr. iv. 29; 51.25–6/III pr. i. 7; 77.26–9/III pr. ix. 22; 78.11–3/III pr. ix. 26; 78.24–6/III pr. ix. 30; 89.23/III met. x. 18; and 149.8/V pr. vi. 48), and another twelve times in passages that have no direct Latin equivalent (27.4–8; 27.8–11; 90.8–12; 90.12–3; 119.33–120.2; 120.13; 137.26–7; 139.16; 143.25; 148.6–10; 148.23–4; and 148.31). *Aeternitas*, on the other hand, only occurs once with no comparable term in the OE in a passage that is translated (141.6–9/V pr. ii. 11) and eight times in passages that are left untranslated (IV met. vi. 16–8; V pr. iii. 5; V pr. iii. 15; V pr. vi. 6; V pr. vi. 8; V pr. vi. 14; V pr. vi. 15; and V pr. vi. 20). *Ece* is also used three times where the Latin contains forms of *mortalis* or *immortalis* (26.11/II pr. iv. 28; 44.8–11/II pr. vii. 14; and 47.1–2/II met. vii. 23–6) and four times where the Latin is formulated solely in negative terms with no specific word for time or eternity (27.21–3/II pr. v. 2; 113.2–4/IV pr. iii. 4; 113.19–20/IV pr. iii. 10; and 113.21–2/IV pr. iii. 11). It is used five times for *aeternitas* or *aeternus* (44.16–27/II pr. vii. 16–8; 118.5/IV pr. iv. 9; 130.28–131.1/IV pr. vi. 17; 147.17–9/V pr. vi. 2; 147.29–148.2/V pr. vi. 4) and twice for *perpetuitas* (10.1–2/I met. v. 1–2 and 92.16–8/III met. xi. 25). The one OE word, then, translates a variety of Latin terms. Other OE expressions appear more rarely; *a* is used once for *aeternitas* (21.8–9/II met. iii. 17–18); *domes dæg* is used once (120.29–31/IV pr. iv. 24); and reformulations about unending time occur twice for *aeternitas*: at 44.12–3/II pr. vii. 15, "ungeendodan" ("unending"); and 44.24–7/II pr. vii. 18, "ne geendað" ("does not end").

84. Some of this material is reiterated elsewhere on 147–8. The added material mostly concerns other qualities of God: that he lacks nothing, seeks nothing, and so forth.

85. See, for instance, Richard Abels, *Alfred the Great: War, Kingship and Culture in Anglo-Saxon England* (New York: Longman, 1999), esp. 180–7; Smyth, *King Alfred the Great,* who discusses Alfred's military, political, and intellectual relations with Mercia in several places; and Pratt, "The Political Thought"; "The Revival of Wisdom as Political Phenomenon," 13–75.

86. Robert Fulk treats in some detail the influence of Mercian dialect on poetry and prose, not only in the work of Alfred's helpers, but even in the texts by Alfred himself, *History of Old English Meter* (Philadelphia: University of Pennsylvania Press, 1992), 297–300. See also Fulk's learned analysis of various dialectal forms in a variety of longer poems, especially "Syncopated Endings of Long-Stemmed Verbs and Other Presumed Indicators of Dialect Origins," 269–347, and "Appendix A: Chronology and Dialect in the Remaining Longer Poems," 393–414.

87. See Gneuss, "The Origin of Standard Old English."

88. See Davis, "National Writing," and my "Alfred's Verse Preface to the *Pastoral Care* and the Chain of Authority," *Neophilologus* 85 (2001): 625–33.

89. His representation of diverse cultures as a single whole functions in rather the same way that later formulators of "the canon" or "Western tradition" constructed a fictitious unity, which John Guillory usefully analyzes in *Cultural Capital.*

Chapter 2

1. Martianus Capella's *De nuptiis Philologiae et Mercurii* might have been known to some Anglo-Saxons at this time; Helmut Gneuss lists four ninth- or early-tenth-century glosses on it (48, 67, 95–6, and 127) in his *Handlist of Anglo-Saxon Manuscripts: A List of Manuscripts and Manuscript Fragments Written or Owned in England up to 1100* (Tempe, AZ: Arizona Center for Medieval and Renaissance Studies, 2001). Janet Bately suggests a "second or even third hand" acquaintance with Plato via "authors such as Macrobius, Martianus Capella, Augustine, Boethius and (via Calcidius' translation of the *Timaeus*) John Scotus Eriugena, and through Latin and OE texts drawing on one or another of these writings," "Boethius and King Alfred," *Platonism and the English Imagination*, ed. Anna Baldwin and Sarah Hutton (Cambridge, UK: Cambridge University Press, 1994), 38–44, at 38. The Neoplatonic *Soliloquia* also presents great difficulties.

2. David Robert Pratt argues that the *De cons* would be a logical next step for readers who had mastered simpler texts such as the Psalms because of its status on the continent: see "The *Consolatio* in the Carolingian World," 249–62, in "The Political Thought of Alfred the Great" (Ph.D. diss., University of Cambridge, England, 1999).

3. For Gregory's influence, see Anton Scharer, *Herrschaft und Repräsentation: Studien zur Hofkultur König Alfreds des Großen* (Munich: R. Oldenbourg Verlag, 2000), esp. chap. 5, "Das Vermächtnis Gregors des Großen:

Einheitsbewußtsein und Zusammenhörigkeitsgeful," 118–33; and my "Influence of Gregory the Great on the Alfredian Social Imaginary," *Rome and the North: The Early Reception of Gregory the Great in Germanic Europe*, ed. Rolf H. Bremmer Jr., Kees Dekker, and David F. Johnson (Leuven, BEL: Peeters, 2001), 67–81. For Augustine, see especially Paul E. Szarmach, "The Meaning of Alfred's *Preface* to the *Pastoral Care*," *Mediaevalia* 7 (1980): 57–86.

4. "Translation and Orality in the Old English *Orosius*," *Oral Tradition* 13 (1998): 377–97.

5. *Language and Symbolic Power*, ed. John B. Thompson and trans. Gino Raymond and Matthew Adamson (Cambridge, MA: Harvard University Press, 1991), 137, emphasis in original.

6. *Language and Symbolic Power*, 138.

7. Bourdieu says, "As a space of potential and active forces, the field is also a *field of struggles* aimed at preserving or transforming the configuration of these forces," Bourdieu and L. J. D. Wacquant, *An Invitation to Reflexive Sociology* (Chicago: University of Chicago Press, 1992), 101. See also *The Rules of Art: Genesis and Structure of the Literary Field*, trans. Susan Emanuel (Stanford, CA: Stanford University Press, 1996), 223–4. Alfred's translations enter into the struggle to define the field of spiritual literature. Although Alfred's setting is very different in its particulars, John Guillory's discussion of the modern canon provides a useful parallel: "The canon achieves its imaginary totality, then, not by embodying itself in a really existing list, but by retroactively constructing its individual texts as a *tradition*, to which works may be added or subtracted without altering the impression of totality or cultural homogeneity. A tradition is 'real,' of course, but only in the sense in which the imaginary is real," *Cultural Capital: The Problem of Literary Canon Formation* (Chicago: University of Chicago Press, 1993), 33, emphasis in original. Alfred's *Boethius* fits into an existing patristic canon while being dramatically new as a vernacular text.

8. Guillory explores how institutions of learning handle struggle and change with the example of women entering the workforce and the canon simultaneously, *Cultural Capital*, 58. (Guillory's reading of change in the Middle Ages, unfortunately, relies on too rigid a notion of feudalism, 70–73.) The *Boethius* both reproduces and attempts to modify social relations by inculcating a Christian habitus that is neither quite a native Anglo-Saxon one nor a truly Boethian one.

9. For Carolingian influence, see Paul E. Szarmach, "Anglo-Saxon Letters in the Eleventh Century," *Acta* (1974): 1–14, and "The Meaning of Alfred's *Preface*"; Thomas A. Shippey, "Wealth and Wisdom in King Alfred's *Preface* to the Old English *Pastoral Care*," *English Historical Review* 94 (1979): 346–55; J. M. Wallace-Hadrill, *Early Germanic Kingship in England and on the Continent* (Oxford: Clarendon Press, 1971), esp. 142–6; Pratt, "The Political Thought"; and Janet L. Nelson, "Power and Authority at the Court of Alfred," in *Essays on Anglo-Saxon and Related Themes in Memory of Lynne Grundy*, ed. Jane Roberts and Janet Nelson (London: Centre for Late Antique and Medieval Studies, King's College London, 2000), 311–37. Alfred P. Smyth treats Carolingian connections at length in his *King Alfred the Great* (Oxford, UK: Oxford University Press, 1995). For the place of the *De cons* among the Carolingians, see John Marenbon, "Carolingian Thought," in *Carolingian Culture: Emulation and Innovation*, ed. Rosamond McKitterick

(Cambridge, UK: Cambridge University Press, 1994), 171–92; and Margaret T. Gibson, "Boethius in the Carolingian Schools," *Transactions of the Royal Historical Society*, 5th series, 32 (1982): 43–56. See also *Boethius: His Life, Thought, and Influence*, ed. Margaret Gibson (Oxford, UK: Basil Blackwell, 1981), and *The Medieval Boethius: Studies in the Vernacular Translations of De Consolatione Philosophiae*, ed. A. J. Minnis (Cambridge, UK: Brewer, 1988). For Alcuin, see Szarmach's "Alfred, Alcuin, and the Soul," in *Manuscript, Narrative, Lexicon: Essays on Literary and Cultural Transmissions in Honor of Whitney F. Bolton*, ed. Robert Boenig and Kathleen Davis (Lewisburg, PA: Bucknell University Press, 2000), 127–48, at 133.

10. See R. Ian Jack's "Significance of the Alfredian Translations," *Australasian Universities Language and Literature Association* (1971): 348–61, for criticism of Alfred's vernacular emphasis. J. M. Wallace-Hadrill discusses both the amount and the variety of vernacular literature the Carolingians produced, including religious and learned works, in *The Frankish Church* (Oxford, UK: Clarendon, 1983), 377–89. Wallace-Hadrill even speculates that "Louis the Pious may have taken some initiative in causing [*Heliand*] to be written," 385. Yet it remains clear that the Carolingians, unlike Alfred, concentrated on Latin.

11. "The Political Ideas of Alfred of Wessex," in *Kings and Kingship in Medieval Europe*, ed. Anne J. Duggan (London: Centre for Late Antique and Medieval Studies, King's College London, 1993), 125–58, at 140.

12. 258.11–32 in the OE, IV.2.1 in the Latin. For more on the activities of Theodore, Hadrian, and their pupils, see Michael Lapidge, "The School of Theodore and Hadrian," *ASE* 15 (1986): 45–72, and *Biblical Commentaries from the Canterbury School of Theodore and Hadrian*, ed. Bernhard Bischoff and Michael Lapidge (Cambridge, UK: Cambridge University Press, 1994).

13. The letter traveled with some manuscripts of the *Historia* and found its way into some chronicles, but it was not translated with the *Historia* into OE. Whether Alfred knew the letter, or knew about Bede's efforts at translation, is unknown. N. R. Ker, *Catalogue of Manuscripts Containing Anglo-Saxon* reprint with supplement (Oxford, UK: Oxford University Press, 1990), lists fourteen copies of the letter (items 88, 104, 110*, 152, 273, 306 art. a, 321, 356, 386; Appendix items 1, 2, 12, 13, and 25 include those copied by foreign scribes). All postdate Alfred, but they hint that it had a wide circulation.

14. See Francis P. Magoun, "Some Notes on King Alfred's Circular Letter on Educational Policy Addressed to His Bishops," *Mediaeval Studies* 10 (1948): 93–107, at 100–1, for speculation about which translations Alfred might have known. Alfred probably had Jerome and the Vulgate in mind, among other things; Albert S. Cook, in "Alfred's 'Word for Word' Translation," *Academy* 30 (1886): 108, cites Jerome the as source for Alfred's "hwilum worde be worde, hwilum andgit of andgiete" ("sometimes word for word, sometimes sense for sense," *PC* 7.19–20).

15. For more details, see my "'Wise wealhstodas': The Prologue to Sirach as a Model for Alfred's Preface to the *Pastoral Care*," *JEGP* 97 (1998): 488–99.

16. Asser informs us immediately after his famous tale of the illiterate young Alfred memorizing a book of English poetry that Alfred went on to learn Psalms and

prayers (24.1–10), and he later adds that Alfred had his advisors read books to him constantly throughout life (77.19–26). The memorization story is fraught with difficulties, not least of which is the fact that the text actually says Alfred "librum... magistrum adiit et legit" ("took the book to his master and read it," 23.13–4). In his edition of Asser, Stevenson takes "legit" to mean something like "learning the contents of the book by rote" (221; his whole note runs 221–5). Simon Keynes and Michael Lapidge agree; alternatively, they suggest "et" should be "qui": "took the book to his master, *who* read it," *Alfred the Great* (New York: Penguin, 1983). Alfred Smyth critiques the tale in his *King Alfred the Great* (Oxford, UK: Oxford University Press, 1995), 181–6. For a detailed rebuttal of many of Smyth's attacks on the *Vita*'s authenticity, see Anton Scharer, *Herrschaft und Repräsentation: Studien zur Hofkultur König Alfreds des Großen* (Munich: Oldenbourg Verlag, 2000), especially "III. Hof und Geschichtsschreibung: Asser *De rebus gestis Aelfredi*," 49–108.

17. Bridget Fowler, *Pierre Bourdieu and Cultural Theory: Critical Investigations* (London: Sage, 1997), 47–48. See also Bourdieu's "Questions of Method" in *Rules*, 179–208.

18. The importance of the Psalms to Anglo-Saxons is clear from the forty manuscripts and fragments still extant, including eleven with thorough glossing, and three more with some glossing, in OE. For details of these manuscripts and their glosses, see Phillip Pulsiano's "Introduction" to his edition, *Old English Glossed Psalters: Psalms 1–50*, Toronto Old English Series 11 (Toronto, ON: University of Toronto Press, 2001), xix–xxxvi. Alfred's translation often diverges both from the Latin and from the (fairly literal) glosses that can be found in OE manuscripts. O'Neill's study of sources in his edition of Alfred's Prose Psalms does not mention OE glosses influencing Alfred's translation (see chap. 3, "The Sources," 31–44).

19. Job, Ecclesiastes, and the Song of Songs are the other three Wisdom Books. Job and Ecclesiastes seem to have had some influence, as will be shown later, but the Song of Songs little or none. For sources of specific passages, see my "Sources of King Alfred's Old English Version of Boethius's *De consolatione philosophiae* (Cameron C.B.9.3)," 2001, *Fontes*, which lists forty-six sources for the *Bo* ranging from certain to possible, including eleven books of the Bible. Malcolm R. Godden lists nineteen sources (including seven Biblical) for *Sol* in "The Sources of King Alfred's Old English Version of Augustine's *Soliloquia* (Cameron C.B.9.4)," 2001, *Fontes*, and J. Hart lists fifty-four sources (of which fifty-three are books of the Bible, as antecedent sources) in "Sources of King Alfred's Old English Version of Gregory's *Pastoral Care* (Cameron C.B.9.3)," 1992, *Fontes*. Proverbs serve no liturgical function but may have appealed to the maxim-loving Anglo-Saxons. Job was one of Gregory's favorites. Ann Astell argues in *Job, Boethius, and Epic Truth* (Ithaca, NY: Cornell University Press, 1994) that the *De cons* was almost always read in the Middle Ages in connection with the book of Job. Although her overall argument may not convince, the similarities she notes between the works are real, as are some of the connections that medieval readers made between the two. She argues that Gregory actually read Job for his *Moralia* partly in terms of Boethius (91 and *passim*). She also notes that Job was cited in the Middle Ages as a prosimetrum, linking it formally with the *De cons*, the best-known non-scriptural prosimetrum (14–7).

20. From the Corpus Christi College manuscript. The translation is fairly close to the Latin; see Prologue, lines 38–43.

21. Malcolm Godden notes that "linguistically and stylistically [the Preface to the *Dial*] shows all the hallmarks of Wærferth's writing rather than Alfred's own" and suggests that Alfred asked Wærferth to write it in his name, "Wærferth and King Alfred: The Fate of the Old English *Dialogues*," in *Alfred the Wise: Studies in Honour of Janet Bately on the Occasion of her Sixty-fifth Birthday*, ed. Jane Roberts and Janet L. Nelson with Malcolm Godden (Cambridge, UK: Brewer, 1997), 35–51, at 36. For the importance of prologues in establishing authority within a field, see Bourdieu, *Rules*, 230. I found one probable use of the *Dialogi* in the *Bo*; see following, and see my *Fontes* entry. Godden lists three possible uses in his *Fontes* entries for the *Sol*.

22. See also 105.20–4, and the opening sections with the prisoner's forgetfulness of Philosophy/Wisdom and his "homeland."

23. The OE is similar though somewhat expanded; see 103.30–104.10.

24. This is a close translation of the Latin; see Psalm 6:7.

25. The final major theme concerns free will, but the *Bo*'s arguments for it are not those of the *De cons*. The point is not that Alfred rejected the argument; he treats it as largely superfluous, substituting a shorter argument of his own; see Kurt Otten, *König Alfreds Boethius*, Studien zur englischen Philologie, neue Folge no. 3 (Tübingen, GER: Max Niemeyer Verlag, 1964), 37–9 and 186, on free will in the *Bo*. Otten stresses the removal of formal logic over what has replaced it.

26. *Language and Symbolic Power*, 54–60, and *Rules*, 289–92. This difference is not necessarily consciously sought; see Bourdieu and Wacquant, *An Invitation*, 100.

27. Although Alfred is now believed not to have translated the *Orosius* himself, it was part of his overall project, and some evidence indicates that it preceded the *Bo*. See Bately's edition of the *Orosius*, "Introduction," lxxxvi–lxxxvii, for evidence that Alfred took the name Rædgota from the *Orosius* for use in the *Bo*. E. Koeppel also dated the *Orosius* before the *Bo* on the basis of the name: "Zur chronologie der übersetzungen des königs Alfred," *Anglia: Beiblatt* 19 (1908), 330–2. My *Fontes* entries detail five possible borrowings from Orosius's *Historiae aduersum paganos* in the *Bo* as well as one probable and one possible borrowing from the OE *Orosius* (the possible also has Orosius's *Historiae* as a possible source). No definite evidence exists to prove a direct connection between the king and the *Bede*, but even if he did not commission it, given his interests, that Alfred would have made the acquaintance of either the Latin or the OE text seems likely. My *Fontes* entries include one possible use of Bede's *Historia ecclesiastica* in the *Bo*, but the OE cannot be securely dated before Alfred's death. See Janet L. Bately, "Old English Prose before and during the Reign of Alfred," *ASE* 17 (1988): 93–138, at 103–4.

28. See especially *PC* 127.8–141.10, chap. 18: "Hu se lareow ne sceal ða inneran giemenne gewanian for ðære uterran abisgunge, ne eft ða uterran ne forlæte he for ðære inneran" ("How the teacher must not decrease his care of inner things for outer cares, nor again relinquish the outer for the inner," 127.8–10), the Latin II.7.

29. The Latin means "rector" or "leader," the OE "the teacher" or "the ruler." See Janet L. Nelson, "The Political Ideas of Alfred of Wessex," in *Kings and Kingship in Medieval Europe*, ed. Anne J. Duggan (London: Centre for Late Antique

and Medieval Studies, King's College London, 1993), 125–58, at 147, for Alfred's broader reading of the term. Nelson argues throughout her article that Alfred's political ideas were specifically Christian but *secular* Christian; she makes some important points, particularly about the shift from bishop to secular ruler, but that Alfred distinguished religious and secular realms as strongly as modern thinkers do is doubtful. See also Wallace-Hadrill, *Early Germanic Kingship*, 143. Teresa Webber places a strong division between religious and secular much later, in the twelfth century, in *Scribes and Scholars at Salisbury Cathedral, c. 1075–c. 1125* (New York: Oxford University Press, 1992), 113 and 129, fn. 58.

30. Gregory also took an active interest in a number of Italian and Merovingian kings, writing letters to encourage them to rectify their behavior and improve the spiritual condition of their subjects. Although Alfred was not necessarily aware of all of Gregory's prodigious correspondence, the theme comes clearly through in many of the pope's writings. See, for instance, Bruno Judic, "Grégoire le Grand et le pouvoir royal," *Studia Patristica* 33 (1997): 434–40.

31. Milton McC. Gatch sees the emphasis on duty in the *Bo* as a crucial shift: "The movement in Alfred, in other words, is always toward the moral obligation of man to respond to the relationship between God and himself, while in Boethius the emphasis is on the orderly functioning (independent of man's response) of a universe governed by a God for whom all things are present," *Loyalties and Traditions: Man and His World in Old English Literature* (New York: Pegasus, 1976), 111.

32. *Language and Symbolic Power*, 139.

33. *Language and Symbolic Power*, 122, 121.

34. David Pratt, "The Illnesses of King Alfred the Great," *ASE* 30 (2001): 39–90, at 44.

35. Pratt, "The Illnesses," 55.

36. See Bourdieu's *Rules* for extended study of modes of reading and interpretation and how they have altered in modern France.

37. Whether homilies were a required part of every liturgy in Alfred's time is not certain. Roy Michael Liuzza notes Gatch's argument that Ælfric made them standard and provided material for them in "Who Read the Gospels in Old English?" in *Words and Works: Studies in Medieval English Language and Literature in Honour of Fred C. Robinson*, ed. Peter S. Baker and Nicholas Howe (Toronto, ON: University of Toronto Press, 1998), 3–24, at 15.

38. The Latin does not really match Alfred's passage: "in somno spiritum ducimus nescientes" ("in sleep we breathe unknowing," III pr. xi. 30).

39. See Malcolm Godden, "Anglo-Saxons on the Mind," in *Learning and Literature in Anglo-Saxon England*, ed. Michael Lapidge and Helmut Gneuss (Cambridge, UK: Cambridge University Press, 1985), 271–98, at 277, for the vocabulary.

40. Corpus Christi has "styrigendlicran 7 ferendran" ("mobile and traveling"). The Corpus text closely translates the Latin (II.22.38–9).

41. Though note that Godden thinks these passages too dissimilar for Gregory to have influenced Alfred here; personal communication, April 25, 2003.

42. The Latin is similar; see III.31.53–8.

43. These ideas can be found throughout both Scripture and the patristics, so Alfred could possibly have drawn on a source other than this passage in the *Regula*

pastoralis. See also Ecclesiastes 9:5–6 for the dead losing their awareness. The New Testament, especially the Pauline epistles, has many references to being dead from sin.

44. Alfred's debt to Augustine goes beyond the *Soliloquia*; Paul E. Szarmach argues for Alfred's knowledge of *De trinitate* and *De doctrina christiana*, or at least of the concept of *sapientia* embodied in them; see his "Meaning of Alfred's *Preface*," 70, and "Anglo-Saxon Letters," 3. These texts, however, may not have been available to Alfred. All of *Fontes* lists only one definite borrowing from *De trinitate*; see R. C. Love, "Sources of Anonymous Latin Charter S1028 (Cameron LS 1028)," 1997. Two probable and one possible use of *De trinitate* appear in Ælfric's *Catholic Homilies* I.20; see Malcolm Godden's "Sources of Ælfric's *Catholic Homilies* 1.20 (Cameron C.B. 1.1.22)," 1996, updated 1998, *Fontes*. Another possible use is recorded by Rohini Jayatilaka in Ælfric's *Supplementary Homilies* 1 "Sources of Ælfric's *Supplementary Homilies* 1 (Cameron C.B. 1.4.1)," 1995, *Fontes*. Gneuss's *Handlist* lists one eighth-century manuscript of *De trinitate* (item 255, fragmentary), and one of *De doctrina* (item 717) from the end of the eleventh century. *Fontes* returns 36 entries for *De doctrina Christiana*, of which 34 are in Bede. Luke M. Reinsma argues that knowledge of this text was lost after Bede, but the method of exegesis survived; see "Rhetoric in England: The Age of Ælfric, 970–1020," *Communication Monographs* 44 (1977): 390–403, especially 393–8. One possible use appears in Ælfric, *Catholic Homilies* 1.31; see Malcolm Godden's "Sources of Ælfric's *Catholic Homilies* 1.31 (Cameron C.B. 1.1.33)," 1989, updated 2002, *Fontes*. M. Griffith records one borrowing from either *De doctrina* or Jerome's Epistle 123 in "Sources of Ælfric's *Preface to Genesis* (Cameron C.B. 1.7.1)," 2000, *Fontes*. No evidence exists of direct borrowing from *De doctrina* in any Alfredian-era texts.

45. See the online Corpus.

46. The word *Dryhten* occurs nine times for God in the *Bo*: 10.17 and .25; 29.6; 57.1; 79.7; 81.32; 82.2 and .6; 136.23.

47. The Latin is similar; see Psalm 8:5–6. O'Neill also uses parenthetical numerals to indicate numbering in the *Gallicanum* Psalter; I have omitted these for ease of reading and refer interested readers to O'Neill's edition.

48. Moreover, Augustine's *De doctrina christiana* is careful not to forget this order of creation (see especially I.23.1–3 and I.30.1–2), as Alfred would have seen if he knew this work, a problem treated near the end of this chapter.

49. Compare III pr. xii. 19 with 98.11–3 and III met. ii .5–6 with 57.7–8. Alfred uses both men and angels as an added example in his explanation of kinds of eternity (148.2) and includes angels in added passages at 141.28–142.22, 143.12–144.12, and 146.3–26.

50. A gloss may also have suggested this change to Alfred; see my Appendix.

51. See Janet M. Bately, "Old English Prose before and during," 103–4.

52. See *Acta sanctorum* 27 May (vol. 19, cols. 694–703) for a detailed *vita* of St. Severinus Boethius, who shares the day and the entry with St. John I (Pope). Both men are described as Christian martyrs slain by the Arian Theodoric. The *Acta sanctorum* entry actually draws on the *De cons* for some of the details of Boethius's trials. Whether Alfred knew this or any related *vita* is unclear. The *vita* in *Acta sanctorum* explains that another man, Albinus Patricius, was falsely accused of sending treasonous letters; Boethius defended him and was then implicated by false witnesses.

Alfred's version of Boethius's downfall is considerably different; see chap. 4. Alfred does appear to have known one or more shorter lives that often accompanied the *De cons*; see my Appendix, my *Fontes* entries, and my "Unauthorized Biographies of Anicius Manlius Severinus Boethius," Dec. 2003, http://www.english.ox.ac.uk/boethius/Symposium2003.html.

53. Luca Obertello emphasizes that the work follows the form of classical philosophy very closely although the content is very different: "L'universo boeziano," *Congresso Internazionale di Studi Boeziani* (Pavia, 5–8 ottobre 1980), ed. Luca Obertello (Rome: Atti, 1981), 157–8. In the same volume, Claudio Moreschini also emphasizes that Boethius used logic but went beyond the purely formal logic of Latin Neoplatonists to return to a more Greek style of work: "Boezio e la tradizione del neoplatonismo latino," 297–310. In his *Poetry of Boethius*, Gerard O'Daly emphasizes the use of rigorous logic in the fifth book in particular (Chapel Hill: University of North Carolina Press, 1991), 12.

54. O'Daly discusses the relationship between the prose and the meters throughout his book. For a classification of the relationships between individual meters and proses, see Bernhard Pabst, *Prosimetrum: Tradition und Wandel einer Literaturform zwischen Spätantike und Spätmittelalter*, vol. 1, Studien zur Literature und Gesellschaft des Mittelalters und der frühen Neuzeit (Cologne, GER: Böhlau Verlag, 1994), 187–94.

55. See in Bieler's edition the notes at the bottom of each page, "Index Locorum Sacrae Scripturae" (109), and "Fontes et Similia" (110–21).

56. See *Language and Symbolic Power*, chap. 6, "Censorship and the Imposition of Form," 137–59, and *Rules*, 289–92. As Bourdieu makes clear, writers need not set out to alienate uninitiated readers, but they write as they learned to read—and if they are initiates of a field, they employ specialized language.

57. See *Language and Symbolic Power*, 151–9, for a more detailed discussion of "internal reading": texts written by and for initiates into a specific discourse. For reading as a cultural practice, see Bourdieu, *Distinction: A Social Critique of the Judgement of Taste*, trans. Richard Nice (Cambridge, MA: Harvard University Press, 1984), 28.

58. See also my chap. 1. Kurt Otten discusses in some detail Alfred's departures from logic, which he credits to a lack of logical terminology in OE; see Otten's chapter "Die Stellung Alfreds zur philosophisch Methode des Boethius," 187–93. To some extent Otten is correct; Alfred lacks some of the purely logical vocabulary Boethius uses. He does employ, however, words such as *racu*: "an exposition, explanation, orderly account, narrative" (Bosworth-Toller, 780) although not as often as he uses the less logically precise *spell* ("saying"). In large measure the shift seems to arise from preference, not necessity. Otten also suggests that Alfred's style of argumentation reflects the actual conditions of the composition of the *Bo*: by dictation, with help from advisors. See also Janet Bately's conclusion that that Alfred generally avoided technical terms in "Uþwita/Philosophus Revisited: A Reflection on OE Usage," in *Essays on Anglo-Saxon and Related Themes in Memory of Lynne Grundy*, ed. Jane Roberts and Janet Nelson (London: Centre for Late Antique and Medieval Studies, King's College London, 2000), 16–36, at 36.

59. For doxa, see the section on "Doxa, orthodoxy, heterodoxy" in Bourdieu's *Language and Symbolic Power*, 159–71; Bourdieu and Wacquant, *Invitation*, 98; and

Bourdieu and Terry Eagleton. "In Conversation: Doxa and Common Life," *New Left Review* 191 (1992): 111–21.

60. *S. Aureli Augustini Hipponiensis Episcopi Epistulae*, ed. Al. Goldbacher, CCSL 57 (Leipzig, GER, Freytag, 1931).

61. For a more thorough list of other sources, see my *Fontes* entries.

62. See Otten, 89–91.

63. For sources and influences, consult the footnotes in the Sources Chrétiennes or Corpus Christianorum Series Latina editions of Gregory's texts.

64. Brian Donaghey first identified the quotation in "The Sources of King Alfred's Translation of Boethius' *De Consolatione Philosophiae*," *Anglia* 82 (1964): 23–57, at 42.

65. See II met. iv: the opposition between the house built on sand and that built on the rock comes clearly from Matthew 7:24–7 (or Luke 6:48–9). See also IV pr i. 6, where the precious and vulgar vessels seem to derive from Romans 9:21–3 or 2 Timothy 2:20, although Boethius changes the meaning of the image, saying that it would be wrong to use vulgar vessels and not precious ones. Chadwick notes other possible Scriptural sources in *Boethius: The Consolations of Music, Logic, Theology, and Philosophy* (Oxford, UK: Clarendon, 1981), 238. Pierre Courcelle allows fewer; see *La Consolation de philosophie dans la tradition littéraire: antécédents et postérité de Boèce* (Paris: Etudes Augustiniennes, 1967), 35. Ann Astell draws connections in *Job, Boethius, and Epic Truth*, 13; see also V. E. Watts in his translation, *The Consolation of Philosophy*, rev. ed. (New York: Penguin, 1999), 81, fn. 15, and esp. Bieler's list of Scriptural parallels, 109.

66. *The Consolations*, 224.

67. *Language and Symbolic Power* 106; emphasis in original.

68. For a similar act of appropriation by Alfred in another text, see my "Alfred's Verse Preface to the *Pastoral Care* and the Chain of Authority," *Neophilologus* 85 (2001): 625–33.

69. Edmund T. Silk, "Boethius' *Consolatione Philosophiae* as a Sequel to Augustine's *Dialogues* and *Soliloquia*," *Harvard Theological Review* 32 (1939): 19–39; Chadwick, *The Consolations*, esp. 249–51 and *in passim*. Joachim Gruber, *Kommentar zu Boethius De Consolatione Philosophiae* (New York: de Gruyter, 1978), 32, rejects the idea of an Augustinian sequel.

70. *PL* 33, col. 597. Recourse to authority undergirds the whole text and can be found throughout.

71. For Alfred's use of commentaries on the *De cons*, see my Appendix.

72. Georgius Thilo and Hermannus Hagen, "Praefatio" to *Servii grammatici qui feruntur in Vergilii carmina commentarii*, vol. 1 (Leipzig, GER: Teubner, 1881), lxxvii. See *Fontes* for two possible borrowings from Servius in the *Bo*, in my entries on that text, and Rohini Jayatilaka, "Sources of the Anonymous Old English Version of Orosius's *History against the Pagans* (Cameron C.B. 9.2)," 2001, *Fontes*, for fifteen possible uses in the *Orosius*.

73. Alfred tends to stay with the moral level of interpretation whereas patristic writers often range more freely among three or four levels of interpretation. For medieval modes of interpretation, see Beryl Smalley's *The Study of the Bible in the Middle Ages*, 2nd ed. (Notre Dame, IN: University of Notre Dame Press, 1964), and

Henri de Lubac, *Medieval Exegesis*, trans. Mark Sebanc (Grand Rapids, MI: Eerdmans, 1998), especially chap. 1, "Theology, Scripture, and the Fourfold Sense," 15–74.

74. See Carnicelli's introduction to *Soliloquies*, 28–9, and Godden's *Fontes* entries for *Sol.*

75. The Latin is similar; see 36.122–4.

76. The Latin is similar; see 9.33–4.

77. Gerard O'Daly argues that the account is not meant to be an allegory in which figures can simply be equated with qualities or things, but a parable whose meaning is more suggestive than exact; see *The Poetry of Boethius*, 192.

78. Modern readers too can disagree. O'Daly sees Orpheus as "the work's symbol of the degradation of poetry" (41), but argues against interpreting Eurydice as the passions, the traditional reading of her character (*The Poetry of Boethius*, 191; his fn. 26 on 191 gives several references to the traditional interpretation).

79. Otten suggests (133) that Alfred may have been guided here by a commentary of the St. Gall type, which comments, "Hoc carmen est fabulosum.... Et admonet ne aliquis inventa luce summi boni iterum redeat ad nequitias tenebrosi orbis ... Qui ad mundi cupiditatem respexerit ... quicquid profecit de eo, perdit ... " ("This song is fabulous.... And admonishes anyone who has found the light of the true good not to return to the evils of the dark world.... Who looks back at worldly desire ... loses whatever he had completed of these things ... "). Alfred may have some verbal echoes of this passage, but in the gloss the emphasis on completion is the good that is completed, and what is to be left behind seems to be as much the world in general as vice.

80. Augustine uses the terms *verus* and *veritas*, *falsus* and *falsitas*, and *fabula*. Alfred uses *soð*, *leasung*, and *spell* ("story"). Boethius uses only *fabula* (III met. xii. 52).

81. Knowing whether the secular songs Aldhelm sang to attract worldly listeners involved Germanic mythology would be helpful, but no detailed account survives. For the story of Aldhelm singing to keep casual churchgoers to stay for the homily, see William of Malmesbury, *De gestis pontificum anglorum*, ed. N. E. S. A. Hamilton, Rolls 52 (London: Longman, 1870), 336. Note too that William attributes the story and the judgments of Aldhelm's activities to Alfred, who may have been influenced by his countryman in the strategies he used to win audiences. See also Jeff Opland's discussion of William's passage and an alternate version of the story, *Anglo-Saxon Oral Poetry: A Study of the Traditions* (New Haven, CT: Yale University Press, 1980), 121–7.

82. See Reinsma 394. Although his arguments concern Ælfric, the same argument can be made for Alfred: he did not need to have read *De doctrina* himself to know its methods.

83. *Scribes and Scholars*, 84. Webber notes only one eleventh-century manuscript of *De doctrina* at Salisbury (Salisbury Cathedral, England, MS 106; Appendix 1, p. 151), but she also finds that Salisbury had numerous works listed in Cassiodorus's *Institutiones* I and Augustine's *Retractiones; De doctrina* is on both lists (38). The Salisbury manuscript of *De doctrina* had annotations of "dignum memorare" ("worthy of committing to memory") which may have been intended for the scribe, for canons studying the text, or for use in sermons. Clearly it was considered

an important text later, although its availability and status in Alfred's time are uncertain. Robert Stanton writes that both Bede and Ælfric drew upon *De doctrina*; see his *Culture of Translation in Anglo-Saxon England* (Cambridge, UK: Brewer, 2002), 147.

84. Augustine mentions specifically Cyprian, Lactantius, Victorinus, Optatus, and Hilary as carriers of gold out of Egypt (II.40.30–2). Augustine himself uses Varro's story of the creation of the statue of the Muses to explain that the concept of nine Muses is a "superstitious" myth and to mention the threefold nature of music (II.17.2–20).

85. The only scientific additions not explicitly covered in Augustine's list are Alfred's additions on elements. Interestingly, Alfred does not generally expand on things that Augustine does not list, although additions on physics, cosmology, and even chemistry could be imagined and can be found in some early commentaries. See, for instance, Stewart's extracts from commentaries of the *De cons* on III met. ix (pp. 30–31), or Silk's on the same meter (pp. 332–9), which expand on cosmology, where Alfred's expansions concern the elements and the soul; Stewart's on V pr. i (p. 39) concerning creation *ex nihilo*, which discusses atoms; and Troncarelli's on Tyrian dye (p. 169). H. F. Stewart, "A Commentary by Remigius Autissiodorensis on the *De consolatione philosophiae* of Boethius," *Journal of Theological Studies* 17 (1916): 22–42; Fabio Troncarelli, the appendix to *Tradizioni Perdute: La "Consolatio philosophiae" nell'alto Medioevo* (Padova, IT: Editrice Antenorei, 1981): 138–96; and Edmund Taite Silk, the appendix to *Saeculi noni auctoris in Boetii consolationem philosophiae commentarius* (Rome: American Academy in Rome, 1935): 305–43. Note Pierre Courcelle's correction to Silk's ascription of his main text, "Étude critique sur les commentaires de la *Consolation* de Boèce (IXe–XVe siècles)," *Archives d'histoire doctrinale et littéraire du moyen âge* 4 (1933): 5–140, at 25.

86. See Brinegar's "'Books Most Necessary': The Literary and Cultural Contexts of Alfred's *Boethius*" (Ph.D. dissertation, University of North Carolina at Chapel Hill, 2000), 154–5. Brinegar emphasizes the religious nature of these additions: Alfred's exploration of their wonders underscores God's role as creator and the awesome power of divine Wisdom to understand such things.

Chapter 3

1. See Gideon Toury, *Descriptive Translation Studies and Beyond* (Philadelphia: Benjamins, 1995), esp. 57 and 70–4.

2. Translators may include some loan-words or nontranslations but select the vast majority of words and phrases according to normal usage in the target language. Ludwig Borinski did an exhaustive study of Alfred's syntax and style in all his translations, *Der Stil König Alfreds: Eine Studie zur Psychologie der Rede* (Leipzig, GER: Bernhard Tauchnitz, 1934). Although he considered the *Orosius* but not the Prose Psalms of the Paris Psalter among Alfred's works, his conclusions are generally sound, and he notes when the *Orosius* appears typical of the others and when it does not. See also William Brown's *Syntax of King Alfred's Pastoral Care* (The Hague: Mouton, 1970), which does not rate Alfred's prose highly, but offers valid observations on specific stylistic traits. Kurt Otten provides a valuable study of several stylis-

tic elements in the *Bo* in his *König Alfreds Boethius*, Studien zur englischen Philologie, neue Folge no. 3 (Tübingen: Max Niemeyer Verlag, 1964), esp. 158–263. All three emphasize that Alfred developed a native prose style that remained largely independent of Latin.

3. *Language and Symbolic Power*, ed. John B. Thompson, trans. Gino Raymond and Matthew Adamson (Cambridge, MA: Harvard University Press, 1991), 76–7.

4. For Bourdieu, every social context is a "market," a place where people exchange language for a variety of benefits. This terminology does not imply a projection of capitalism onto precapitalist societies. See *Outline of a Theory of Practice*, trans. Richard Nice (Cambridge, UK: Cambridge University Press, 1977), for an introduction. Indeed, John Guillory criticizes Bourdieu for using capitalism solely as a model and not engaging the contemporary economic system itself; see "Bourdieu's Refusal," *Modern Language Quarterly* 58 (1997): 367–98.

5. *Language and Symbolic Power*, 77.

6. Gideon Toury writes that doublets occur "usually not as a mere case of 'hendiadis,'... but rather as a submission to a target pole overall norm of 'acceptability,'" *In Search of a Theory of Translation* (Tel Aviv: Porter Institute for Poetics and Semiotics, 1980), 130. Most Anglo-Saxonists, however, see them as means to cover inadequacies in OE. P. Fijn van Draat set the tone in "The Authorship of the Old English *Bede*," writing that translators usually resorted to them when a single word could not accurately render the original, but also to give one literal and one figurative rendering, to offer different dialect forms, to show cause and effect or stages of action, and "in hundreds of instances... simply due to... garrulous longwindedness," *Anglia* 39 (1916): 319–46, at 322. Mary Catherine Bodden addresses the use of doublets to cover gaps between OE and Latin ranges of meaning in "Anglo-Saxon Self-Consciousness in Language," *English Studies* 1 (1987): 24–39, especially 31–2. Inna Koskenniemi's *Repetitive Word Pairs in Old and Early Middle English Prose*, Annales Universitatis Turkuensis Series B, vol. 107 (Turku, FIN: Turun Yliopiston Julkaisuja, 1968), however, treats word pairs as a stylistic choice to meet audience expectations. Janet Bately also notes that Alfredian doublets often translate one Latin word, but sometimes they simply reorder Latin elements; see "Old English Prose before and during the Reign of Alfred," *ASE* 17 (1988): 93–138, at 126. Most work on doublets remains impressionistic, selecting (often atypical) examples instead of studying all doublets in a particular text. Even Koskenniemi's count of doublets is surprisingly low: in 13 texts (including the *Bede*, in which she counted more than 300), she found a total of 939 pairs (including antitheses). I count nearly that many doublets and antitheses in the *Bo* alone.

7. For example, in "andwyrde 7 cwæð" ("answered and said"), both verbs share one subject and communicate similar ideas. (Koskenniemi defines "word pairs" similarly but includes antitheses, 11.) Doublets do not include parallel words with different meanings: "sio eorðe is dryge 7 ceald, 7 þæt wæter wæt 7 ceald" ("The earth is dry and cold, and the water wet and cold," 80.6) has pairs of words, but no doublets.

8. I have not considered the four doublets or two antitheses found in the closing prayer of MS B (149.11–26) because it is probably not Alfred's work; see my Introduction.

9. For example: "deglu ðing tæcan 7 selðcuð" (127.1–2 for "miraculum," IV pr. vi. 1), "indicate each hidden and wonderful thing," for "wonder."

10. Eighty-six of these are Latin doublets, twenty-four other kinds of Latin word pairs (usually juxtaposed without a conjunction). Among these are OE doublets that differ in meaning from a Latin word pair, so the breakdowns of doublets total more than 745.

11. By comparison, in the Meters, where OE prose is "translated" into OE alliterative verse, doublets are added much less frequently (15.7 percent) and their meaning rarely differs from the source text (3.6 percent). See my Introduction for questions surrounding the Meters.

12. Only in eighteen cases does a doublet in Latin not lead to one in OE. In six of these the phrase is not translated (II pr. ii. 4, II pr. iii. 2, II pr. iv. 3, II pr. v. 4, II pr. v. 9, and II pr. v. 34); in another eight, a doublet in the Latin becomes an OE singlet that is part of a larger parallelism or antithesis (10.29–11.1/I pr. v. 1; 17.25/II pr. ii. 8; 54.24–6/III pr. ii. 10; 82.11/II met. ix. 24; 88.4/III pr. x. 37; 104.20–1/IV pr. i. 7; 123.25–7/IV pr. iv. 40; and 130.30–1/IV pr. vi. 17). In one (88.4/III pr. x. 37) the Latin supplies a specific parallelism that the OE then covers with a blanket term. In one case the Latin doublet becomes a more complicated phrase that still contains two members but is not a doublet or parallelism (35.31–2/II pr. vi. 4). Only in three cases does a Latin doublet become an English singlet without being part of a larger repetitive construction (compare I pr. v. 2, with two doublets, with 11.3–4, and II pr. v. 2 with 27.20). Alfred almost never entirely eliminates Latin doublets, though he may change their form.

13. At least thirty-two of the 204 doublets that match one Latin word involve Latin words that Alfred has elsewhere translated with a single word.

14. Other explanations scholars (such as Van Draat) advance prove unhelpful. In a text that asserts that true good is divinity and earthly goods merely partial goods, that proximity to God is health and distraction by the world is illness, identifying doublets that have one literal and one metaphorical term is often impossible. Of those few doublets that seem clearly half literal and half metaphorical, most do not correspond to any specific Latin word, and others reproduce a mixed doublet in the source. Doublets that combine Latinate and OE words, express a range of time, describe stages in an process, or involve differences between Anglo-Saxon and Roman life (for example, adding "snow" to "rain" at 52.5) are all insignificant (1 percent or less).

15. Lists various scholars compiled from other texts include 42 different doublets appearing nearly 100 times in the *Bo.* See A. P. McD. Orchard, "Crying Wolf: Oral Style and the 'Sermones Lupi,'" *ASE* 21 (1992): 239–64; Figure 5, "Some of Wulfstan's favorite words and phrases," contains an antithesis used in the *Bo.* Dorothy Bethurum, in "Stylistic Features of the Old English Laws," *Modern Language Review* 27 (1932): 263–79, lists thirty-eight alliterative "formulas" from the laws of Æthelred (272), which include twenty-three doublets and eleven antitheses; two of the doublets and one antithesis are in the *Bo.* G. Kotzor, ed., *Das altenglische Martyrologium,* Phil.-Hist Klasse, Neue Forschung 88 (Munich: Bayerische Akademie der Wissenschaften, 1981), 422–3, lists thirty-eight doublets, of which two appear thirty-five times in the *Bo*; both also appear in Koskenniemi's list. Paul Gonser, "Übersetzungstechnik," *Das Angelsächsische Prosa-Leben des Hl.*

Guthlac (Heidelberg, GER: Carl Winter's Universitätsbuchhandlung, 1909), 52–94, lists ninety-three doublets (at 77–81), of which three appear nine times in the *Bo*; one (with four occurrences) overlaps with Koskenniemi's list. H. Hecht's list of 416 doublets for the *Dial (Bischof Wærferths von Worcester Übersetzung*, 96–7) includes eleven that occur once each in the *Bo*; one overlaps with Koskenniemi. Koskenniemi's list, the most inclusive, contains fourteen doublets found in the *Bo* a total of sixty-nine times (120–62). A list of OE alliterative formulas includes 474 doublets in J. P. Oakden with Elizabeth R. Innes, *Alliterative Poetry in Middle English: A Survey of the Traditions* (Manchester, UK: Manchester University Press, 1935): 199–232; sixteen of these appear in Alfred. Twelve of them are not on the other lists and add thirteen instances of doublets in the *Bo* that occur elsewhere.

16. 357 (47.9 percent) were repeated in whole (318) or in part (39), as when the triplet "ælcere *fullfremed*nesse 7 ælces *god*es 7 ælcere gesælðe" (84.9–10) appears as the doublet "þæt fulle *good* 7 þæt *fullfremede*" ("each perfection and each good and each happiness" and "that full good and that perfection," 83.5–6; emphasis added).

17. The Latin is "nostris educatus alimentis" ("brought up on our foods," I pr. ii. 2). Repetition within the work may also help unify the text, as Pierre-Eric Monnin says doublets in the Meters do; see "Poetic Improvements in the Old English *Meters of Boethius," English Studies* 60 (1979): 346–60, at 352.

18. If only the seventy-four OE antitheses that match one or more words of Latin are examined, the figure rises to 50 percent. All Latin antitheses were reproduced by OE antitheses.

19. Janet Bately comments that they are relatively rare in the *Martyrology*, "Old English Prose," 135, but she finds both native origins for doublets (124–8) and models in the more prestigious Latin (132–6). For similar figures, see Bede's *De Schematibus et Tropis* on zeugma, schesis onomaton, and hypozeuxis, illustrated from the Psalms and Pauline Epistles: Bede, *Opera Didascalica pars I* CCSL vol. 123A (Turnhout, BEL: Brepols, 1975): 144–5, 148. The pseudo-Ciceronian *Ad Herennium* (ed. Harry Caplan, Loeb Classical Library; Cambridge, MA: Harvard University Press, 1989) explains antithesis (IV.15 and IV.45), and synonymy (IV.28). See also Jackson J. Campbell, "Knowledge of Rhetorical Figures in Anglo-Saxon England," *Journal of English and Germanic Philology* 66 (1967): 1–20; and "Adaptation of Classical Rhetoric in Old English Literature," in *Medieval Eloquence: Studies in the Theory and Practice of Medieval Rhetoric*, ed. James J. Murphy (Berkeley: University of California Press, 1978), 173–97. Campbell demonstrates Anglo-Saxon knowledge of classical rhetoric and vernacular adaptations, but he cautions against interpreting every figure as evidence of classical training, listing "multiple appositives"—doublets—as a technique that "existed in the Old English poetic style independent of Latin learning" (191). Koskenniemi believes the Psalms influenced doublets in English and other languages (24 and 27). Although Alfred may not have read Latin rhetorical handbooks, he might have been influenced by those who did or by the Scriptures. The most common doublets in the *Bo, andwyrde 7 cwæð* (ten occurrences, plus one of *andwyrde 7 sæde) and andswarode 7 cwæð* (thirty-one occurrences) seem to reflect the Vulgate's *respondit dicens* and variations, as Paul E. Szarmach noted (conversation, July 1999). This construction appears most in

Matthew, followed in frequency by Luke and Mark, and rarely in John (who uses "respondit et dixit," a construction even closer to "andswarode 7 cwæð").

20. 170 (22.8 percent) of the doublets alliterate. Of these, 125 (16.7 percent) have a fully alliterating pair and forty-five (6 percent) have alliteration in two of three or more elements. Twenty-five (15 percent) of the antitheses involve alliteration (all have two elements). Thirty-three percent of the doublets in the Meters alliterate, by contrast, whereas the A text of the *Chronicle* through 896 has doublets but only displays alliteration in 9.8 percent. For the influence of poetry on Alfred's writing, see Peter Clemoes, "King Alfred's Debt to Vernacular Poetry: The Evidence of *ellen* and *cræft*," in *Words, Texts and Manuscripts: Studies in Anglo-Saxon Culture Presented to Helmut Gneuss*, ed. Michael Korhammer with Karl Reichl and Hans Sauer (Cambridge, UK: Brewer, 1992), 213–38.

21. Cynewulf, the only known author of a section of the poem, has been dated to the late eighth or early ninth century. See, for instance, Daniel G. Calder, *Cynewulf* (Boston: Twayne, 1981), 11, and Earl R. Anderson, *Cynewulf: Structure, Style, and Theme in His Poetry* (London: Associated University Presses, 1983), 17. Patrick W. Conner has challenged Cynewulf's dates, arguing that *Christ II* must date to after 875, the continental origin of its source text, and most likely it could not be earlier than the mid-tenth century; "On Dating Cynewulf," in *Cynewulf: Basic Readings*, ed. Robert E. Bjork, Basic Readings in Anglo-Saxon England, vol. 4 (New York: Garland, 1996), 23–55. R. D. Fulk's essay in the same volume, "Cynewulf: Canon, Dialect, and Date" (3–21), groups Alfredian and Cynewulfian poetry together on the basis of metrical similarities, 16–9. The few securely dated poems extant in OE appear well after Alfred's time, but *Christ* most likely covers a range of dates that extend both before and after Alfred's.

22. Doublets vary in frequency among the three sections: I has one doublet every 23.7 lines, II every 25.8 lines, and III more frequently, every 18.5 lines. Antitheses show great divergence: one every 87.8 lines in I, every 53.3 lines in II, and every 48.63 lines in III. (These samples, particularly the antitheses, are too small to support conclusions about the style or authorship of the sections.)

23. Three are antitheses: "dædum ond wordum" appears at *Christ* 429, 1367, and 1582, and at *Bo* 141.8; "sunne ond mona" appears at *Christ* 606 and 694 and *Bo* 126.14; "innan and utan" appears at *Christ* 1004 and *Bo* 36.9 and 36.12. One doublet, "deora ond fugla," appears at *Christ* 982 and *Bo* 121.15 and 124.7–8. *Christ* has Latin source texts, but poetry that is not translated contains doublets as well; the *Wanderer* has only 115 lines, but one antithesis ("feor oþþe neah," 26) and four doublets, two of which alliterate. I have not counted other pairs, such as "selesecgas ond sincþege" (34) and "sorg ond slæp" (39), that make more of a distinction in sense, and four runs of repeated phrases with one or two words changed, although these are essentially doublets without a connecting "ond"; see lines 66–9, 92–3, 94–5, and 108–10. These phrases all contain some alliteration. Further examination of the poetic corpus would turn up variation in individual practices but many more doublets in many more poems.

24. *Language and Symbolic Power*, 67.

25. See also II pr. vii. 2/41.23 and II pr. vii. 8/43.8. As noted previously, a reference to Aristotle's *Physics* is explicit at V pr. i. 12; the OE adds the word "bec,"

140.8–9. One reference to Plato does not explicitly mention books in either version (III pr. xii. 38/101.13–8).

26. Each copy of Alfred's translation of the *PC* was to travel with an extremely valuable gold *æstel*, and the verse preface to the *PC* refers to Gregory's "searoðonca hord" ("hoard of clever thoughts"). See also my "Wealth and Wisdom: Symbolic Capital and the Ruler in the Translational Program of Alfred the Great," *Exemplaria* 13 (2001): 111–45 for the symbolic value of books.

27. See Seth Lerer, *Boethius and Dialogue: Literary Method in the Consolation of Philosophy*, esp. chap. 4: "Readings and Rewritings in Book Four" (Princeton, NJ: Princeton University Press, 1985), 166–202.

28. The Latin text's own stated disregard for the spiritual and intellectual condition of others must be taken with a degree of caution. If it were literally true that only the understanding of Boethius himself were at stake, the text would never have been written and copied. The *De cons* is too polished and rigorous a work to have been simply the journal of a prisoner awaiting execution. See my chaps. 2 and 4 for more detailed discussions of the differing positions on the responsibility for educating others that the Latin and the OE texts take. Boethius's veiled use of Scripture hints that the audience includes both Christians and non-Christians: the former will appreciate allusions to the Bible, which the latter may overlook, persuaded instead by logic.

29. For Bourdieu's "internal reading," see my chap. 2, and his chap. 6, "Censorship and the Imposition of Form," *Language and Symbolic Power*, 137–59.

30. See *Bo* 73.13–6; 94.11–2; 95.31–2; 96.3; 97.19; 98.4–5; 109.21–2; 112.4–7; 113.12–5; 118.12; 143.22–3; 148.4–6.

31. *Language and Symbolic Power*, 79–81.

32. Alfred might have noted the self-consciousness of the Epistles, which refer back to the Gospels, the prophets, and occasionally themselves or previous epistles. II Corinthians makes several references to I Corinthians; 3 John 9 refers to John's previous letter. Yet these Scriptural cross-references are limited to one genre, and it is not the genre of the *Bo*. Alfred's use of citation is also different than those in most Latin works. The self-consciousness of the *Bo* is much closer to Anglo-Saxon norms.

33. See, for instance, Riddles 26 (book), 47 (bookworm), 51 (pen and fingers?) 67 (Bible?), 93 (inkhorn?). For the Riddles and details about their solutions, see ASPR III.

34. Asser tells of Alfred memorizing a book of poems that his mother has promised to the son who can first recite it; Alfred is clearly quite young at the time (chap. 23). See chap. 2, 16, for problems with the story and references on it.

35. See my Introduction and notes on problems of authorship of poetry and order of composition.

36. Borinski notes the shift at the verbal level, 129–32; Otten extends the observation to cover larger passages, 241–58.

37. Alfred omits II met. i, which personifies Fortune in a quick succession of images and allusions; much of the personification of Philosophy (now Wisdom) at the start of the text; I met. iii personifying night and day; V met. i, a vivid image of rivers wreaking havoc whose connection to the argument about law and chance is somewhat obscure; V met. iii, which relies heavily on substantives and generalized imagery of light and darkness; and V met. iv, which rejects the Stoic notion of a *tabula rasa*—a

corrective Anglo-Saxons presumably did not need. In other cases, Alfred merely omits parts of meters, including dense allusions from III met. x. 7–11 and IV met. vii. 1–31. Sometimes he does omit concrete passages; I met. vi is drastically shortened, and V met. ii and V met. v are condensed, but these come from portions that Alfred has greatly condensed overall.

38. The OE versions of I met. i (8.6–14) and II met. ii (19.1–10) are also significantly more narrative and less allusive than the Latin; II met. iii (21.1–9), II met. iv (26.22–27.13), IV met. iii (115.12–116.34), and IV met. vi (135.23–136.31) are handled similarly, although to varying extents. The most dramatic transformation occurs in Alfred's version of the Orpheus meter (the bulk of which is translated only into prose), III met. xii; see Joseph S. Wittig's detailed discussion, "King Alfred's Boethius and Its Latin Sources: A Reconsideration," *ASE* 11 (1983): 157–98, "The Orpheus Meter," 163–80. Alfred explains many details in additions of varying length and makes the passage from 102.9–103.13 much more narrative than the corresponding Latin (III met. xii. 13–51). The repetition of *ða* ("then") eighteen times in the space of thirty-eight printed lines in Sedgefield's edition emphasizes the piling of event on event much more strongly than the terse, allusive Latin. Boethius's pithy conclusion "uidit, perdidit, occidit" ("He looked, he lost, he killed," III met. xii. 51) becomes the more prosaic: "Ða he furðum on ðæt leoht com, ða beseah he hine underbæc wið ðæs wifes; ða losade hio him sona" ("When he came further into that light, then he looked behind himself at his wife; then she was lost to him at once," 103.12–3). Although less succinct, the OE makes more sense to neophytes.

39. A search of the online Corpus produces ninety-three occurrences of "gigant-" and "ent-."

40. Along the same lines, in the image of a man leaving home and finding his reputation worthless in foreign lands (63.11–27/II pr. iv. 11–3), Alfred specifies the cause of the departure where the Latin does not (III pr. iv. 11) and replaces the verb "uanescunt" ("vanish," III pr. iv. 13) with "hi losiað swa swa sceadu oððe smec" ("they are lost just as shadows or smoke," 63.26–7). See also 30.14–9/II pr. v. 16; 36.28–37.10/II pr. vi. 10–1; 42.9–10/II pr. vii. 5; 49.11–3 (added before II met. viii. 3); 49.18–20 (added before II met. viii. 5); 62.16–26/III pr. iv. 2); and 92.1–11 (expands III pr. xi. 22). Sometimes Alfred simply drives the point home. Where the Latin says children may become a torment for their parents (III pr. vii. 5), the OE adds, "forðæmþe manig wif forswilt for hire bearne ær heo hit brengan mæge" ("because many a woman dies for her child before she can bring it forth," 70.21–2), then a story about sons conspiring against their father (70.22–7). Although readers are certainly capable of providing their own examples of parental suffering, Alfred's vivid words bring realism and pathos to the passage.

41. Similarly, Boethius's example of a person who cannot walk on his feet but must go on his hands (IV pr. ii. 28–9) becomes in OE that of a child who cannot yet walk (108.8–26).

42. Likewise, people do not generally walk on their hands even if they cannot use their legs. My undergraduates sometimes insist that Boethius has it backward: clearly someone who can walk on his or her hands is *more* powerful than those who simply use their feet.

43. See Otten's discussion of the difference between the images and the implications this has for the philosophical ideas illustrated, 246–7. See also F. Anne Payne, *King Alfred and Boethius: An Analysis of the Old English Version of the Consolation of Philosophy* (Madison: University of Wisconsin Press, 1968), 98–9, and Jerold Frakes, "Die Rezeption der Neuplatonischen Metaphysik des Boethius durch Alfred und Notker," *Beiträge zur Geschichte der deutschen Sprache und Literatur* 106 (1984): 51–74, at 63.

44. Alfred sometimes adds entirely new images: the earth's place in the universe as "rondbeag on scelde" ("a boss on a shield," 41.25–6), the perfect good as the sea (53.3–8). Later, the *Bo* supplements the idea of power as a partial good (IV pr. ii. 43) with the image that all goods are rooted and culminate in God just as the walls of a house are bound by both floor and roof (110.22–5). All of these illustrations are both specific and concrete.

45. Otten thinks that this drive for concreteness is unique to Alfred, 256–8. It certainly appears in his other works, but it is not confined to them. In his *PC*, for instance, Alfred changes Gregory's image of ship unable to stand still (*Regula pastoralis* 508.79–82) by pointing out that a ship has an anchor and that one can row against the current (445.9–14). See also Roy Ray Moye, Jr. "Alfred's Method of Translation in the Old English 'Pastoral Care'" (Ph.D. diss. University of North Carolina at Chapel Hill, 1993), chap. 3, "Embellishment of Imagery" (74–107). The *Sol* begin with Alfred's own preface of gathering wood and building a house (47.1–49.12). Soon thereafter, Alfred translates Ratio's example of finding just "aliquid" ("something," I.1) to the image of a hoard: "Gyf ðu enigne godne heorde hæbbe . . . " ("If you have any good hoard . . . " 49.7). Later he adds extended seasonal imagery (53.9–22) to Augustine's mention of the change of seasons (I.4). Dorothy Whitelock traces the tendency to Alfred's exposure to Gregory; see "The Prose of Alfred's Reign," in *Continuations and Beginnings: Studies in Old English Literature*, ed. E. G. Stanley (London: Nelson, 1966), 67–103, at 79–80 and 95.

46. 2.18–21, 94.12–23, 179.1–5, 260.1–5.

47. Compare II iv. 1–5 (88–9); II vi. 1–12 (94–7); III xi. 1 (155–6); and IV vi. 11–3 (219–20); *Pauli Orosii Historiarum aduersum paganos*, ed. Carolus Zangemeister, CSEL 5 (Vienna: C. Geroldi Filium Bibliopolam Academiae, 1882).

48. David Pratt also notes this tendency, which he ascribes to "Alfred's didactic purpose," "The Political Thought of Alfred the Great" (Ph.D. diss., University of Cambridge, UK 1999), 310–1.

49. See for instance III pr. xii. 30, where the narrator complains about the way he is being led.

50. Likewise, the idea that misunderstanding God's knowledge is sinful not only appears at III pr. x. 15 or 84.31–2 in the OE, but is also anticipated by Alfred at 84.18–21.

51. See my *Fontes* entries for the repetition of earlier passages.

52. *Orality and Literacy: The Technologizing of the Word* (New York: Methuen, 1982), 49. See also Brian Stock, *The Implications of Literacy: Written Language and Models of Interpretation in the Eleventh and Twelfth Centuries* (Princeton, NJ: Princeton University Press, 1983), 40.

53. See the collapse of the argument about virtue and vice, IV pr. vii. 15 and 138.9–12. Other omitted arguments include: Boethius's rejection of hope and prayer, V pr. iii. 33–6 (which may have been dangerously near the sin of despair); Philosophy's argument that observation of present or future does not affect free will, V pr. iv. 2–13; her distinction between opinion and fact, V pr. iv. 21–3; her idea that the superior can comprehend the inferior but not vice versa and discussion of the abilities of reason and the limits of knowing, V pr. iv. 28–39; and the whole technical discussion of conditional and simple necessity, V pr. vi. 12–37. Alfred replaces V pr. vi. 38–45 on free will with a different argument leading to the same conclusion. Payne argues that Alfred's *Bo* sometimes does not make sense because Alfred rejects Boethius's view of an ordered world and therefore rejects Boethian logic (135–8 and 144). Borinski comments that Alfred often replaces a logical progression with an "unlogischer Ausdruck" ("illogical expression," 227), and Otten maintains that OE lacked logical or systematic language, resulting in a loss of clarity and the destruction of syllogisms (186–92). Otten also observes that Alfred is interested in truth, not logic, and his use of authority over logic is justified by Augustine (191–3). Milton McC. Gatch defends Alfred's style of argumentation while agreeing that the king is illogical because formal logic was foreign to the Anglo-Saxon mind-set; see "King Alfred's Version of Augustine's *Soliloquia*: Some Suggestions on Its Rationale and Unity," in *Studies in Earlier Old English Prose*, ed. Paul E. Szarmach (Albany: State University of New York Press, 1986), 17–45, at 33, and *Loyalties and Traditions*, 108–12.

54. "Ac onget ðæt nauht nis betere on þis andweardum life" is from MS B. Malcolm Godden writes that the passage "makes very poor sense and syntax" in the C manuscript and that the B reading "is clearly correct," "Editing Old English and the Problem of Alfred's *Boethius*," in *The Editing of Old English: Papers from the 1990 Manchester Conference*, ed. Donald G. Scragg and Paul E. Szarmach with Helene Scheck and Holly Holbrook (Cambridge, UK: Brewer, 1994), 163–76, at 170.

55. In one passage, the OE reduces the Latin argument almost to a tautology when an argument is shortened too much; compare III pr. x. 18–9 with 85.27–9. (Compare also the logic of IV pr. ii. 2–3 to 106.4–9.) More often, the reasoning has been heavily abbreviated, such as at 140.8–17/V pr. i. 11–9 and 144.12–24/V pr. iv. 3–23, where much of the argumentation has been left out and the conclusions cannot truly be said to follow necessarily. Abbreviated arguments sketch out reasons, and authority compensates for the rest.

56. Pierre Riché, in *Écoles et Enseignement dans le Haut Moyen Age: Fin du Ve siècle—Milieu du XIe siècle* (Paris: Picard, 1989), 261–6, argues that dialectic was scarce between the sixth and tenth centuries: Bede and Aldhelm avoided it as heresy (261), and Alcuin did not employ it either (262). However, John J. Contreni argues for "intense study of dialectic and the application of dialectic to the problems intellectuals debated in the Carolingian realms" in the ninth century, "The Carolingian Renaissance: Education and Literary Culture," in *The New Cambridge Medieval History: Volume II c. 700—c. 900*, ed. Rosamond McKitterick (Cambridge, UK: Cambridge University Press, 1995), 737. Some Continental intellectuals might have studied dialectic, but how far this penetrated is not clear. Furthermore, Stock argues that formal logic is only possible in a written culture;

writing helps support this particular structure of thought, 18. Ong also writes that formal or syllogistic logic simply does not function in oral societies, and that members of them may even be incapable of following such reasoning, 52–3. In *The Psychology of Literacy* (Cambridge, MA: Harvard University Press, 1981), Sylvia Scribner and Michael Coles report that less educated or even illiterate subjects were not incapable of completing syllogisms, but they did not recognize the form; success often depended on what they did just before they were tested on logic. Subjects of all types of literacy and education also tended to concentrate more on content than on form to complete syllogisms empirically rather than logically (126–8)—both of which Alfred sometimes does. Jack Goody writes, "The syllogism, as we know it, was a particular invention of a particular place and time," *The Interface between the Written and the Oral* (New York: Cambridge University Press, 1987), 221.

57. Michael Clanchy, *From Memory to Written Record: England, 1066–1307* (Cambridge, MA: Harvard University Press, 1993), 125–6.

58. Katherine O'Brien O'Keeffe, *Visible Song: Transitional Literacy in Old English Verse*, Cambridge Studies in Anglo-Saxon England 4 (Cambridge, UK: Cambridge University Press, 1990), 83–5.

59. See chap. 6, "Censorship and the Imposition of Form," 137–59, and my chap. 2.

60. See Janet Bately's conclusion that Alfred generally avoided technical terms in "Uþwita/Philosophus Revisited: A Reflection on OE Usage," in *Essays on Anglo-Saxon and Related Themes in Memory of Lynne Grundy*, ed. Jane Roberts and Janet Nelson (London: Centre for Late Antique and Medieval Studies, King's College London, 2000), 16–36, at 36.

61. For example, III pr. x. 17 and 85.6; IV pr. iii. 8 and 113.85.

62. For example, 119.1/IV pr. iv. 15; 147.12–7/V pr. vi. 1; 88.32/III pr. x. 43; and 119.26–8/IV pr. iv. 22–3.

63. See, for instance, 86.9–12/III pr. x. 26, for *spell* and 101.6–13/III pr. xii. 38 for *bispell* and *bisn.*

64. *Language and Symbolic Power*, 48.

65. *Language and Symbolic Power*, 58–9.

66. *Language and Symbolic Power*, 59–62.

67. For a different perspective on the shift from oral norms of speaking to literate forms of reference, see Brenda Danet and Bryna Bogoch's "Orality, Literacy, and Performativity in Anglo-Saxon Wills" in *Language and the Law*, ed. John Gibbons (London: Longman, 1994), 100–35. They find much of the phrasing in wills personal and circumstantial: omitting dates while referring to people or property in ways useful only to local contemporaries, addressing recipients as if they were present, and offering evaluative or qualifying remarks.

68. Sometimes this change merely intensifies what is already present in the Latin: in I met. vii Philosophy invokes "tu" only once, in line 20, whereas Wisdom addresses the whole meter to the narrator (14.9–25); likewise, in IV met. i, only line 27 has a second-person pronoun, but the OE meter employs the second person throughout (105.7–28). Compare also the second person references in both II pr. vii. 19 and 44.28–30.

69. Payne thinks that Wisdom has less authority than Philosophy and is merely an equal of the narrator, 116. Otten, on the other hand, writes that because Wisdom is in charge of goods, he has even more authority than his Latin counterpart, whereas the less important narrator can only submit and not argue with the superior Wisdom, 88–91. What Otten sees as narratorial submissiveness and Payne sees as a closer relationship are different readings of a less argumentative characterization.

70. "Tone in Alfred's Version of Augustine's *Soliloquies*," in *Studies in Earlier Old English Prose*, ed. Paul E. Szarmach (Albany: State University of New York Press, 1986), 47–85, at 48. David Pratt also writes, "In both [*Bo* and *Sol*] it is far easier for the reader to empathise with the respective human interlocutors, than with the Prisoner of circumstance in the original *Consolatio*," "The Political Thought," 276. I agree, with the caveat that the narrator of the *Bo* does not appear very sympathetic at the start; see following.

71. When Asser tells of young Alfred memorizing the book of poems, he mentions a *magister* who helps Alfred. Whether all of Asser's details are correct, the tale must have appeared plausible to the original audience: Alfred's mother encouraged and helped all her sons to learn, but Alfred also had a *magister* (chap. 23), as did Alfred's youngest son (chap. 75). Most teaching of children older than age seven at this time was done in external monastic or episcopal schools; see Pierre Riché, *Education et culture dans l'Occident barbare, VIe–VIIIe siècle* (Paris: Editions du Seuil, 1962), 511.

72. In I pr. iv. 20–2 the Latin narrator declares that he has been rightly accused of wanting the Senate's safety; perhaps Alfred took this as an admission of guilt, although he did not translate the passage. Peiper's *Vitae* I and VI, two of six *vitae* that often prefaced manuscripts of the *De cons*, say that Boethius sent the letters, and V declares that he defended liberty. Rudolfus Peiper, *Anicii Manlii Severini Boethii Philosophiae consolationis libri quinque* (Leipzig, GER: Teubner, 1881). Alfred may have seen some *vitae*; for details, see my *Fontes* entries for 7.1–24 and my "Unauthorized Biographies of Anicius Manlius Severinus Boethius," presented at the Alfredian Boethius Project First Annual Symposium, Oxford University, England, July 2003 (on the Boethius Project Web site at http://www.english.ox.ac.uk/boethius/Symposium2003.html).

73. As Rosemary Woolf comments, most martyrs suffer "spectacular tortures which are related zealously and in detail. These are borne by the martyrs with insolent contempt." "Saints' Lives," in *Continuations and Beginnings: Studies in Old English Literature*, ed. E. G. Stanley (London: Nelson, 1966), 37–66, at 43.

74. Mod addresses his answer (or lack thereof) to the second person dual because he is answering both Wisdom and "þæm woruldsælðum" ("those worldly goods," 19.11), which Wisdom has been impersonating.

75. For the benefits of a strategy of condescension, see Bourdieu, *Language and Symbolic Power*, 68–9.

76. See also the note on *Ælfric's Colloquy* following, which also features emotional involvement. The master sympathizes with the farmer's hard work (34), for instance.

77. Riché, *Écoles et Enseignement*, 527. Although masters might be abrupt and even harsh, students were expected to submit humbly, not to question or object (527–8).

78. For comparison, see *Ælfric's Colloquy*, ed. G. N. Garmonsway (New York: Appleton-Century-Crofts, 1966). Although the *Colloquy* has close ties to Latin learning, its tone is very different than that of classical dialogues. The master in both the OE and Latin versions fires questions rapidly at the students, but they answer in a leisurely way, and both sides of the conversation are personal. The master pauses to bargain with the fowler for a hawk (lines 132–6), and the participants argue over whose work is most important (217–33). The master receives permission to beat the students (7–10), yet the exchanges have a very un-Boethian informality.

79. *Language and Symbolic Power*, 80.

80. Alfred's alterations of the theme of friendship have also been noted by Allan J. Frantzen, *King Alfred*, Twayne's English Authors Series (Boston: Twayne, 1986), 54–6; Rebecca Thomas, "The Binding Force of Friendship in King Alfred's *Consolation* and *Soliloquies*," *Ball State University Forum* 29 (1988), 5–20, at 10; and Otten, 112–8. For friendship and alliance in Carolingian and Alfredian circles, see Janet L. Nelson, "Alfred's Carolingian Contemporaries," in *Alfred the Great: Papers from the Eleventh-Centenary Conferences*, ed. Timothy Reuter, Studies in Early Medieval Britain 3 (Aldershot, UK: Ashgate, 2003), 293-310.

81. Charlton T. Lewis and Charles Short note under the first sense, "friendship," "very freq. in Cic., occurring more than 200 times," *A Latin Dictionary* (Oxford, UK: Clarendon, 1879), 105.

82. See III pr. ii. 9/54.6–15 and the echo of this passage at 54.15–20; compare also 48.17–20 with II pr. viii. 7 and 49.33–50.3 with II met. viii. 22–7.

83. Otten, 112, 117.

84. Alfred's dual role as translator and king and his "kingly concerns" as expressed in the *Bo* have often been discussed, but treatments vary. For kingship as an image that Alfred develops, see Gatch, *Loyalties and Traditions*, 34, 37, and Waterhouse, "Tone in Alfred's Version," 68–71. For intersections between policy and translation, see Pratt, "The Political Thought." Others view Alfred's treatment more as an individual's meditations; see Janet Bately, "Boethius and King Alfred," in *Platonism and the English Imagination*, ed. Anna Baldwin and Sarah Hutton (Cambridge, UK: Cambridge University Press, 1994), 38–44, at 40; Nelson, "The Political Ideas," 145; Payne, especially 128–30; Otten, especially 100–18; and J. M. Wallace-Hadrill, *Early Germanic Kingship in England and on the Continent* (Oxford, UK: Clarendon, 1971), 144. Allen Frantzen adds a consideration of audience, *King Alfred*, 48.

85. *The Poetry of Boethius* (Chapel Hill: University of North Carolina Press, 1991), 85–6.

86. See especially *Language and Symbolic Power*, 77–8.

87. Malcolm Godden argues that Alfred keeps his persona separate from the figures of the narrators in the *Boethius* and *Soliloquies* and that Alfred's treatment of kingship is more what one would expect from a courtier. He suggests that perhaps courtiers did some of the actual translation, or they at least that they influenced Alfred's thinking on kingship strongly. See his "Player King: Identification and Self-Representation in King Alfred's Writings," in *Alfred the Great: Papers from the Eleventh-Centenary Conferences*, ed. Timothy Reuter, Studies in Early Medieval Britain 3 (Aldershot, UK: Ashgate, 2003), 137-50. I would argue that Alfred associates himself more closely

with his narrators than Godden would allow, and yet the *Boethius* clearly does consider kingship not only from the point of view of a king, but from the perspective of those who serve him.

88. The Latin has: "Quos quidem regia potestas saepe incolumis, saepe autem lapsa prosternit," III pr. v. 9. ("Indeed, royal power often ruins [intimates of the king] while it is still unharmed and often ruins them as it falls.")

89. Alfred omits references to two kings (Paulus and Perses) at II pr. ii. 12, probably because his audience would not be familiar with them and Alfred has already glossed other stories in this section, expanding the prose greatly. Other references are kept or explained.

90. Nero is the subject of II met. vi and III met. iv and is mentioned at III pr. v. 10.

91. At 34.22–7 he remarks on the conflict between virtue and office. Allusions to Tarquin (II pr. vi. 2), Busirides (II pr. vi. 10), Regulus (II pr. vi. 11), and the sword of Damocles (III pr. v. 6) become narratives (34.30–35.6, 36.28–37.5, 37.5–10, and 65.27–66.1, respectively).

92. Brian Donaghey thinks the substitution of Theodoric for Decoratus is a mistake, but notes that Schepss deems it a deliberate change. See Donaghey's "The Sources of King Alfred's Translation of Boethius' *De Consolatione Philosophiae*," *Anglia* 82 (1964): 23–57, at 39, and Georg Schepss, "Zu König Alfreds 'Boethius,'" *Archiv für das Studium der neueren Sprachen und Literaturen* 94 (1895): 149–60, at 155.

93. Jane Chance quotes the moral but insists that Alfred makes Orpheus a hero who is not condemned but who can be equated with wisdom. Alfred's ambivalence toward the figure seems to have misled her. See *Medieval Mythography: From Roman North Africa to the School of Charters, AD 433–1177* (Gainesville: University Press of Florida, 1994), 211–2.

94. Klaus Grinda reads the OE version of the story as an allegory of the danger of excessive love: "Zu Tradition und Gestaltung des Kirke-Mythos in König Alfreds *Boethius*," in *Motive und Themen in englischsprachiger Literatur als Indikatoren literaturgeschichtlicher Prozesse*, ed. Heinz-Joachim Müllenbrock and Alfons Klein (Tübingen, GER: Max Niemeyer Verlag, 1990), 1–23, at 16–20. See also David Pratt, "The Illnesses of King Alfred the Great," *ASE* 30 (2001): 39–90, esp. 80–83, and my chap. 1, n. 27.

95. Janet Nelson notes that Boethius's image of the mouse ruling other mice derides kingship in general; kings are as ridiculous and insignificant as the mouse. In Alfred's translation, however, "Lawgiving and tax-taking are not ludicrous in human communities precisely because a man with a discerning mind can exercise authority successfully" ("The Political Ideas," 146–7).

96. MS B has "ungecyndlicre," "unnatural." Either is plausible here.

97. Much work has been done on kingship in *Beowulf*, but the topic is still hotly debated. Some scholars assert that the poem lavishes praise on Beowulf and Hrothgar, giving a straightforward account of good kings (opposed by bad kings such as Heremod). Others read the kings as figures of pride. For a good recent treatment with references to both sides of the argument, see Scott DeGregorio, "Theorizing Irony in *Beowulf*: The Case of Hrothgar," *Exemplaria* 11 (1999), 309–43.

Chapter 4

1. *Language and Symbolic Power*, ed. John B. Thompson, trans. Gino Raymond and Matthew Adamson (Cambridge, MA: Harvard University Press, 1991), 40–54.

2. *Language and Symbolic Power*, 61.

3. *Language and Symbolic Power*, 66; emphasis in original.

4. *Language and Symbolic Power*, 76–7.

5. See Janet M. Bately, "The Literary Prose of King Alfred's Reign: Translation or Transformation?" Inaugural Lecture in the Chair of English Language and Medieval Literature delivered at University of London King's College on March 4, 1980; reprinted as *Old English Newsletter Subsidia*, vol. 10 (1984), 12. Allen Frantzen sees the change from Philosophy to Wisdom as the internalization of the dialogue to match the *Sol*; in his view, Wisdom is an aspect of the narrator's own mind, *King Alfred* (Boston: Twayne, 1986), 50. Yet Wisdom is explicitly not just part of the mind but "heofoncund Wisdom" (8.16), "*heavenly* Wisdom," and at 143.22–30, Wisdom makes an argument based on what God would do in certain situations. F. Anne Payne argues that Wisdom has much less authority and is closer to the narrator's level, but she has overlooked some of the details in Wisdom's description, especially those connecting Wisdom with God; see *King Alfred and Boethius: An Analysis of the Old English Version of the Consolation of Philosophy* (Madison: University of Wisconsin Press, 1968), esp. 113–22.

6. Paul writes "Christum Dei virtutem et Dei sapientiam" ("Christ the virtue of God and the wisdom of God," I Cor. 1:24). Wisdom is also a gift of the Spirit at I Cor 12:8; references to the Spirit of Wisdom could be taken as anticipating the third person of the Trinity.

7. Alfred translates this fairly closely; see 121.4–8.

8. *PC* 247.16–249.2 (Latin chap. 36.13–9) in a passage ultimately from Proverbs 1:24–6, 28.

9. Courcelle, *La Consolation de philosophie dans la tradition littéraire: antécédents et postérité de Boèce* (Paris: Etudes Augustiniennes, 1967), 33–46. The prologue to the *Grammatica* is in the *Patrologia Latina* 101, cols. 349–54.

10. All data on OE word frequencies in this chapter come from the online Corpus.

11. See Janet Bately's "Uþwita/Philosophus Revisited: A Reflection on OE Usage," in *Essays on Anglo-Saxon and Related Themes in Memory of Lynne Grundy*, ed. Jane Roberts and Janet Nelson (London: Centre for Late Antique and Medieval Studies, King's College London, 2000), 16–36.

12. See *Bo* 45.5, .10, .12, and .15 (all part of the same anecdote, II pr. vii. 20), where Alfred translates Boethius's "philosoph–" with "uðwit–." At 81.17, the word translates "philosophi" from Alcuin's *De anime ratione* (*PL* 101, 639A); see Malcolm Godden, "Anglo-Saxons on the Mind," in *Learning and Literature in Anglo-Saxon England*, ed. Michael Lapidge and Helmut Gneuss (Cambridge, UK: Cambridge University Press, 1985), 271–98, esp. 272–4. At 46.24 the word may translate "philosophus" if Alfred is using a gloss to II met. vii. 16; see my Appendix. The word is also used for Epicurus at 55.8; Seneca at 66.25; Aristotle at 73.1; Plato at 79.4 and

95.20; and Cicero at 143.5–7, although Boethius does not call them philosophers (III pr. ii. 12, III pr. v. 10, III pr. viii. 10, III pr. ix. 33, III met. xi. 15, and V pr. iv. 1, respectively). The word occurs in an added passage at 85.24.

13. Bosworth-Toller, 1145–6.

14. Bately, "Uþwita," 18.

15. "Uþwita," 20–1.

16. Bately finds that *uþwita* occurs primarily where a title would be expected. She suggests in her conclusion that the OE *uþwita* may predate conversion as a native title "for a member of that select band of people who were the repository of special knowledge," "Uþwita," 36.

17. For "pupillo tu eris adiutor" ("you shall be the helper for the poor child," 9:35).

18. The major difference between Alfred and his source text and these Old Testament texts is gender: *philosophia* and *sapientia* are both grammatically feminine and personified as female figures. Alfred's *Wisdom* is grammatically masculine although not always biologically male; Alfred almost always uses a masculine pronoun for Wisdom but also characterizes him as a mother. The feminine *Gesceadwisnes* would avoid this conflict. Wisdom is called "se Wisdom 7 seo Gesceadwisnes" at 9.15, 10.28, 21.18–9, 23.17, 27.14, and 29.15–6, but obviously Alfred is not using *Gesceadwisnes* here to make the gender feminine. The figure is simply "seo Gesceadwisnes" at 29.11, 33.20, 40.6–7, 41.7–8, 51.11, 51.18, and 52.28, but none of these passages invokes any other specifically feminine attribute or pronoun. Moreover, *Gesceadwisnes* had a restricted meaning, "discernment" (see, for instance, *Pastoral Care*, 65.21–2). Bosworth-Toller offers the Latin "discretio" as a synonym and defines the word as "I. Discretion, prudence" and "II. discrimination" (401). Alfred seems not to have thought of grammatical gender as being strongly related to sex (perhaps not surprising considering that the primary word for woman in OE, "wif," is neuter). He betrays no discomfort juxtaposing masculine nouns and pronouns with the words "fostermodor" and "modor," and he does not use *Gesceadwisnes* to avoid gender clashes; we have no indication he ever considered gender a problem. Alfred would also have found justification for a masculine Wisdom elsewhere in the Book of Wisdom. At the very start of the book, the feminine Wisdom is momentarily replaced by the spirits of discipline and wisdom, grammatically masculine in Latin (1:4–6). Later in the book a masculine craftsman teaches wisdom (7:21). The Wisdom Books offered precedent both for changing the gender of a personification and for equating wisdom and learning with male figures. The gender problem is even more marked in the *Sol*, where Augustine characterizes *sapientia* as a woman to be passionately loved and embraced, I.22. Alfred expands eight lines of suggestive Latin into an even more suggestive forty-two lines of OE, 75.16–77.2, while leaving the OE grammatical gender of *Wisdom* intact. Thus the male narrator looks at and embraces a male naked body in a text that later prohibits any kind of gender bending. That Alfred omits Augustine's passage condemning men who dress as women, II.30, is perhaps for the best.

19. V. E. Watts takes *confiteri* as "admit," *The Consolation of Philosophy*, rev. ed. (New York: Penguin Books, 1999), 113, and I think the meaning implied is "to oneself," not "to others." Yet this is not explicit in the Latin, leaving Alfred free to interpret it as he does.

20. *Boethius and Dialogue: Literary Method in the Consolation of Philosophy* (Princeton, NJ: Princeton University Press, 1985), 84, and see 213–4 for *De cons.*

21. Compare also "me inscitiam meam fuisse confessum" (III pr. xii. 3; "I confessed my own ignorance") and "Ic geman genog geara min agen dysig" (96.6; "I recall well enough my own foolishness").

22. Titus 3:3–4 offers similar hope. Compare the *Bo*'s attitude at 31.12–3 with the Paris Psalter 32.15. The way to God in the Psalms, as in the *Bo*, is to avoid being *dysig* (39.4). Moreover, as in the *Bo*, the narrator of the Psalms is sometimes *dysig* (37.5). There is hope for the *dysig.*

23. *Dysig* often appears in OE Psalter glosses on these words as well; see the online Corpus and Phillip Pulsiano, *Old English Glossed Psalters: Psalms 1–50*, Toronto Old English Series 11 (Toronto, ON: University of Toronto Press, 2001).

24. For Alfred's primary source, see *Le psautier romain et les autres anciens psautiers latins*, ed. Robert Weber, Collectanea Biblica Latina 10 (Rome: Abbaye Saint-Jerome, 1953). Patrick P. O'Neill identifies the *Romanum* as Alfred's main source, *King Alfred's Old English Prose Translation of the First Fifty Psalms* (Cambridge, MA: Medieval Academy of America, 2001), esp. 31–4.

25. The *Orosius* uses *dysig* twice, but with no Latin equivalent; the Latin text is also not concerned with *stulti* or *insipientes.* Forms of *dysig* occur in *Bede* at 76.4 (for I.27, p. 90); 112.9 (II.5, 152); 136.27 (II.13, 184); 136.30 (II.13, 184); 304.3 (IV.23, 374); 362.9 (IV.27, 432), all for forms of *stultus* except for 136.30 and 304. 3, which are for *superstitione.* The word appears at *Dial* 46.7 (for I.5.39); 111.17 (for II.4.7); 121.19 (for II.8.99); 143.20 (Hatton with no corresponding Latin); 174.24 (no corresponding Latin); 210.2 (for III.15.139); 266.23 (for IV.4.61); and 340.16 (for IV.53.5). (Those not specified as from the Hatton manuscript are from the Corpus.) Where Latin occurs, it is a form of *stultus. Dysig* occurs for *stultus* in the *Pastoral Care* at 203.19–205.2 (for III.6.14–8, from I Cor. 3:18); 220.9–11 (III.9.71–3; Prov. 29:11); 265.24–267.2 (III.13.39–42; Prov. 27:22); 306.11–4 (III.18.17–8; Prov. 15:7); and 387.34–5 (III.26.29; Prov. 1:32). It occurs for *improbus* ("unwise") at 371.6–7 (III.24.71–3); 405.18–23 (III.28.41–5); and 407.15–9 (III.28.71–4). It occurs for *insanientes* ("raging") at 355.16–7 (III.22.125–7); and for *bruta audentium corda* ("brute hearts of the listeners"), at 459.25–7 (III.39.20–1). David Pratt argues that Alfred's whole program, from literary works to artifacts such as the candle lanterns and Fuller Brooch, offers hope for the unlearned that they may gain wisdom, "Persuasion and Invention at the Court of King Alfred the Great," in *Court Culture in the Early Middle Ages: The Proceedings of the First Alcuin Conference*, ed. Catherine Cubitt (Turnhout, BEL: Brepols, 2003), 189–221.

26. The Latin is similar; see II.13, 184.

27. *Language and Symbolic Power* 151–9; see also my chaps. 2 and 3.

28. Several scholars have noted differences between Alfred's views of worldly goods and Boethius's: see Payne, 62; Thomas A. Shippey, "Wealth and Wisdom in King Alfred's *Preface* to the Old English *Pastoral Care*," *English Historical Review* 94 (1979): 346–55; W. F. Bolton, "How Boethian Is Alfred's *Boethius*?" in *Studies in Earlier Old English Prose*, ed. Paul E. Szarmach (Albany: State University of New York Press, 1986), 153–68, at 156; Katherine Proppe, "King Alfred's *Consolation of Philosophy*," *Neuphilologische Mitteilungen* 74 (1973): 646–48; and Janet L. Nelson,

"Wealth and Wisdom: The Politics of Alfred the Great," in *Kings and Kingship*, ed. J. Rosenthal, State University of New York Acta, 11 (Binghamton, NY: CEMERS, State University of New York at Binghamton, 1986), 31–52.

29. *The Fate of Fortune in the Early Middle Ages: The Boethian Tradition* (New York: Brill, 1988), 81.

30. See *Bo* 20.7–17. Payne, 63, and Otten, *König Alfreds Boethius*, Studien zur englischen Philologie, neue Folge no. 3 (Tübingen, GER: Max Niemeyer Verlag, 1964), 23–4, also note the change, and Frakes emphasizes it further. See also David Robert Pratt, "The Political Thought of Alfred the Great" (Ph.D. diss., University of Cambridge, UK, 1999), 279.

31. Frakes, *Fate of Fortune*, 81.

32. "Frumenti uini et olei sui multiplicati sunt" ("the fruit of the vine and his oil are multiplied," 4:8).

33. Otten, 31. See also 30–5 and 60–70 in his chap. 1, "Zum Inhalt."

34. Bourdieu, *Language and Symbolic Power*, 121.

35. See my discussion of Gregory's influence on Alfred in chap. 2. Milton McC. Gatch sees the emphasis on duty in the *Bo* as a crucial shift, *Loyalties and Traditions: Man and His World in Old English Literature* (New York: Pegasus, 1976), 111. See also my "Influence of Gregory the Great on the Alfredian Social Imaginary," in *Rome and the North: The Early Reception of Gregory the Great in Germanic Europe*, ed. Rolf H. Bremmer (Leuven, BEL: Peeters, 2001), 67–81.

36. Calhoun, "Habitus, Field, and Capital: The Question of Historical Specificity," in *Bourdieu: Critical Perspectives*, ed. Craig Calhoun, Edward LiPuma, and Moishe Postone (Cambridge, UK: Polity Press, 1993), 61–88, esp. 72–82.

37. Astell comments that Gregory feels even moderate sadness over lost goods is allowable; *Job, Boethius, and Epic Truth* (Ithaca, NY: Cornell University Press, 1994), 93.

38. Alfred goes out of his way to deny that they are the one good. Philosophy concludes at III pr. ii. 20 that the fact that all seek partial goods shows them to be good. Alfred seems to fear that his readers will mistake the partial good for the true because he drops the idea that in loving the partial goods people are in fact loving the complete good and adds a clear warning that true good is not to be found in this life; see 56.24–30.

39. This speech also presents the model of the three orders; on this topic, see Timothy E. Powell's "The 'Three Orders' of Society in Anglo-Saxon England," *ASE* 23 (1994): 103–32.

40. The *Moralia in Job* was popular both in England and on the Continent, and Helmut Gneuss finds three seventh- or eighth-century, probably Northumbrian, manuscripts or fragments (840.5, 858, and 865.5), one late eighth-century southern English or Mercian manuscript (946.5), and possibly a later-ninth-century manuscript (564: "perh. E France, prov. England before 1100 possible"); *Handlist of Anglo-Saxon Manuscripts: A List of Manuscripts and Manuscript Fragments Written or Owned in England up to 1100* (Tempe, AZ: Arizona Center for Medieval and Renaissance Studies, 2001). If Alfred knew the *Moralia*, he might note that Gregory reads these passages both as an allegory of the Church's charity (XIX.29–31 and 38–45, XXVI.64–77) and an example of how just men behave (XX.32–7); *Moralia in*

Job, ed. Marcus Adriaen, Corpus Christianorum Series Latina 143–143B (Turnhout, BEL: Brepols, 1979 and 1985).

41. 141–7 and 387–93 in the OE, chaps. 19 and 50 in the Latin.

42. The Latin has a different emphasis: "Sed quia auctore Deo ad religionis reuerentiam omne iam praesentis saeculi culmen inclinatur, sunt nonnulli qui intra sanctam Ecclesiam per speciem regiminis gloriam affectant honoris . . ." ("But because with God as author all the height of this present era is turned to reverence for religion, there are no few who in holy Church attain the glory of honor through the appearance of governance . . ." 1.10–3). Gregory's main point is that the honor now given to religion can attract the wrong people to office; his comment that religion is so honored is secondary. Alfred does pick up the main point immediately following the previous quotation, but he has separated the secondary point and made it a primary one as well.

43. For the Latin, see 19.58–68; perhaps from Paul, who in I Timothy 3.7 says that bishops must have good reputations.

44. Compare also II pr. v. 6 with 28.10–21. Otten writes that Alfred reads *uox* as *fama* to present a more positive view of fame, 102. Although the subject of the comparison, as in the source text, is primarily discourse or the word, Alfred links it at the start of this passage to reputation or fame. The contrast with violence underscores the power of words.

45. Despite the qualifiers, Proppe reads the passage as an attack on fame in general, but she notes that fame is praised at 139.7–15. She concludes:

> Alfred is using the old vocabulary of eagerness for fame and pride to exhort his people to study. Never mind the contradictions, it is rather a question of compromise. My purpose here has not been to point out petty inconsistencies but to show the semi-emergent Roman conception of Christianity, rationality, humility and renunciation lying side by side with tenacious old Anglo-Saxon emotions. (648)

46. As Otten notes, 108.

47. Asser asserts Alfred's importance from his birth, presenting him as the heir apparent despite his older brothers. Asser's lists of Welsh kings (chap. 80) and other foreigners who submitted to Alfred (76), and of his ties with the pope (71) and Carolingian rulers (70), all underscore Alfred's stature. Asser describes Alfred's use of a long list of riches in chaps. 98–103.

48. Alfred does not translate this passage directly, but he has already moderated Augustine's previous absolute rejection of these things into a rejection of excess.

49. *Language and Symbolic Power*, 76–7. Proppe believes that Alfred despised worldly goods and made compromises based on calculations of audience needs and desires (646–8), but his personal stand cannot be known with certainty. And, as Bourdieu reminds us, early experiences have a lasting effect on the habitus. Alfred may well have shared his contemporaries' high estimation of riches, at least in part. See Bourdieu and L. J. D. Wacquant, *An Invitation to Reflexive Sociology* (Chicago: University of Chicago Press, 1992), 133.

50. Kurt Otten attributes the image to commentaries, but his illustrative quotation, "lumina eius scilicet *cordis* eius" ("his eye, namely, of his *heart*"), does not use quite the same image; 146, emphasis added. For further discussion of commentaries, see my Appendix.

51. See 54.18–21 in the OE (I.5 in the Latin), 66.6–9 (I.12–13), 67.1–5 (I.13), 71–2 (I.16–7), and 76.25–79 (I.23).

52. For other passages where Alfred translates "eye" as "mind's eye," see Psalm 12.4 in the OE (also 12.4 in the Latin), 13.8 (13.3), and 16.10 (16.11). The Psalter glosses in Pulsiano, *OE Glossed Psalters*, merely translate *oculos*; they do not explicate the metaphor.

53. For straightforward eye imagery without explicit mention of the mind, see for instance *Regula pastoralis* 29.8–9 (Latin I.1.44), 29.16 (I.1.51), 65.5–9 (I.11.13–6), 413.15 (III.29.12), and 415.27 (III.29.58).

54. Alfred translates the first as "modes eagum," (270.3), the second as "eage heora modes" (272.2), and again as "eagan þæs modes" (272.4) when Alfred repeats the phrase instead of using a pronoun.

55. Bosworth-Toller's definition IIa. for *seon* is the metaphorical sense of "to see," and III. is "to see, perceive, discern, understand" (864–5).

56. Lerer argues that references to hunting in the letter that prefaces Alfred's translation of the *Regula pastoralis* and Asser's *Life* "draw on a set of images developed in the *Consolation of Philosophy*," but they are actually given very little space in the source text. He does not supply any references but probably includes IV met. iv. 2–6 (discussed following); *Literacy and Power in Anglo-Saxon Literature* (Lincoln: University of Nebraska Press, 1991), 78.

57. Charlton T. Lewis and Charles Short define *peto*: "I. To fall upon any thing. A. Lit. 1. In a hostile sense, to rush at, attack, assault, assail; to let fly at, aim a blow at, thrust at, etc.... 2. Without the notion of hostility... II. Trop. A. To attack, assail one with any thing... B. To demand, seek, require...." These notions can be associated with hunting, but the verb does not carry with it the necessary connotations of hunting or tracking that *vestigo* or *venari* would. *A Latin Dictionary* (Oxford, UK: Clarendon, 1879), 1364–5.

58. 41.16–8 (II pr. vi. 3); 78.19–20 (III pr. ix. 28); 99.21–5 (III pr. xii. 25); 101.6–13 (III pr. xii. 38); 109.6–8 (IV pr. ii. 31); 118.9–17 (IV pr. iv. 11); 118.18–20 (IV pr. iv. 12); and 120.19–20 (IV pr. iv. 23). In four of these Latin passages, terms such as *rationes* or *necessarium* appear (III pr. xii. 25, III pr. xii. 38, IV pr. iv. 11, and IV pr. iv. 12); hunting imagery helps Alfred avoid technical language.

59. The Latin in this passage contains technical language as well, all of which Alfred omits. For other changes to hunting imagery, see 36.4–6 (II pr. vi. 5); 131.20–1 (IV pr. vi. 22); and 135.12–5 (IV pr. vi. 56).

60. For other additions of hunting imagery, see 27.20–1, 72.9–13, and 121.19–29.

61. Lerer explains the imagery in terms of Alfred's defense of himself and of the activity of reading from charges of effeminacy or weakness (see *Literacy and Power*, chap. 2: "The Beautiful Letters: Authority and Authorship in Asser and King Alfred," 61–96, esp. 78). However, whether the victorious war leader Alfred, or the

activity of reading, faced such charges is not clear. Lerer cites Procopius's history of the Gothic wars for "old Germanic mistrust" of education (Lerer's footnote 21, 216–7), but that is far removed from Alfred's time and place. For Shippey, see 348.

62. See also 14:22–3.

63. Why Alfred omits the passage is unclear. It is very near the end of the work. Alfred's haste to finish the *Bo* can be seen in the text both explicitly in Wisdom's desire to finish (148.4–6), and implicitly in the increasing omissions. Perhaps as he neared the end of the *Regula pastoralis*, an even longer work, he also omitted more.

64. The two dozen uses of forms of *–hunt–* and *–spyr–* in laws, charters, and the Anglo-Saxon Chronicle can only begin to suggest the importance of hunting for a noble Anglo-Saxon male.

65. "Evidence for Knowledge of Latin Literature," 43.

66. Samuel Kroesch, "The Semantic Development of OE *Cræft*," *Modern Philology* 26 (1928–9): 433–41, sketches the word's overall development. Susan J. Hitch treats it briefly in "Alfred's *Cræft*: Imagery in Alfred's Version of Augustine's Soliloquies," *Journal of the Department of English, University of Calcutta* (1986–7): 130–47; see esp. 144–5. Peter Clemoes treats the term in more detail in "King Alfred's Debt to Vernacular Poetry: The Evidence of *ellen* and *cræft*," in *Words, Texts and Manuscripts: Studies in Anglo-Saxon Culture Presented to Helmut Gneuss on the Occasion of His 65th Birthday*, ed. Michael Korhammer with Karl Reichl and Hans Sauer (Cambridge, UK: Brewer, 1992), 213–38. Elizabeth Baldwin Stevens Girsch's "A Semantic Analysis of the Old English *Cræft* and Related Words" (Ph.D. diss., University of Toronto, ON, 1988) offers an extensive study of the word's long history. The remainder of this chapter is adapted with permission from Cambridge University Press from my "Power, Skill and Virtue in the Old English *Boethius*," *ASE* 26 (1997): 81–108.

67. *Outline of a Theory of Practice*, trans. Richard Nice (Cambridge, UK: Cambridge University Press, 1977), 21.

68. *Language and Symbolic Power*, 141.

69. *DOE*, Fascicle C (Toronto, 1988), 837. All *DOE* citations in this chapter are from this fascicle.

70. *DOE*, 837–8. Subdivisions of definitions will be mentioned as they arise. These definitions indicate the range of meanings but not how common each was because the senses are in logical order, not order of frequency (personal communication from Antonette diPaolo Healey, 1995).

71. The *DOE* lists "ca. 650" occurrences, 837. My count differs partly because I consider some variants between manuscripts of the same text different enough to be counted separately and partly because some occurrences that appear as two separate words in the Corpus are listed as compounds in the *Dictionary*, and so they are entered under a different headword (personal communication from Antonette diPaolo Healey, 1995). My work on the word *cræft* was first done with *The Microfiche Concordance to Old English*, ed. Antonette diPaolo Healey et al. (Toronto, ON: PIMS, 1980), and I have updated it using the newer online Corpus.

72. *Ælfric's Lives of Saints*, ed. Walter W. Skeat, EETS 76, 82, 114, 94 (London: N. Trübner, 1881–1900). More specialized meanings account for many

occurrences, however: "I.c.i: medicine, medical recipe," 837, is employed forty-two times in *Bald's Leechbook* alone.

73. It occurs repeatedly in the *Orosius* and the metrical *Solomon and Saturn.* Although *Solomon and Saturn* cannot be dated precisely, general consensus places it at the end of the ninth century or start of the tenth century; see Robert J. Menner, *The Poetical Dialogues of Solomon and Saturn* (New York: Modern Languages Association, 1941), 16–7, and ASPR VI, lix–lx. See also Patrick P. O'Neill's "On the Date, Provenance and Relationship of the 'Solomon and Saturn' Dialogues," *ASE* 26 (1997): 139–68, which links the texts to Alfred's circle.

74. Kroesch distinguishes mental and physical skills and argues that the former sense came first (440), but his arguments rely on unsupported assumptions about dating and his evidence is thin. Girsch argues that the distinction between physical and mental skills is not productive (89–90). Bourdieu argues more generally that mental and physical labor are not strongly separated until the modern era; see *The Rules of Art: Genesis and Structure of the Literary Field,* trans. Susan Emanuel (Stanford, CA: Stanford University Press, 1996), 290–312.

75. *Dictionary,* 841. The OE and the Latin are identical in Modern English both here and in the next quotation.

76. *The Sermones Catholici or Homilies of Ælfric,* ed. Benjamin Thorpe (London, 1844–6; reprint New York: Johnson Reprint Corp., 1971).

77. Alfred's works contain the vast majority of occurrences of the word *cræft* in this sense, both in its broadest definition and in its first three subdivisions: "3.a.i. *gastlic cræft* 'spiritual strength, spiritual discipline'"; "3.a.ii. *gecynde cræft* 'natural disposition'"; "3.b. in plural: (*gode*) *cræftas* rendering *virtutes* 'virtue.'" *Virtus* itself, of course, is not identical to modern "virtue." Lewis and Short define it in their *Latin Dictionary*: "manliness, manhood . . . strength, vigor; bravery, courage; aptness, capacity; worth, excellence, virtue, etc.," 1997. The Latin *virtus* thus overlaps with other senses of *cræft*: power and talent. Late-antique and early-medieval works tend to use *virtus* more in its moral sense than for manliness or physical strength or courage (see Kroesch on its use in Christian literature, 437); in Gregory's *Dialogi* and *Regula pastoralis,* the word clearly means right conduct, and in the *De cons,* the primary sense is also that of moral and intellectual rectitude. The overlap between multiple senses of *virtus* and *cræft* makes it all the more surprising that Alfred is the only one to translate the former by the latter. Other uses for "spiritual or mental merit" occur in "The Death of Edgar," the metrical portion of the Paris Psalter, *Andreas,* and *Daniel.*

78. *DOE,* 843–4. Kroesch, while saying "it regularly translates the Lat. *virtus,*" also gives examples only from the *Pastoral Care* and *Bo,* 437. Girsch is inconsistent on the matter. Throughout she deems the usage typical of Alfred (esp. 124, 799–800). She mentions other writers employing the usage, but her specific examples are unpersuasive, and for each she offers an alternative translation (see 124, 301, 363–4, 471–2, 516, and 767). Girsch herself seems unconvinced of these readings, for she concludes that only Alfred and the *Dial* have the special usage (800)—but the body of the dissertation never mentions this usage in the *Dial.* No convincing evidence exists that any other OE writer used the word *cræft* to mean "virtue" or translate *virtus.*

79. They occur in poetry, but Ælfric displays particular fondness for these senses, using them more than two dozen times in his homilies and saints' lives. See Girsch, esp. 262–311, on Ælfric.

80. Girsch notes that Alfred avoids negative senses of the word, in contrast to most prose writers and even the translators and writers working under his patronage (see 256 and 772–3).

81. It appears only once in poetry, in *Christ and Satan; mægen* and *miht* seem to have been preferred in verse.

82. Ælfric's *Grammar* and Byrhtferth's *Manual* contain most of these; the others come primarily from glosses on Latin texts.

83. The usage appears in so few texts that dating it conclusively is difficult; the earliest appearances seem to be in the *Martyrology* and Alfred's works, and most come from later OE. The sense may have originated in translation, spreading only to a few works with strong ties to Latin, and it does not seem ever to have been highly influential.

84. For an example of "power," see 108.27–9; for physical and mental skill, 40.12–41.1, 46.17–20 and 72.13–15; for God's creation, 80.22–4. Other examples could be given as well. Girsch notes that "Alfred uses nearly the full range of *cræft*" (158).

85. *The Dictionary* mentions only the use of plural forms of *cræft* to represent plural forms of *virtus*, but Alfred uses the singular forms for virtue as well. In 62.21–4, 133.21–7, and 134.2–4 he translates a singular form of *virtus* with the singular form *cræft*. Several of the additions also seem to have the meaning "virtue" for a singular form of *cræft*, as at 62.24, "Swa swa wisdom is se hehsta *cræft*" ("Just as wisdom is the highest virtue"). More than half of the occurrences of *cræft* in the *Bo* are not translations of any specific word from the Latin. Of those that are, *virtus* is the most common Latin word, translated by *cræft* fifteen times. Other words *cræft* translates are *vis*, which *cræft* translates four times, and *potentia* and *vigor*, twice each. *Cræft* translates *virtus* in these passages: 10.19–21, 22.6–10, 44.31–45.3, 45.7–8, 61.7–9, 62.21–4, 69.11–5, 104.4–9, 104.18, 108.29–30, 133.7–8, 133.21–7, 134.2–4, 138.21–4, 149.5–7. It appears for *vis* at 18.5–11, 106.1–4, 108.27–9, and 110.1–4; *potentia* at 37.10–13 and 110.19–22; *vigor* at 116.29–30 and 116.30–2. It is added to 30.7–10, 30.22–3, 35.13–5, 37.30–38.2, 38.9–11, 40.12–4, 40.14–5, 40.18, 40.25–7, 40.27–41.1, 41.1–3, 45.22–4, 46.17–20, 54.20–2, 61.9–15, 62.24–6, 62.29–31, 63.29–64.2, 69.1–4, 79.4–6, 72.6–13, 72.13–5, 80.22–4, 81.23–5, 87.7–9, 93.3–6, 109.3, 10.6–8, 122.1–4, 122.4–10, 127.10–4, 132.9–10, 132.10–3, 141.13–6. By contrast, the two instances of *cræft* in the *Bede* translate *peritia* (304.10) and *ars* (328.8). In *Or*, it translates *vis* three times (31.2–10, 34.21–4, and 42.22–4), *virile* (33.4–9), *victoria* (51.24–5), and *ingenio* (103.8–12) once each; eight times it does not translate any Latin word (23.27–30, 30.12–6, 30.24–8, 30.33–31.2, 33.11–2, 42.28–30, 51.19–24, and 85.12–9). In the *GD* the word translates *ars* six times (counting one Hatton occurrence with its corresponding Cotton occurrence), 62.7–16, Hatton 73.28–74.6 and Cotton 73.29–74.7, 180.21–2, 180.22–4, 342.3–7, and 342.11–4. It translates *arx* once (188.16–9). (Kroesch suggests that the translation for *arce* arose from the misreading *arte*, or from a flawed exemplar; a Verona manuscript of Gregory's works has *arte* here. 440, fn. 2.) David Yerkes's *Two Versions of*

Wærferth's Translation of Gregory's Dialogues: An Old English Thesaurus (Toronto, ON: University of Toronto Press, 1979), supports my findings that no systematic substitution among *cræft, mægen*, and *miht* occurs in that text.

86. *Cræft* occurs for *virtus* in these passages: 41.9–10, 53.5–8, 59.11–4, 163.1–3, 163.5–9 (in the same passage it is used again with *mægen*), 220.25–222.3, 222.18–22, 251.2–6 (twice), 289.12–4, 291.9–12, 307.10–3, 345.7–10, 347.9–13, 347.15–7, 359.18–21, 359.21–3, 359.23–4 (twice), 383.36–385.5, 385.7–9, 433.27–8, 447.15–7, 463.21–2, 463.23–6, 463.23–6, 465.6–9, 465.20–2, 465.30–3, 467.8–10, and 467.10–4. It is an addition to the text in these: 226.5–6, 227.5–10, 231.7–8, 231.9–10, 269.2–4, 345.23–347.2, 385.26–9, 409.19–22, 463.5–9 (twice; also in the same passage, *mægen & cræft* appears for *virtus*), and 463.11–5. Alfred is less consistent in the Psalms, where he uses the word *cræft* for *virtus* but prefers *mægen*. He uses the doublet *mægen 7 cræft* for *virtus* twice in Psalm 17 (17.31 and 17.37) and *mægen* alone several times (20.1, 30.12, 32.14, 45.1, 45.6, 45.10, and 48.6). He uses *cræft* alone once (32.15). For Alfred's authorship of the text, see O'Neill, *King Alfred's Old English Prose Translation of the First Fifty Psalms*, 73–96, and his references. Without knowing when Alfred worked on the *Psalter*, we cannot tell whether it was before or after he had established a consistent usage in the *Bo*.

87. Twenty times *mægen* alone translates *virtus*: 83.9–13, 83.22–85.1, 87.3–5, 87.21–5, 95.15–9, 101.1–3, 149.3–4, 163.14–8, 163.23–4, 215.15–21 (twice), 220.18–22, 233.14–6, 311.9–10, 311.12–3, 313.3–6, 315.8–12, 321.25–323.3, 323.3–6, and 443.3–6. In seven other passages, *mægen 7 cræft* together render *virtus*: 27.15–9, 41.11–3, 163.5–9, 463.5–7, 463.15–9, 465.3–6, and 467.5–6.

88. *Mægen* appears for *virtus* at 21.10. *Cræft* appears for *virtus* in: 10.19–21, 22.6–10, 44.31–45.3, 45.7–8, 61.7–9, 62.21–4, 69.11–5, 104.4–9, 104.18–24, 108.29–30, 133.7–8, 133.21–7, 134.2–4, 138.21–4, and 149.5–7.

89. Clemoes, 236.

90. Bosworth-Toller defines the word primarily as "custom, usage," and so forth (1042–3). J. R. Clark Hall gives "usage, custom, habit, conduct, disposition . . . (in pl.) virtues, (good) manners, morals, morality," *A Concise Anglo-Saxon Dictionary*, with supplement by Herbert D. Meritt (Toronto, ON: University of Toronto Press, 1991), 356. Ferdinand Holthausen includes "Tugenden" in his translations for the plural, *Altenglisches Etymologisches Wörterbuch* (Heidelberg, GER: Carl Winters Universitätsbuchhandlung, 1934), 361. The definition Bosworth-Toller gives for *unþeaw* includes "vice" (1132). See also Alfred's own Preface to the *Regula pastoralis*: "ðone naman anne we lufodon ðætte we Cristne wæren, & swiðe feawe ða ðeawas" (5.6–8; "the name alone we loved, that we were Christians, and very few of the virtues"). In the *Regula pastoralis* he occasionally uses *ðeaw* for *virtus*; see 81.24, where he substitutes *weorcum 7 ðeawum* for *morum uirtute*, and 149.2 and 149.4, where *gode ðeawas* translates *virtutes*; see also 18.5–6.

91. See Hans Käsmann, *Studien zum kirchlichen Wortschatz des Mittelenglischen 1100–1350: Ein Beitrag zum Problem der Sprachmiscung* (Tübingen, GER: Niemeyer, 1961), 243; Clemoes, 224–6. Helmut Gneuss, *Lehnbildungen und Lehnbedeutungen im Altenglishen* (Berlin: Erich Schmidt Verlag, 1955), offers *megen, mægen* as the usual translation for *virtus* and does not mention *cræft* (72); he also discusses *mægen* and *miht* as translations for *virtus* in "The Origin of Standard

Old English and Æthelwold's School at Winchester," *ASE* 1 (1972), 63–83, especially 76–9. See also Mechtild Gretsch, *Die Regula Sancti Benedicti in England* (Munich: Wilhelm Fink Verlag, 1973), 347–9. Bosworth-Toller includes the definition "virtue" for these latter two words and gives examples of each as translations; *mægen*, 655; *meaht*, 672–3. Clark Hall also gives "virtue" as a definition for these (see 224 for *mægen* and 237 for *miht*). Holthausen gives "Tüchtigkeit" as one of the definitions for both (210 for *mægen*, 216 for *meaht*). The online Corpus also shows these to be the common translations.

92. See Pulsiano, *OE Glossed Psalters*, xxi; Neil R. Ker, *Catalogue of Manuscripts Containing Anglo-Saxon*, reprint with supplement (Oxford, UK: Oxford University Press, 1990), item 203; and Gneuss, *Handlist*, item 381. *Mæht* or *miht* occurs more than 175 times and the pair *mægen 7 miht* translates *virtus* another three dozen times. Occasionally other terms appear, such as *strengð* and pairings of *strengð* with *mægen* or *miht*.

93. Only once does he use it to translate *uirtus* in *Bo*, at 21.10–1; it occurs for *fortitudo* at 38.2–4 and for *potentia* at 67.4–6. The other four occurrences of the word do not correspond to any Latin word (41.9–12, 53.16–8, 112.30–1, and 147.10–3), but context makes it clear that each means *strength* or *power* (as in the first definition of *cræft*) rather than *virtue*.

94. *Mægen* is overwhelmingly used in these two works for *virtus*: forty-seven of its fifty-two occurrences in *Bede* are for *virtus* (along with three for *vis* and one each for *auxiliarii* and *signum*), as are twenty-six of the thirty-two occurrences in the Hatton manuscript of *GD* and eighty-six of the one hundred fifteen in the Cotton manuscript. (Most Hatton occurrences are duplicated by Cotton occurrences.) In *Or*, *mægen* occurs only six times, once each for *virtus*, *auxilium*, and *strenus*, and three times without a Latin equivalent but where the word clearly means virtue. *Miht* occurs once in *Bo*, four times in *GD*, three times in *Or*, and twice in *Bede*, but never for *virtus* and always in the more general sense of power; it was apparently not considered a synonym for *virtus* by these translators as it was by some of the Psalter glossators.

95. See *Language and Symbolic Power*, 52–65, and my treatment in earlier chapters.

96. Clemoes, 232.

97. "Alfred's *Cræft*," 145.

98. For more details, see Allen J. Frantzen, *The Literature of Penance in Anglo-Saxon England* (New Brunswick, NJ: Rutgers University Press, 1983).

99. Clemoes, 237.

100. Clemoes gives as evidence primarily *Elene* and *Guthlac*. Only *Elene* even approaches Alfred's usage, but there it seems clear that *cræft* is merely the first step to true wisdom and that it can even be a hindrance. Judas possesses *cræft* long before the poem begins, but only after threats, torture, and conversion does he use that *cræft* properly. Elene and Constantine use theirs properly, but again, the faculty seems to be an intellectual one and not virtue itself. *Guth* uses *cræft* to indicate strength of mind, a unified intellectual and martial strength. Alfred's conception of *cræft* may have been partly inspired by poems, but it goes well beyond the poetic tradition.

101. As noted previously, *virtus* itself can mean physical strength, and the word carries these implications even though Boethius does not explore them fully, using *potentia* for power instead. Moreover, as Ann Astell notes, at IV pr. vii. 19 Philosophy gives an etymology deriving *virtus* from *vis*, virtue from strength; *Job, Boethius*, 43.

102. The Latin word that most closely matches *cræft* in this passage is *uiribus*, but a simple translation of *cræft* here is difficult.

103. Dismissing the distinction between *anweald* and *cræft* in this passage as insignificant, or saying that this is merely a doublet or word pair, might be tempting. Yet formally it does not look like a doublet, and not all doublets are tautologous; see chap. 3.

104. For the sources of details in this passage and further references, see my entries in "The Sources of King Alfred's Old English Version of Boethius's *De consolatione philosophiae* (Cameron B.9.3)," 2001, *Fontes*. Alfred was highly selective in his borrowings here, crafting diverse sources into a concise elaboration on Boethius's text unparalleled in any one source.

105. The compound *drycræft* does occur three times, 98.102, 116.14, and 116.27, and *drycræftig* once, at 116.3, but the simplex *cræft* is never used for trick or vice in the text.

106. This idea may seem strange and even un-Christian, but Alfred may have found precedent in Augustine's *De civitate Dei*, ed. Bernhard Dombart and Alfonse Kalb, 2 vols. CCSL 47–8 (Turnhout, BEL: Brepols, 1955), X.1.273: "... qui verus est Deus facitque suos cultores deos" ("who is true God and makes his worshippers gods"); see Otten, 85–6.

107. Clemoes, 232–3.

108. On this passage, see also Proppe, esp. 647–8, and Otten, 101.

109. Bourdieu, *Language and Symbolic Power*, 141.

110. *Language and Symbolic Power*, 142, emphasis in original.

111. Alfred softens the passage to say that goods come "sometimes" to the wicked instead of "more richly" to them.

112. *Language and Symbolic Power*, 143.

113. O'Daly, *The Poetry of Boethius* (Chapel Hill: University of North Carolina Press, 1991), 44.

114. Hitch, "Alfred's *Cræft*," 144.

115. Augustine might also be cited, but his influence is more problematic; see my discussion of Alfred's knowledge of Augustine in chap. 3.

116. Here *cræft* translates *ars* (see 1.4–5 in the Latin).

117. Nor can the influence of Gregory's imagery be discounted. The familiar image of the shepherd pervades the *Regula pastoralis* and links physical, mental, and spiritual care.

118. For Carolinginan education, see Pierre Riché, *Education et culture dans l'Occident barbare, VIe–VIIIe siècle* (Paris: Editions du Seuil, 1962), and the essays in *Carolingian Culture: Emulation and Innovation*, ed. Rosamond McKitterick (Cambridge, UK: Cambridge University Press, 1994). For Alfred's use and adaptation of Carolingian models, see Janet L. Nelson, "Power and Authority at the Court of Alfred," in *Essays on Anglo-Saxon and Related Themes in Memory of Lynne*

Grundy, ed. Jane Roberts and Janet Nelson (London: Centre for Late Antique and Medieval Studies, King's College London, 2000), 311–37, and Pratt, "The Political Thought."

119. See esp. Janet L. Nelson, "The Political Ideas of Alfred of Wessex," in *Kings and Kingship in Medieval Europe*, ed. Anne J. Duggan (London: Centre for Late Antique and Medieval Studies, King's College London, 1993), 129. For Alfred's use of Carolingian precedents, see Frantzen, *King Alfred*, 20–1. For his recruitment of Continental scholars, see Simon Keynes and Michael Lapidge's "Introduction," in *Alfred the Great: Asser's Life of King Alfred and Other Contemporary Sources* (New York: Penguin, 1983), 26–8. Alfred P. Smyth treats Carolingian connections at length in his *King Alfred the Great* (Oxford, UK: Oxford University Press, 1995). W. F. Bolton, "How Boethian Is Alfred's *Boethius*?" in *Studies in Earlier Old English Prose*, ed. Paul E. Szarmach (Albany: State University of New York Press, 1986), 153–68, maintains that Alfred was well aware of the details of the program and particularly Alcuin's role in it, and specifically imitated the thinking of his expatriate countryman. See also Paul E. Szarmach, "Alfred, Alcuin, and the Soul," in *Manuscript, Narrative, Lexicon: Essays on Literary and Cultural Transmissions in Honor of Whitney F. Bolton*, ed. Robert Boenig and Kathleen Davis (Lewisburg, PA: Bucknell University Press, 2000), 127–48.

120. MGH, *Legum Sectio II: Capitularia Regum Francorum*, Tomus I, ed. Alfredus Boretius (Hanover, GER: Supersis Bibliopolii Hahniani, 1883), 58.

121. MGH, 79.

122. MGH, 79.

123. Hitch, "Alfred's *Cræft*," 144.

124. *Language and Symbolic Power*, 52.

125. See Nelson, "Power and Authority"; and Keynes and Lapidge's "Introduction" to *Alfred the Great*, 16–8, and (in the same volume) Alfred's Will, 174–7, which is somewhat defensive about the settlement of the inheritance. For the OE text of Alfred's Will see Florence E. Harmer, *Select English Historical Documents of the Ninth and Tenth Centuries* (Cambridge, UK: Cambridge University Press, 1914), 15–9. See also the *Anglo-Saxon Chronicle* entry for 900 in Janet M. Bately, ed., *The Anglo-Saxon Chronicle: A Collaborative Edition*, vol. 3: MS A (Cambridge, UK: Brewer, 1986): the revolt of Alfred's nephew probably occurred because of resentment over what was seen as Alfred's usurpation in making his own sons heirs.

126. *Rules*, 261–2, emphasis in original.

Conclusion

1. The *PC* has been studied more extensively than the Prose Psalms of the Paris Psalter. See especially Simeon Potter, "The Old English *Pastoral Care*," *Transactions of the Philological Society* 46 (1947): 114–25; William H. Brown, Jr., "Method and Style in the Old English *Pastoral Care*," *Journal of English and Germanic Philology* 68 (1969): 666–84, and his *Syntax of King Alfred's Pastoral Care* (The Hague: Mouton, 1970); Roy Ray Moye, Jr., "Alfred's Method of

Translation in the Old English Pastoral Care" (Ph.D. diss., University of North Carolina at Chapel Hill, 1993); David Robert Pratt, "The Political Thought of Alfred the Great" (Ph.D. diss., University of Cambridge, UK, 1999), esp. chap. 3, "The *Hierdeboc* as a Treatise on Power," 76–135; and Kathleen Davis, "National Writing in the Ninth Century: A Reminder for Postcolonial Thinking about the Nation," *Journal of Medieval and Early Modern Studies* 28 (1998): 611–37. For sources, see J. Hart, "Sources of King Alfred's Old English Version of Gregory's *Pastoral Care* (Cameron C.B.9.3)," 1992, *Fontes.* Alfred's introductions to the Psalms introduced explicit references to Christ into the Old Testament text; see Patrick P. O'Neill, "The Old English Introductions to the Prose Psalms and the Paris Psalter: Sources, Structure, and Composition," *Studies in Philology* 78 (1981): 20–38. O'Neill's new edition of the prose Psalms offers a detailed account of the manuscript, sources, methods, language, and authorship; see his "Introduction," 1–96. For further bibliography on these or other topics, see my "King Alfred: A Bibliography, with Special Attention to Literature," in *Basic Readings in Old English Prose,* ed. Paul E. Szarmach, Basic Readings in Anglo-Saxon England Series, vol. 5 (New York: Garland, 2000), 463–502, and Greg Waite, *Old English Prose Translations of King Alfred's Reign,* Annotated Bibliographies of Old and Middle English Literature, vol. 6 (Rochester, NY: Brewer, 2000).

2. The most recent work on the *Sol* includes Malcolm R. Godden, "The Sources of King Alfred's Old English Version of Augustine's *Soliloquia* (Cameron C.B.9.4)," 2001, *Fontes*; Pratt's chapter on the *Sol,* "Seeing God as He Is," 316–56 in his "Political Thought"; Eugene Green, "Speech Acts and the Question of Self in Alfred's *Soliloquies,*" in *Interdigitations: Essays for Irmengard Rauch,* ed. Gerald F. Carr, Wayne Harbert, and Lihua Zhang (New York: Peter Lang, 1998), 211–8; Prodosh Bhattacharya, "An Analogue, and Probable Source, for a Metaphor in Alfred's Preface to the Old English Translation of Augustine's *Soliloquies,*" *Notes and Queries,* 233, new series 45 (1998): 161–3; and Michael Treschow, "Echoes of the Periphyseon in the Third Book of Alfred's *Soliloquies,*" *Notes and Queries* 238, ns 40 (1993): 281–6.

3. *The Culture of Translation in Anglo-Saxon England* (Cambridge, UK: Brewer, 2002), 99.

4. See, for instance, Malcolm R. Godden, "Ælfric and the Vernacular Prose Tradition," in *The Old English Homily and Its Backgrounds,* ed. Paul E. Szarmach and Bernard F. Huppé (Albany: State University of New York Press, 1978), 99–117; W. F. Bolton, "The Alfredian Boethius in Ælfric's 'Lives of Saints' I," *Notes and Queries* 217, ns 19 (1972): 406–7; Bernard F. Huppé, "Alfred and Ælfric: A Study of Two Prefaces," in *The Old English Homily and Its Backgrounds,* ed. Paul E. Szarmach and Bernard F. Huppé (Albany: State University of New York Press, 1978) 119–37; and Jeremy J. Smith, "Alfred and Ælfric: Wisdom and Poetry in Anglo-Saxon Education," *Revista canaria de estudias ingleses* 16 (1988): 9–20. For Alfred's influence on specific passages in Ælfric (and perhaps on other authors), see *Fontes.*

5. See the notes to chap. 1 for lists of names Alfred uses and other texts in which they appear.

6. *The Rules of Art: Genesis and Structure of the Literary Field,* trans. Susan Emanuel (Stanford, CA: Stanford University Press, 1996), 292.

7. Pratt, "The Political Thought," 314–5.

8. Brian S. Donaghey, "Nicholas Trevet's Use of King Alfred's Translation of Boethius, and the Dating of His Commentary," in *The Medieval Boethius: Studies in the Vernacular Translations of De Consolatione Philosophiae*, ed. A. J. Minnis (Cambridge, UK: Brewer, 1987), 1–31.

9. He adds, "The entire difference between utopianism and realism is to be found here." *Language and Symbolic Power*, ed. John B. Thomson and trans. Gino Raymond and Matthew Adamson (Cambridge, MA: Harvard University Press, 1991), 188–9.

10. *Rules*, 58.

11. Donaghey, "Nicholas Trevet's Use."

12. "King Alfred and the Tenth-Century Reform of the English Church," in his *Wessex and England from Alfred to Edgar: Six Essays on Political, Cultural, and Ecclesiastical Revival*, Studies in Anglo-Saxon History, vol. 3 (Woodbridge, NY: Boydell Press, 1992): 185–205.

13. Roy Michael Liuzza, "Who Read the Gospels in Old English?" in *Words and Works: Studies in Medieval English Language and Literature in Honour of Fred C. Robinson*, ed. Peter S. Baker and Nicholas Howe (Toronto, ON: University of Toronto Press, 1998), 3–24, at 6.

14. Helmut Gneuss, *Handlist of Anglo-Saxon Manuscripts: A List of Manuscripts and Manuscript Fragments Written or Owned in England up to 1100* (Tempe, AZ: Arizona Center for Medieval and Renaissance Studies, 2001), 4–5.

15. "National Writing," 628.

16. "Power and Authority at the Court of Alfred," in *Essays on Anglo-Saxon and Related Themes in Memory of Lynne Grundy*, ed. Jane Roberts and Janet Nelson (London: Centre for Late Antique and Medieval Studies, King's College London, 2000), 311–37, at 336–7.

17. *Language and Symbolic Power*, 68–9.

Appendix

1. "Zu König Alfreds 'Boethius,'" *Archiv für das Studium der neueren Sprachen und Literaturen* 94 (1895): 149–60.

2. Bolton, "The Study of the Consolation of Philosophy in Anglo-Saxon England," *Archives d'histoire doctrinale et littéraire du moyen âge* 44 (1977): 33–78, esp. Appendix II, "Mythological Glosses in Remigian Manuscripts," 60–78; and Otten, *König Alfreds Boethius*, Studien zur englischen Philologie, neue Folge no. 3 (Tübingen, GER: Max Niemeyer Verlag, 1964), esp. 125–41.

3. "King Alfred's *Boethius* and Its Latin Sources: a Reconsideration," *ASE* 11 (1983): 157-98.

4. For two recent dissertations, see David R. Pratt, "The Political Thought of Alfred the Great" (Ph.D. diss., University of Cambridge, UK, 1999), esp. the section on "The *Consolatio* in the Carolingian World," 249–62, and John H. Brinegar, "'Books Most Necessary': The Literary and Cultural Contexts of Alfred's Boethius" (Ph.D. diss., University of North Carolina at Chapel Hill, 2000). See also my *Fontes*

entries, which identify specific possible borrowings from commentaries and *vitae.* I have identified no certain borrowings, but 19 probable or possible uses (as well as several analogues in a commentary attributed to Remigius) out of the 742 total entries for the *Bo.* In a more narrowly focused study, Paul E. Szarmach attempted to identify the source of Alfred's comments on the cardinal virtues at *Bo* 62.21–9. Szarmach could not identify any source text, although he suggested that a diagram of the virtues could have influenced Alfred. He concludes that, "the more information scholarship has brought to bear on the Alfredian *Boethius,* the more it seems to stress Alfredian independence and elusiveness" (234), "Alfred's *Boethius* and the Four Cardinal Virtues," in *Alfred the Wise: Studies in Honour of Janet Bately on the Occasion of Her Sixty-Fifth Birthday,* ed. Jane Roberts and Janet L. Nelson with Malcolm Godden (Cambridge, UK: Brewer, 1997), 223–35. More recently, Szarmach identifies material in Kk.3.21 (fol. 49v) that may have influenced the translation of *Meter 20*; the added material can also be found in the prose, at 81.15–6, a passage I had matched independently with the comment in Kk.3.21. See Szarmach, "The *Timaeus* in Old English," in *Lexis and Texts in Early English: Studies Presented to Jane Roberts,* ed. Christian J. Kay and Louise M. Sylvester, Costerus ns 133 (Amsterdam: Rodopi, 2001), 255–67, at 263; his "Alfred, Alcuin, and the Soul," in *Manuscript, Narrative, Lexicon: Essays on Literary and Cultural Transmissions in Honor of Whitney F. Bolton,* ed. Robert Boenig and Kathleen Davis (Lewisburg, PA: Bucknell University Press, 2000), 127–48, esp. 138–40; and my *Fontes* entry for the prose passage.

5. "The 'Remigian' Glosses on Boethius' *Consolatio Philosophiae* in Context" is forthcoming in a festschrift for Thomas D. Hill edited by Charles D. Wright. I am grateful to Joseph Wittig for providing me with a copy of his work before publication.

6. The understanding of how names work is different here; whether that is because the commentary was not actually Alfred's source or simply because Anglo-Saxons did not fully understand Roman names is not clear.

7. Brinegar traces other possible sources for many of Alfred's additions in his "'Books Most Necessary'": for Cicero, see 112–3; for Brutus and Cato, 114–7; and for Circe, 93.

Bibliography

Primary Sources

Ælfric. *Ælfric's Colloquy*. Ed. G. N. Garmonsway. New York: Appleton-Century-Crofts, 1966.

Alfred, King. *King Alfred's Old English Prose Translation of the First Fifty Psalms*. Ed. Patrick P. O'Neill. Cambridge, MA: Medieval Academy of America, 2001.

———. *King Alfred's Old English Version of Boethius De Consolatione Philosophiae*. Ed. Walter John Sedgefield. Oxford, UK: Clarendon Press, 1899.

———. *King Alfred's Version of St. Augustine's Soliloquies*. Ed. Thomas A. Carnicelli. Cambridge, MA: Harvard University Press, 1969.

———. *King Alfred's West-Saxon Version of Gregory's Pastoral Care*. Ed. Henry Sweet. EETS 45, 50. London: N. Trübner, 1871.

———. "Will of King Alfred." *Select English Historical Documents of the Ninth and Tenth Centuries*. Ed. Florence E. Harmer. Cambridge, UK: Cambridge University Press, 1914. 15–9.

Das altenglische Martyrologium. Ed. G. Kotzor. Phil.-Hist Klasse, Neue Forschung 88. Munich, GER: Bayerische Akademie der Wissenschaften, 1981.

Anglo-Saxon Chronicle: A Collaborative Edition, The. Gen. eds. David Dumville and Simon Keynes. Cambridge, UK: Brewer, 1986–.

Anglo-Saxon Poetic Records, The. Ed. George Phillip Krapp and Elliott Van Kirk Dobbie. 6 vols. New York: Columbia University Press, 1931–53.

Asser. *Asser's Life of King Alfred Together with the Annals of Saint Neots*. Ed. with commentary by William Henry Stevenson and article by Dorothy Whitelock. Oxford, UK: Clarendon Press, 1959.

Augustine, Bishop of Hippo. *De doctrina christiana*. Ed. J. Martin. CCSL 32. Turnhout, BEL: Brepols, 1962.

———. *Soliloquies and Immortality of the Soul.* Ed. and trans. Gerard Watson. Warminster, UK: Aris and Phillips, 1990.

Bede. *Bede's Ecclesiastical History of the English People.* Ed. and trans. Bertam Colgrave and R. A. B. Mynors. Oxford, UK Clarendon, 1969.

Biblia sacra iuxta vulgatam versionem. Ed. Robert Weber et al. Stuttgart, GER: Deutsche Bibelgesellschaft, 1969.

Boethius, Anicius Manlius Severinus. *Anicii Manlii Severini Boethii Philosophiae Consolatio.* Ed. Ludwig Bieler. Corpus Christianorum Series Latina 94. Turnhout, BEL: Brepols, 1957.

———. *Anicii Manlii Severini Boethii Philosophiae consolationis libri quinque.* Ed. Rudolfus Peiper. Leipzig, GER: Teubner, 1881.

CETEDOC Library of Christian Texts on CD-ROM. Turnhout, BEL: Brepols, 1991.

"A Commentary by Remigius Autissiodorensis on the *De consolatione philosophiae* of Boethius." Ed. H. F. Stewart. *Journal of Theological Studies* 17 (1916): 22–42.

Dictionary of Old English Corpus online. http://ets.umdl.umich.edu/o/oec/; access restricted to subscribers.

Gregory the Great. *Dialogues.* Ed. Adalbert de Vogüé and trans. (into French) Paul Antin. Sources Chrétiennes vols. 251, 260, 265. Paris: Les Éditions du Cerf, 1980.

———. *Moralia in Job.* Ed. Marcus Adriaen. Corpus Christianorum Series Latina 143–143B. Turnhout, BEL: Brepols, 1979 and 1985.

———. *Règle Pastorale.* Ed. Floribert Rommel with introduction, notes, and index by Bruno Judic and trans. (into French) Charles Morel. Sources Chrétiennes vols. 381–2. Paris: Éditions du Cerf, 1992.

Old English Glossed Psalters: Psalms 1–50. Ed. Phillip Pulsiano. Toronto Old English Series 11. Toronto, ON: University of Toronto Press, 2001.

Old English Orosius, The. Ed. Janet Bately. EETS ss 6. London: Oxford University Press, 1980.

Old English Version of Bede's Ecclesiastical History of the English People, The. Ed. and trans. Thomas Miller. EETS 95–6, 110–1. London: Trübner, 1890.

Orosius, Paulus. *Pauli Orosii Historiarum aduersum paganos.* Ed. Carolus Zangemeister. CSEL 5. Vienna: C. Geroldi Filium Bibliopolam Academiae, 1882.

Psautier romain et les autres anciens psautiers latins, Le. Ed. Robert Weber. Collectanea Biblica Latina 10. Vatican City: Libreria Vaticana, 1953.

Saeculi noni auctoris in Boetii consolationem philosophiae commentarius. Ed. Edmund T. Silk. Rome: American Academy in Rome, 1935. 305–43.

Wærferth, Bishop. *Bischof Wærferths von Worcester Übersetzung der Dialoge Gregors des Grossen.* Ed. H. Hecht. Leipzig, 1900–7, reprint Darmstadt, GER: Wissenschaftliche Buchgesellschaft, 1965.

William of Malmesbury. *De gestis pontificum anglorum.* Ed. N.E.S.A. Hamilton, Rolls 52. London: Longman, 1870.

Secondary Sources

Abels, Richard. *Alfred the Great: War, Kingship and Culture in Anglo-Saxon England.* New York: Longman, 1999.

Astell, Ann. *Job, Boethius, and Epic Truth.* Ithaca, NY: Cornell University Press, 1994.

Bately, Janet M. "The Alfredian Canon Revisited: One Hundred Years On." In *Alfred the Great: Papers from the Eleventh-Centenary Conferences.* Ed. Timothy Reuter. Studies in Early Medieval Britain 3. Aldershot, UK: Ashgate, 2003. 107–120.

———. "An Alfredian Legacy? On the Fortunes and Fate of Some Items of Boethian Vocabulary in Old English." *From Anglo-Saxon to Early Middle English: Studies Presented to E. G. Stanley.* Ed. Malcolm Godden, Douglas Gray, and Terry Hoad. Oxford, UK: Clarendon, 1994. 8–32.

———. "Boethius and King Alfred." *Platonism and the English Imagination.* Ed. Anna Baldwin and Sarah Hutton. Cambridge, UK: Cambridge University Press, 1994. 38–44.

———. "Evidence for Knowledge of Latin Literature in Old English." *Sources of Anglo-Saxon Culture.* Ed. Paul E. Szarmach with Virginia Darrow Oggins. Studies in Medieval Culture, vol. 20. Kalamazoo: Medieval Institute Publications, Western Michigan University, 1986. 35–51.

———. "Lexical Evidence for the Authorship of the Prose Psalms in the Paris Psalter." *ASE* 10 (1982): 69–95.

———. "The Literary Prose of King Alfred's Reign: Translation or Transformation?" Inaugural Lecture in the Chair of English Language and Medieval Literature Delivered at University of London King's College on March 4, 1980. Reprint *Old English Newsletter Subsidia* 10 (1984).

———. "Old English Prose before and during the Reign of Alfred." *ASE* 17 (1988): 93–138.

———. "Those Books that Are Most Necessary for All Men to Know: The Classics and Late Ninth-Century England, A Reappraisal." *The Classics in the Middle Ages: Papers of the 20th Annual Conference of the Center for Medieval and Early Renaissance Studies.* Ed. Aldo

S. Bernardo and Saul Levin. Binghamton, NY: Center for Medieval and Early Renaissance Studies, 1990. 50–65.

———. "Uþwita/Philosophus Revisited: A Reflection on OE Usage." *Essays on Anglo-Saxon and Related Themes in Memory of Lynne Grundy*. Ed. Jane Roberts and Janet Nelson. London: Centre for Late Antique and Medieval Studies, King's College London, 2000. 16–36.

Bethurum, Dorothy. "Stylistic Features of the Old English Laws." *Modern Language Review* 27 (1932): 263–79.

Bodden, Mary Catherine. "Anglo-Saxon Self-Consciousness in Language." *English Studies* 1 (1987): 24–39.

Boethius Project, The. Dir. Malcolm R. Godden. Oxford University, UK. http://www.english.ox.ac.uk/boethius/index.html.

Bolton, Diane K. "The Study of the Consolation of Philosophy in Anglo-Saxon England." *Archives d'histoire doctrinale et littéraire du moyen âge* 44 (1977): 33–78.

Bolton, W. F. "How Boethian is Alfred's *Boethius*?" *Studies in Earlier Old English Prose*. Ed. Paul E. Szarmach. Albany: State University of New York Press, 1986. 153–68.

Borinski, Ludwig. *Der Stil König Alfreds: Eine Studie zur Psychologie der Rede*. Leipzig, GER: Bernhard Tauchnitz, 1934.

Bosworth, Joseph. *An Anglo-Saxon Dictionary*. Ed. and enlarged by T. Northcote Toller. Oxford, UK: Clarendon, 1921.

Bourdieu, Pierre. *Distinction: A Social Critique of the Judgement of Taste*. Trans. Richard Nice. Cambridge, MA: Harvard University Press, 1984.

———. *The Field of Cultural Production*. Ed. Randal Johnson. New York: Columbia University Press, 1993.

———. *Language and Symbolic Power*. Ed. John B. Thomson and trans. Gino Raymond and Matthew Adamson. Cambridge, MA: Harvard University Press, 1991.

———. *Outline of a Theory of Practice*. Trans. Richard Nice. Cambridge, UK: Cambridge University Press, 1977.

———. *The Rules of Art: Genesis and Structure of the Literary Field*. Trans. Susan Emanuel. Stanford, CA: Stanford University Press, 1996.

———. and L. J. D. Wacquant. *An Invitation to Reflexive Sociology*. Chicago: University of Chicago Press, 1992.

Brinegar, John. "Books Most Necessary': The Literary and Cultural Contexts of Alfred's *Boethius*." Ph.D. diss., University of North Carolina at Chapel Hill, 2000.

Brown, William H., Jr. "Method and Style in the Old English *Pastoral Care.*" *Journal of English and Germanic Philology* 68 (1969): 666–84.

———. *A Syntax of King Alfred's Pastoral Care.* The Hague: Mouton, 1970.

Busse, Wilhelm G. "Die 'karolingische' Reform König Alfreds." *Karl der Große und das Erbe der Kulturen.* Ed. Franz-Reiner Erkens. Berlin, GER: Akademie Verlag, 2001, 169–84.

Calhoun, Craig. "Habitus, Field, and Capital: The Question of Historical Specificity." *Bourdieu: Critical Perspectives.* Ed. Craig Calhoun, Edward LiPuma, and Moishe Postone. Cambridge, UK: Polity Press, 1993. 61–88.

Campbell, Jackson J. "Adaptation of Classical Rhetoric in Old English Literature." *Medieval Eloquence: Studies in the Theory and Practice of Medieval Rhetoric.* Ed. James J. Murphy. Berkeley: University of California Press, 1978. 173–97.

———. "Knowledge of Rhetorical Figures in Anglo-Saxon England." *Journal of English and Germanic Philology* 66 (1967): 1–20.

Chadwick, Henry. *Boethius: The Consolations of Music, Logic, Theology, and Philosophy.* Oxford, UK: Clarendon, 1981.

Clanchy, Michael. *From Memory to Written Record: England, 1066–1307.* Cambridge, MA: Harvard University Press, 1993.

Clark Hall, J. R., with supplement by Herbert D. Meritt. *A Concise Anglo-Saxon Dictionary.* Toronto, ON: University of Toronto Press, 1991.

Clemoes, Peter. "King Alfred's Debt to Vernacular Poetry: The Evidence of *ellen* and *cræft.*" *Words, Texts and Manuscripts: Studies in Anglo-Saxon Culture Presented to Helmut Gneuss.* Ed. Michael Korhammer with Karl Reichl and Hans Sauer. Cambridge, UK: Brewer, 1992. 213–38.

Codices Boethiani: A Conspectus of Manuscripts of the Works of Boethius. Vol. I: Great Britain and the Republic of Ireland. Ed. M. T. Gibson and Lesley Smith with Joseph Ziegler. Warburg Institute Surveys and Texts 25. London: Warburg Institute, University of London, 1995.

Cook, Albert S. "Alfred's 'Word for Word' Translation." *Academy* 30 (1886): 108.

Courcelle, Pierre. *La Consolation de philosophie dans la tradition littéraire: antécédents et postérité de Boèce.* Paris: Études Augustiniennes, 1967.

———. "Étude critique sur les commentaires de la *Consolation* de Boèce (IXe–XVe siècles)." *Archives d'histoire doctrinale et littéraire du moyen âge* 4 (1933): 5–140.

Davis, Kathleen. "National Writing in the Ninth Century: A Reminder for Postcolonial Thinking about the Nation." *Journal of Medieval and Early Modern Studies* 28 (1998): 611–37.

———. "The Performance of Translation Theory in King Alfred's National Literary Program." *Manuscript, Narrative, Lexicon: Essays on Literary and Cultural Transmission in Honor of Whitney F. Bolton.* Ed. Robert Boenig and Kathleen Davis. Lewisburg, PA: Bucknell University Press, 2000. 149–70.

Dictionary of Old English. Ed. Antonette DiPaolo Healey et al. Toronto, ON: PIMS, 1986–.

Discenza, Nicole Guenther. "Alfred's Verse Preface to the *Pastoral Care* and the Chain of Authority." *Neophilologus* 85 (2001): 625–33.

———. "The Influence of Gregory the Great on the Alfredian Social Imaginary." *Rome and the North: The Early Reception of Gregory the Great in Germanic Europe.* Ed. Rolf H. Bremmer Jr., Kees Dekker, and David F. Johnson. Leuven, BEL: Peeters, 2001. 67–81.

———. "King Alfred: A Bibliography, with Special Attention to Literature." *Basic Readings in Old English Prose.* Ed. Paul E. Szarmach. Basic Readings in Anglo-Saxon England Series. New York: Garland, 2000. 463–502.

———. "The Old English *Bede* and the Construction of Anglo-Saxon Authority." *ASE* 31 (2002): 69–80.

———. "Power, Skill and Virtue in the Old English *Boethius.*" *ASE* 26 (1997): 81–108.

———. "The Sources of King Alfred's Old English Version of Boethius's *De consolatione philosophiae* (Cameron B.9.3)." 2001, *Fontes.*

———. "Unauthorized Biographies of Anicius Manlius Severinus Boethius." Presented at the Alfredian Boethius Project First Annual Symposium, Oxford University, England July 2003. http://www.english.ox.ac.uk/boethius/Symposium2003.html.

———. "Wealth and Wisdom: Symbolic Capital and the Ruler in the Translational Program of Alfred the Great." *Exemplaria* 13 (2001): 433–67.

———. "'Wise wealhstodas': The Prologue to Sirach as a Model for Alfred's Preface to the *Pastoral Care.*" *JEGP* 97 (1998): 488–99.

Donaghey, Brian S. "Nicholas Trevet's Use of King Alfred's Translation of Boethius, and the Dating of His Commentary." *The Medieval Boethius: Studies in the Vernacular Translations of De Consolatione Philosophiae.* Ed. A. J. Minnis. Cambridge, UK: Brewer, 1987. 1–31.

———. "The Sources of King Alfred's Translation of Boethius' *De Consolatione Philosophiae.*" *Anglia* 82 (1964): 23–57.

Donoghue, Daniel. "Word Order and Poetic Style: Auxiliary and Verbal in *Metres of Boethius.*" *ASE* 15 (1986): 167–96.

Dubois, Jacques. "Pierre Bourdieu and Literature." Trans. Meaghan Emery with Pamela Sing. *SubStance* 93 (2000): 84–102.

Dumville, David. "King Alfred and the Tenth-Century Reform of the English Church." *Wessex and England from Alfred to Edgar: Six Essays on Political, Cultural, and Ecclesiastical Revival.* Studies in Anglo-Saxon History 3. Woodbridge, NY: Boydell Press, 1992. 185–205.

EBoethius. Dir. Kevin Kiernan. University of Kentucky. http://beowulf.engl.uky.edu/~kiernan/eBoethius/mainpage.html.

Fehlauer, Friedrich. *Die englischen Übersetzungen des Boethius 'De Consolatione Philosophiae," I. Die alt- und mittelenglischen Übersetzungen.* Berlin: Emil Felber, 1909.

Fischer, Olga. "A Comparative Study of the Philosophical Terms in the Alfredian and Chaucerian Boethius." *Neophilologus* 63 (1979): 622–39.

Fontes Anglo-Saxonici: World Wide Web Register. http://fontes.english.ox.ac.uk/ or CD-ROM version 1.1 (Oxford, UK: Fontes Anglo-Saxonici Project, 2002).

Foot, Sarah. "The Making of *Angelcynn*: English Identity before the Norman Conquest." *TRHS* 6th ser. 6 (1996): 25–49.

Fowler, Bridget. *Pierre Bourdieu and Cultural Theory: Critical Investigations.* London: Sage Publications, 1997.

Frakes, Jerold. *The Fate of Fortune in the Early Middle Ages: The Boethian Tradition.* New York: Brill, 1988.

———. "Die Rezeption der Neuplatonischen Metaphysik des Boethius durch Alfred und Notker." *Beiträge zur Geschichte der deutschen Sprache und Literatur* 106 (1984): 51–74.

Frantzen, Allen J. "The Form and Function of the Preface in the Poetry and Prose of Alfred's Reign." In *Alfred the Great: Papers from the Eleventh-Centenary Conferences,.* Ed. Timothy Reuter. Studies in Early Medieval Britain 3. Aldershot, UK: Ashgate, 2003. 121–36.

———. *King Alfred.* Twayne's English Authors Series. Boston: Twayne Publishers, 1986.

Gatch, Milton McC. "King Alfred's Version of Augustine's *Soliloquia*: Some Suggestions on Its Rationale and Unity." *Studies in Earlier Old English Prose.* Ed. Paul E. Szarmach. Albany: State University of New York Press, 1986. 17–45.

———. *Loyalties and Traditions: Man and His World in Old English Literature.* New York: Pegasus, 1976.

Gibson, Margaret T., ed. *Boethius: His Life, Thought, and Influence.* Oxford, UK: Basil Blackwell, 1981.

———. "Boethius in the Carolingian Schools." *TRHS* Fifth Series, 32 (1982): 43–56.

Girsch, Elizabeth Baldwin Stevens. "A Semantic Analysis of the Old English *Cræft* and Related Words." PhD diss., University of Toronto, ON, 1988.

Gneuss, Helmut. *Handlist of Anglo-Saxon Manuscripts: A List of Manuscripts and Manuscript Fragments Written or Owned in England up to 1100.* Tempe, AZ: Arizona Center for Medieval and Renaissance Studies, 2001.

———. *Lehnbildungen und Lehnbedeutungen im Altenglishen.* Berlin: Erich Schmidt Verlag, 1955.

———. "The Origin of Standard Old English and Æthelwold's School at Winchester." *ASE* 1 (1972): 63–83.

Godden, Malcolm R. "Anglo-Saxons on the Mind." *Learning and Literature in Anglo-Saxon England.* Ed. Michael Lapidge and Helmut Gneuss. Cambridge, UK: Cambridge University Press, 1985. 271–98.

———. "Editing Old English and the Problem of Alfred's *Boethius.*" *The Editing of Old English: Papers from the 1990 Manchester Conference.* Ed. Donald G. Scragg and Paul E. Szarmach with Helene Scheck and Holly Holbrook. Cambridge, UK: Brewer, 1994. 163–76.

———. "King Alfred's Boethius." *Boethius: His Life, Thought, and Influence.* Ed. Margaret Gibson. Oxford, UK: Basil Blackwell, 1981. 419–24.

———. "The Player King: Identification and Self-Representation in King Alfred's Writings." In *Alfred the Great: Papers from the Eleventh-Centenary Conferences.* Ed. Timothy Reuter. Studies in Early Medieval Britain 3. Aldershot, UK: Ashgate, 2003. 137–50.

———. "The Sources of King Alfred's Old English Version of Augustine's *Soliloquia* (Cameron B.9.4)." 2001, *Fontes.*

———. "Wærferth and King Alfred: The Fate of the Old English *Dialogues.*" *Alfred the Wise: Studies in Honour of Janet Bately on the Occasion of Her Sixty-Fifth Birthday.* Ed. Jane Roberts and Janet L. Nelson with Malcolm Godden. Cambridge, UK: Brewer, 1997. 35–51.

Grinda, Klaus. "Zu Tradition und Gestaltung des Kirke-Mythos in König Alfreds *Boethius.*" *Motive und Themen in englischsprachiger Literatur als Indikatoren literaturgeschichtlicher Prozesse.* Ed. Heinz-Joachim Müllenbrock and Alfons Klein. Tübingen, GER: Max Niemeyer Verlag, 1990. 1–23.

Gruber, Joachim. *Kommentar zu Boethius De Consolatione Philosophiae.* New York: de Gruyter, 1978.

Guillory, John. "Bourdieu's Refusal." *Modern Language Quarterly* 58 (1997): 367–98.

———. *Cultural Capital: The Problem of Literary Canon Formation.* Chicago: University of Chicago Press, 1993.

Hart, J. "Sources of King Alfred's Old English Version of Gregory's *Pastoral Care* (Cameron C.B.9.3)." 1992, *Fontes.*

Hartmann, K. A. Martin. "Ist König Alfred der Verfasser der alliterierended Übertragung der Metra des Boetius?" *Anglia: Zeitschrift für englische Philologie* 5 (1882): 411–50.

Hitch, Susan J. "Alfred's *Cræft*: Imagery in Alfred's Version of Augustine's Soliloquies." *Journal of the Department of English, University of Calcutta* (1986–7): 130–47.

Holthausen, Ferdinand. *Altenglisches Etymologisches Wörterbuch.* Heidelberg, GER: Carl Winters Universitätsbuchhandlung, 1934.

Holton, Robert. "Bourdieu and Common Sense." *SubStance* 26 (1997): 38–52.

Hubbard, Frank G. "The Relation of the 'Blooms of King Alfred' to the Anglo-Saxon Translation of Boethius." *Modern Language Notes* 9 (1894): 161–71.

Irvine, Susan. "Ulysses and Circe in King Alfred's *Boethius:* A Classical Myth Transformed." In *Studies in English Language and Literature: 'Doubt wisely': Papers in honour of E. G. Stanley.* Ed. M. J. Toswell and E. M. Tyler. London: Routledge, 1996. 387–401.

———. "Wrestling with Hercules: King Alfred and the Classical Past." In *Court Culture in the Early Middle Ages: The Proceedings of the First Alcuin Conference.* Ed. Catherine Cubitt. Turnhout, BEL: Brepols, 2003. 171–88.

Jack, R. Ian. "The Significance of the Alfredian Translations." *Australasian Universities Language and Literature Association* (1971): 348–61.

Jayatilaka, Rohini. "Sources of the Anonymous Old English Version of Orosius's *History against the Pagans* (Cameron C.B.9.2)." 2001, *Fontes.*

Käsmann, Hans. *Studien zum kirchlichen Wortschatz des Mittelenglischen 1100–1350: Ein Beitrag zum Problem der Sprachmiscung.* Tübingen, GER: Niemeyer, 1961.

Ker, N. R. *Catalogue of Manuscripts Containing Anglo-Saxon.* Reprint with supplement. Oxford, UK: Oxford University Press, 1990.

Keynes, Simon. "The Power of the Written Word: Alfredian England 871–899." In *Alfred the Great: Papers from the Eleventh-Centenary Conferences.* Ed. Timothy Reuter. Studies in Early Medieval Britain 3. Aldershot, UK: Ashgate, 2003. 175–97.

Keynes, Simon, and Michael Lapidge, trans. *Alfred the Great.* New York: Penguin, 1983.

Kiernan, Kevin S. "Alfred the Great's Burnt *Boethius.*" *The Iconic Page in Manuscript, Print, and Digital Culture.* Ed. George Bornstein and Theresa Tinkle. Ann Arbor: University of Michigan Press, 1998. 7–32.

Koeppel, E. "Zur chronologie der übersetzungen des königs Alfred." *Anglia: Beiblatt* 19 (1908): 330–2.

Koskenniemi, Inna. *Repetitive Word Pairs in Old and Early Middle English Prose.* Annales Universitatis Turkuensis Series B, vol. 107. Turku, FIN: Turun Yliopiston Julkaisuja, 1968.

Kroesch, Samuel. "The Semantic Development of OE *Cræft.*" *Modern Philology* 26 (1928–9): 433–41.

Lerer, Seth. *Boethius and Dialogue: Literary Method in the Consolation of Philosophy.* Princeton, NJ: Princeton University Press, 1985.

———. *Literacy and Power in Anglo-Saxon Literature.* Lincoln: University of Nebraska Press, 1991.

Lewis, Charlton T., and Charles Short. *A Latin Dictionary.* Oxford, UK: Clarendon, 1879.

Liuzza, Roy Michael. "Who Read thc Gospels in Old English?" *Words and Works: Studies in Medieval English Language and Literature in Honour of Fred C. Robinson.* Ed. Peter S. Baker and Nicholas Howe. Toronto, ON: University of Toronto Press, 1998. 3–24.

McKitterick, Rosamond, ed. *Carolingian Culture: Emulation and Innovation.* Cambridge, UK: Cambridge University Press, 1994.

Magoun, Francis P. "Some Notes on King Alfred's Circular Letter on Educational Policy Addressed to His Bishops." *Mediaeval Studies* 10 (1948): 100–1.

Metcalf, Allan A. "On the Authorship and Originality of the *Meters of Boethius.*" *Neuphilologische Mitteilungen* 71 (1970): 185–7.

The Microfiche Concordance to Old English. Ed. Antonette diPaolo Healey et al. Toronto, ON: PIMS, 1980.

Minnis, A. J., ed. *The Medieval Boethius: Studies in the Vernacular Translations of De Consolatione Philosophiae.* Cambridge, UK: Brewer, 1988.

Monnin, Pierre-Eric. "Poetic Improvements in the Old English *Meters of Boethius.*" *English Studies* 60 (1979): 346–60.

Moreschini, Claudio. "Boezio e la tradizione del neoplatonismo latino." *Congresso Internazionale di Studi Boeziani* (Pavia, 5–8 ottobre 1980). Ed. Luca Obertello. Rome: Atti, 1981. 297–310.

Moye, Roy Ray, Jr. "Alfred's Method of Translation in the Old English *Pastoral Care*." Ph.D. diss., University of North Carolina at Chapel Hill, 1993.

———. "Boethius and King Alfred." *Platonism and the English Imagination*. Ed. Anna Baldwin and Sarah Hutton. Cambridge, UK: Cambridge University Press, 1994. 38–44.

Napier, Arthur S. "Bruchstück einer altenglischen Boethiushandschrift." *Zeitschrift fur deutsches Altertum und deutsche Literatur* 31 (1887): 52–4.

Nelson, Janet L. "Alfred's Carolingian Contemporaries." In *Alfred the Great: Papers from the Eleventh-Centenary Conferences*. Ed. Timothy Reuter. Studies in Early Medieval Britain 3. Aldershot, UK: Ashgate, 2003. 293–310.

———. "The Franks and English in the Ninth Century Reconsidered." *The Preservation and Transmission of Anglo-Saxon Culture*. Ed. J. Rosenthal and P. Szarmach. Kalamazoo: Medieval Institute Publications, Western Michigan University, 1997. 141–58.

———. "'A King across the Sea': Alfred in Continental Perspective." *TRHS*, 5th series 36 (1986): 45–68.

———. "The Political Ideas of Alfred of Wessex." *Kings and Kingship in Medieval Europe*. Ed. Anne J. Duggan. London: Centre for Late Antique and Medieval Studies, King's College London, 1993. 125–58.

———. "Power and Authority at the Court of Alfred." *Essays on Anglo-Saxon and Related Themes in Memory of Lynne Grundy*. Ed. Jane Roberts and Janet Nelson. London: Centre for Late Antique and Medieval Studies, King's College London, 2000. 311–37.

———. "Wealth and Wisdom: The Politics of Alfred the Great." *Kings and Kingship*. Ed. J. Rosenthal, Center for Medieval and Early Renaissance Studies, State University of New York, Acta 11. Binghamton, NY: State University of New York at Binghamton, 1984. 31–52.

Obertello, Luca. "L'universo boeziano." *Congresso Internazionale di Studi Boeziani* (Pavia, 5–8 Ottobre 1980). Ed. Luca Obertello. Rome: Atti, 1981. 157–68.

O'Brien O'Keeffe, Katherine. *Visible Song: Transitional Literacy in Old English Verse*. Cambridge Studies in Anglo-Saxon England 4. Cambridge, UK: Cambridge University Press, 1990.

O'Daly, Gerard. *The Poetry of Boethius*. Chapel Hill: University of North Carolina Press, 1991.

O'Neill, Patrick P. "The Old English Introductions to the Prose Psalms and the Paris Psalter: Sources, Structure, and Composition." *Studies in Philology* 78 (1981): 20–38.

Ong, Walter. *Orality and Literacy: The Technologizing of the Word.* New York: Methuen, 1982.

Otten, Kurt. *König Alfreds Boethius.* Studien zur englischen Philologie, neue Folge no. 3. Tübingen, GER: Max Niemeyer Verlag, 1964.

Pabst, Bernhard. *Prosimetrum: Tradition und Wandel einer Literaturform zwischen Spätantike und Spätmittelalter.* Vol. 1, Studien zur Literature und Gesellschaft des Mittelalters und der frühen Neuzeit. Cologne, GER: Böhlau Verlag, 1994.

Payne, F. Anne. *King Alfred and Boethius: An Analysis of the Old English Version of the Consolation of Philosophy.* Madison: University of Wisconsin Press, 1968.

Potter, Simeon. "The Old English *Pastoral Care.*" *Transactions of the Philological Society* 46 (1947): 114–25.

Powell, Timothy E. "The 'Three Orders' of Society in Anglo-Saxon England." *ASE* 23 (1994): 103–32.

Pratt, David Robert. "The Illnesses of King Alfred the Great." *ASE* 30 (2001): 39–90.

———. "Persuasion and Invention at the Court of King Alfred the Great." In *Court Culture in the Early Middle Ages: The Proceedings of the First Alcuin Conference.* Ed. Catherine Cubitt. Turnhout, BEL: Brepols, 2003. 189–221.

———. "The Political Thought of Alfred the Great." Ph.D. diss., University of Cambridge, UK, 1999. Forthcoming as *The Political Thought of King Alfred the Great.* Cambridge Studies in Medieval Life and Thought. Cambridge, UK: Cambridge University Press, 2004.

Proppe, Katherine. "King Alfred's Consolation of Philosophy." *Neuphilologische Mitteilungen* 74 (1973): 635–48.

Reinsma, Luke M. "Rhetoric in England: The Age of Ælfric, 970–1020." *Communication Monographs* 44 (1977): 390–403.

Riché, Pierre. *Écoles et Enseignement dans le Haut Moyen Age: fin du Ve siècle–milieu du XIe siècle.* Paris: Picard, 1989.

———. *Education et culture dans l'Occident barbare, VIe–VIIIe siècle.* Paris: Éditions du Seuil, 1962.

Robinson, Fred. *Beowulf and the Appositive Style.* Knoxville: University of Tennessee Press, 1985.

Scharer, Anton. *Herrschaft und Repräsentation: Studien zur Hofkultur König Alfreds des Großen.* Munich: R. Oldenbourg Verlag, 2000.

Schepss, Georg. "Zu König Alfreds 'Boethius.'" *Archiv für das Studium der neueren Sprachen und Literaturen* 94 (1895): 149–60.

Scribner, Sylvia, and Michael Coles. *The Psychology of Literacy*. Cambridge, MA: Harvard University Press, 1981.

Shippey, Thomas A. "Wealth and Wisdom in King Alfred's *Preface* to the Old English *Pastoral Care*." *English Historical Review* 94 (1979): 346–55.

Silk, Edmund T. "Boethius' *Consolatione Philosophiae* as a Sequel to Augustine's *Dialogues* and *Soliloquia*." *Harvard Theological Review* 32 (1939): 19–39.

Sisam, Kenneth. "The Authorship of the Verse Translation of Boethius' Metra." *Studies in the History of Old English Literature*. Oxford, UK: Clarendon Press, 1953. 293–7.

Smith, Jeremy J. "Alfred and Ælfric: Wisdom and Poetry in Anglo-Saxon Education." *Revista canaria de estudias ingleses* 16 (1988): 9–20.

Smyth, Alfred P. *King Alfred the Great*. Oxford, UK: Oxford University Press, 1995.

Stanton, Robert. *The Culture of Translation in Anglo-Saxon England*. Cambridge, UK: Brewer, 2002.

———. "The (M)other Tongue: Translation Theory and Old English." *Translation Theory and Practice in the Middle Ages*. Ed. Jeanette Beer, Studies in Medieval Culture 38. Kalamazoo: Medieval Institute Publications, Western Michigan University, 1997. 33–46.

———. "Rhetoric and Translation in Ælfric's Prefaces." *Translation and Literature* 6 (1997): 135–48.

Stock, Brian. *The Implications of Literacy: Written Language and Models of Interpretation in the Eleventh and Twelfth Centuries*. Princeton, NJ: Princeton University Press, 1983.

Szarmach, Paul E. "Alfred, Alcuin, and the Soul." *Manuscript, Narrative, Lexicon: Essays on Literary and Cultural Transmissions in Honor of Whitney F. Bolton*. Ed. Robert Boenig and Kathleen Davis. Lewisburg, PA: Bucknell University Press, 2000. 127–48.

———. "Alfred's *Boethius* and the Four Cardinal Virtues." *Alfred the Wise: Studies in Honour of Janet Bately on the Occasion of Her Sixty-Fifth Birthday*. Ed. Jane Roberts and Janet L. Nelson with Malcolm Godden. Cambridge, UK: Brewer, 1997. 223–35.

———. "Anglo-Saxon Letters in the Eleventh Century." *Acta* (1974): 1–14.

———. "The Meaning of Alfred's *Preface* to the *Pastoral Care*." *Mediaevalia* 7 (1980): 57–86.

———. "*Meter 20*: Context Bereft." *ANQ* 15.2 (2002): 28–34.

———. "The *Timaeus* in Old English." *Lexis and Texts in Early English: Studies Presented to Jane Roberts*. Ed. Christian J. Kay and Louise M. Sylvester, Costerus ns 133. Amsterdam: Rodopi, 2001. 255–67.

Thomas, Rebecca. "The Binding Force of Friendship in King Alfred's *Consolation* and *Soliloquies*." *Ball State University Forum* 29 (1988): 5–20.

Toller, T. Northcote. *Supplement to An Anglo-Saxon Dictionary.* With enlarged addenda and corrigenda by Alistair Campbell. Oxford, UK: Clarendon, 1898.

Troncarelli, Fabio. *Traditione Perduti.* Medioevo e umanismo 42. Padua, IT: Antenore, 1981.

Toury, Gideon. *Descriptive Translation Studies and Beyond.* Philadelphia: John Benjamins, 1995.

———. *In Search of a Theory of Translation.* Tel Aviv: Porter Institute for Poetics and Semiotics, 1980.

VanderBilt, Deborah. "Translation and Orality in the Old English *Orosius*." *Oral Tradition* 13 (1998): 377–97.

van Draat, P. Fijn. "The Authorship of the Old English *Bede*." *Anglia* 39 (1916): 319–46.

Waite, Greg. *Old English Prose Translations of King Alfred's Reign.* Annotated Bibliographies of Old and Middle English Literature 6. Rochester, NY: Brewer, 2000.

Wallace-Hadrill, J. M. *Early Germanic Kingship in England and on the Continent.* Oxford, UK: Clarendon, 1971.

Waterhouse, Ruth. "Tone in Alfred's Version of Augustine's *Soliloquies*." *Studies in Earlier Old English Prose.* Ed. Paul E. Szarmach. Albany: State University of New York Press, 1986. 47–85.

Watts, V. E., trans. *The Consolation of Philosophy.* Rev. ed. New York: Penguin, 1999.

Webber, Teresa. *Scribes and Scholars at Salisbury Cathedral, c. 1075–c. 1125.* New York: Oxford University Press, 1992.

Whitelock, Dorothy. "The Old English Bede." *Proceedings of the British Academy* 48 (1962): 57–90.

———. "The Prose of Alfred's Reign." *Continuations and Beginnings: Studies in Old English Literature.* Ed. Eric Gerald Stanley. London: Nelson, 1966. 67–103.

Wittig, Joseph S. "King Alfred's Boethius and Its Latin Sources: A Reconsideration." *ASE* 11 (1983): 157–198.

———. "The 'Remigian' Glosses on Boethius' *Consolatio Philosophiae* in Context." In festschrift for Thomas D. Hill, ed. Charles D. Wright. Forthcoming.

Yerkes, David. *Two Versions of Wærferth's Translation of Gregory's Dialogues: An Old English Thesaurus.* Toronto, ON: University of Toronto Press, 1979.

Index of Manuscripts

Index of Scriptural Citations

GENERAL INDEX